INTRODUCING THOMISTIC PHILOSOPHY

[being the fifth edition, revised and enlarged of a
Philosophy for Living:
A Sketch of Aquinate Philosophy]

by
JOHN-EMERY KONECSNI

D1509009

1

TABLE OF CONTENTS

TO ANY PROFESSOR WHO PICKS THIS UP
APOLOGIA PRO OPERE MEO

The life span of books on Thomas Aquinas is indeed brief. Catholic colleges which once required 20 credits of Thomism for everybody in 1960 now offer a choice of any 3 to 12 and Aquinas might never appear to the student.

The Thomas who does appear is a truncated beast: only his psychology, or only the theology, only the logic or only the metaphysics. Father Walter Farrell's "Companion to the Summa" was long out of print and his "My Way of Life" tends to raise the hackles of theology departments at religious colleges and eyebrows from chairmen at secular colleges. It is out of sheer despair at finding a one-volume survey of Aquinas which concentrates strictly on his philosophy and yet is readable to the non-philosopher which has driven me to write this little book.

Corrections of content are always welcomed: They can only make this a better book. I can only hope it pleases you and informs your students.

Acknowledgments [1977] are also in order at this point. My thanks to Mr. James Edward Lyons at the University Press of America for his helpful suggestions and direction in the presentation of this book's first edition while it was still in the manuscript stages.

Especial thanks must go to Thomas J. Delendick of the New York Botanical Garden for bringing his taxonomist's eye to the task of proof-reading; to Gail DiLeonardo of New York Hospital/Cornell Medical Center for all of the helpful precision which made the final copy into a presentable child; to the late Harold Zajac; to Deborah Streleck for her reading and criticism; and to Joanne Ryan, Academic Dean, and M. Anne J. O'Laughlin, D.L.Sc., President of my former College, for gracious support in providing the time and money which made the publication of this book possible.

A BRIEF WORD FOR THE SECOND EDITION [1987]

The temptation to pun the title, playing off brevity against the lawyer's lengthy documents must be resisted but the pun is valid: much of the `detachment' of philosophy is advocacy under other guises. Sometimes there is a pre-existing commitment or involvement which makes the philosopher's `objectivity' suspect. As you can see I have already set off in single quotes those words about which specialists disagree.

Nine years ago, I chose to pass over in silence those multiple arguments which give students the impression that philosophers do split hairs for a living. (Of course we split hairs but the technical vocabulary is no worse than physicists discussing quarks which are `strange' or `charming').

My choice to emphasize basics I still consider sound: playing piano or painting in oils (without numbers!) deepen one's appreciation of the fine arts but for many the merest survey may create the desire. That desire is what I wish to stimulate.

Thomas Aquinas worked to bring all truths together so they could function harmoniously, each in its own sphere of expertise. His sanity and balance constitute a high-wire act of the mind which is elaborated in the following pages.

Nine years have created new debts which I herewith discharge in part (`in part' only because I owe everyone and memories are not under conscious control):

The Very Reverend Joseph T. Cahill C.M. and Andrew J. Bartilucci encouraged my stay in the classroom. James Byrne and Arthur Gianelli kept my "hand in" philosophy. Martha L. Mackey and Irene Delaney, who made this readable. Gail DiLeonardo Konecsni, who made this possible.

THE THIRD EDITION 1997: Very Reverend President Donald J Harrington, Provost Tony H. Bonaparte, and Dean Thomas H. Wiser have permitted this bureaucrat the opportunity to continue in the classroom and Philosophy Chairman Arthur Gianelli is overwhelmingly owed for 30 years of kindness and support

Fourth Edition 2000: With the WEBCT publication of edition three `doing the possible' becomes more probable, so my first thanks go to Mary Macedonio and her WEB team at SJU

Information Technology. The players change; the gratitude remains: to the central administration, the liberal arts college, and the philosophy department for their indulgence and Dean Robert Mangione for his positive support of even mere administrators teaching. Daniel Derrett, The Churchills, Steven Jay Gould, and the neurophilosophy and cognitive science philosophy folks have recently provided the stimulus to rethink certain of the chapters that follow. As my daughter has said quoting a catalog Tee shirt: I'm lost in thought.... its unfamiliar territory.

FIFTH EDITION 2012: Professor Paul Gaffney is now Chair of Philosophy, Rev. Donald Harrington CM still presides over my university, and Professor Robert J Mangione continues as Dean of the College of Pharmacy and Health Sciences and all three have continued to permit me to haunt the classroom. John-Luke Konecsni, novelist, has contributed significantly to making this intelligible to those born in the last decade of the last millennium. Margaret and Gail Konecsni have contributed editorial and proof-reading skills which I lack

ABBREVIATIONS FOUND IN FOOTNOTES
[if you don't read footnotes, skip this]

PLATO: quoted by dialogue name followed by STEPHANUS number: Symposium178e: p178, bottom fifth of the page

ARISTOTLE: Meta., vi, 1,982a10: is a standard way of citing Metaphysics book six, chapter one, followed by the standard BEKKER edition referring to page 982 left hand column, line ten.

PL or PG: Migne's edition of the Latin(PL) or Greek (GK) Fathers of the Christian Church

WORKS BY THOMAS AQUINAS:

ST: Summa Theologiae is structured as the record of a debate:

First, a question is posed, then the objections [objecta, ideas thrown-out for consideration] are listed, a quote from some authority (introduced by the phrase sed contra)may be cited for counterbalance; then, comes the reply (sometimes called the body of the article or c. for corpus); finally answers are given to the objections (ad.2 means answer to objection 2).

In other words, you don't read this book but must think through it with Thomas.

Footnotes are quoted as part, question, article, reply. II-II,110,3,2 means that the quote can be found in the second half of part two, the 110th question, article three, response to objection two.

CG: Summa contra Gentes quoted a book 1, 2, 3,or 4, then the chapter number Commentaries on Scriptures (lecturae or expositiones): In Psal, eg, refers to the Commentray on the Psalms quoted by chapter, verse, lecture

COMMENTARIES ON THE WORKS OF ARISTOTLE: In Periherm is the commentary on PERI HERMENEIAS; In Post on the logic text POSTERIOR ANALYTICS; In Physic on PHYSICS; In De Cael from DE CAELO ET MUNDO. DE GENERATIONE ET CORRUPTIONE's commentary is cited as In de Gen; METEOROLOGICA's commentary is In Meteor; DE ANIMA, Aristotle's treatise on life is commented on in In De Anima.In de sensu comments on DE SENSU ET SENSATO. In de Memor.on DE MEMORIA ET REMINISCENTIA and in Meta on Aristotle's METAPHYSICS.

INTRODUCTION: WHERE NO ONE HAS GONE BEFORE?

"I think Hesiod no poor genealogist when he made Iris (the rainbow) the daughter of Thaumas (the wonderer)"
Plato Theaetetus, 155d

PHILOLOSPHY BEGINS IN WONDER ... and comedian Robin Williams is a philosopher. Whether he is playing Peter Pan or standing on a bare stage talking about his newborn child, this man expresses a sense of wonder at the closely-seen marvels of new life and a sense of the absurd about grown-ups. Wonder is special domain of children and those souls who-may-grow-old-but-refuse-to-grow-up in our daily-increasing, global-conformity, peer-pressure world of standardized expectations.

Robin Williams and Jesus of Nazareth--now there's a pair! But "unless you become like these little children, you shall not enter the Kingdom of Heaven" sounds like a blessing or a threat on Man's style of living. [Capital 'M' in Man is shorthand for males and females of the human species, so feel free to substitute the above longhand wherever 'Man' appears in the text.]

Style or manner of living (Not the tired cliché of 'life-styles' as applied any year's politically protected perversions) goes to the heart of being human. Consider:

The inanimate world does not seem to possess a style or a set of mannerisms. Rather, our experience of it is as a lump of something that we manipulate in chemistry lab or woodworking class. The evolutionary folks like I. A. Oparin teach about atoms evolving greater stability as they grow to mega-molecule virus size and make evolution understandable on the level of chemistry--- and it still looks like a lump.

The plant world does not have a style: for the most part, it just sits there and takes it: rain, hail, wind, sunshine all appear to be one and the same to it. But look very closely: even the single-celled creatures [eucaryotes] are light-years beyond rock crystals in its dynamic activities of nutrition, growth, and reproducing its offspring out of a piece of itself. Daniel Derrett [in *Darwin's Dangerous Ideas*] nicely smoothes out the edges of the dramatic difference between living and non-living. He describes a Darwinian mechanism wherein a prokaryote swallows a bacterial forerunner of the cell nucleus to become a real cell, an eukaryote. A biologist's whole life can be devoted to just one aspect of 'cell biology' like microbial genetics or plant cell physiology.

At the level of 'higher' life forms, brute animals do not have a style. [a parenthetical remark to Darwinians: despite Charles Darwin's admonitory note to himself to eschew the use of 'higher' and 'lower', this book uses the term descriptively: animals do more than plants.] Lassie, Flipper, Benji and all the other animals in the Screen Actors Guild are a tribute to the human trainers who have taught these appealing actors to mimic human behavior. Darwin notwithstanding, oaks make acorns which make other oaks; dogs breed dogs, not horses; each species of bird builds nests just like all others birds of the same species; novelty, freedom, new arrangements (also called creativity), are just not there. Where Darwin is right and his critics wrong is on the entire notion of species or essences

Man is the miracle. More beastly than any beast: only humans and rats kill their own kind, but rats have no Hitler, Stalin, Mao, Pol Pot or Ayatollah to exterminate their own by the millions. The only wild animal: no other animal has freedom, is capable of variety, is unpredictable, has made art, literature, music, science, technology, and is capable of being opened to even higher things. ONLY MAN HAS A STYLE AND NEEDS ONE. The rest of the attached is merely a cartoon-sketch of an introduction to the basic style which humans must choose in order to be truly and permanently happy.

The structure of the text may be considered secular Thomism: a rational philosophy which appeals to no evidence higher than reason and ordinary experience for its metaphysics, philosophy of nature, philosophy of Man, and its ethics, whether personal, social, or political. It is open to revelation but does not require it, just as eyesight in brute animals does not require the radical upgrading caused by contact with intellect in Man. Finally "philosophy is not the study of the philosophers but of truth"-- Being able to footnote who said what is only important for tests. Only truth is important for becoming wise

CHAPTER I
IT ALL BEGINS WITH THE SENSES

A list of defined terms usually opens textbooks. In dramatic cases like chemistry consider the International Union of Pharmacists and Chemists which creates unambiguous nomenclature like acetylsalicylic acid [aspirin]. It all seems designed to befuddle students to lose them in woods of words. Since the philosophy of Thomas Aquinas provides a real framework for handling the problems of living, and since Aquinas used no technical vocabulary at all, I shall play fast and loose with traditional Thomistic terminology in an effort to make what follows as alive to the reader as it is in itself. There really is such a thing as a living philosophy, and it is quite different from the philosophies of the merely living.

When most people use the word philosophy, they mean one of two things Either it is a sort of "grin and bear it" *Stoicism* held by the permanently depressed, or they mean the pure pleasure *hedonism* philosophy, which gets a trifle manic around the edges in the world of AIDS.

For those even less intelligent, philosophy becomes a collection of half-baked clichés somewhere between The Simpsons and President Obama. Cliché-collecting goes back to Ancient Romans like Cicero and can be deeply embarrassing when you discover that two or more of your clichés contradict each other. That is one of the constant dangers of *eclecticism*.

Systematic philosophy is nothing less than the attempt to find a framework which is broad enough to encompass all that we have or could experience. It is the skeleton on which all other courses will build their muscles, sinews, and organs.

Actually, the skeleton is a poor example. A skeleton is something hidden which can be reached only after we have removed all the muscle and fat of the other sciences. The problem is the sheer vividness and largeness of the obvious. The "master of those who know," Aristotle, expressed it best: "We are like owls blinded by the noon sun." The topics to be considered are almost too obvious for comment.

"Too obvious" is a dangerous expression. How often have we been surprised by a close friend, who looks like us, talks like us, and then does something which is all out of character, like voting for the loser in the last election. Therefore, let's start with the Tale of the Orange.

Put down this book and go get a piece of fruit. Nutritionists say it is good for you, is usually low calories and we need it for what is to follow.

Got your fruit? Good! DO NOT TOUCH IT! (Not yet, we can get to that later.) For the sake of argument, let's say that it is an orange.

Look at it. What color is it? Orange? Look again: see those little spots of yellow and green and brown? There you see the difference between seeing and observing; the difference is between something we do naturally and something we have to train ourselves to do. But this trained sense of observation is something which comes later.

Big deal! Your orange has spots of other colors. It is at this point that philosophy starts making a pest of itself. The Socratic method of asking annoying questions designed to unsettle our too-easy assumptions earned Socrates the reputation of the gad-fly and resulted in his death as a traitor to civic conformity of ancient Athens. Plato credits Socrates as saying that "the unexamined life is not worth living." History warns us that the examination is not without risks.

How do you know that what you see is what there is? At first glance, that is a dumb question. You know what it is, because that is what you see. Well, how do you know that what you see is what there is? We're not talking about a man that is color-blind. He obviously has problems of his own: a disease or condition. But what about us "normal" people?

Before you rule out the problem of those who are color-blind, how do you know that the color-blind are so exceptional? Let me take a more sophisticated example. If you take a piece of paper soaked in phenolphthalein and stick it on your tongue, it will cause different reactions. For some it will have no taste at all; for others it will have a bitter taste.

This is the type of problem that drove the old Romans to coin the phrase, *"de gustibus non disputandum est."* (Concerning taste, there can be no arguments.) It is an elegant answer: it allows us to make up our own minds or to delegate the job to the *arbiter elegantiarum*, the taste maker, like the entertainment critic, restaurant reviewer, the predigested political columnist, and the art critic, people whose blog tell us what to see and do, what to like and dislike.

This is the preference of the lazy but some still suffer from the ideal once shared by university professors: that educated people should be able to think for themselves. Aquinas makes a statement that *the argument from authority* is the weakest which human reason can use. It is no argument to say, "I believe the moon is made of green cheese because Teacher X of Harvard says so" (Not Professor X; after all, Professor X is played by Patrick Stewart, and his expertise is in other areas). For all of what follows, then, the only guides are our experience and our naked intelligence.

Some organized religions claim a revelation from a personal God to Moses, Mahomet, or the Mormons are a different case. Even if Jesus is "the way, the truth, and the light," a philosopher is still entitled to ask "may I see your credentials?"

(What has St. Thomas Aquinas got to do with this? Thomists are disciples of that great man, because there is much to learn from him. Discipleship is not an argument from authority. Aquinas is simply another participant in the discussion. How else can you use an authority who does not wish to be used as an authority but merely a conveyor of truths? We now return to your original program already in progress)

When you throw people back on their own resources so

abruptly, they usually resort to another excuse. Man is the only animal that makes excuses, or needs to. This time the excuse is more imaginative, however. It is the contention that "you can't be sure about anything." This view, or rather lack of vision, is called *skepticism*. Like a good pre-packaged thought, it comes in three sizes: small, medium and large.

Large-size skepticism is also known as *absolute* skepticism. It asserts that "you cannot be certain of anything." If I am certain that I cannot be absolutely certain about anything, then absolute skepticism defeats itself on its own terms. I can't even be certain about not being certain.

Medium sized skepticism says, "I am reasonably sure that you cannot be certain of anything." Now that is a reasonable opinion. But, like political opinions, it is a matter on which one can disagree with another. So we must trust to the reasonable person to keep acting reasonably. Philosophy has nothing to fear from truly reasoning people. When the 'reasonable' skepticism hides a combination of fear and laziness, when it is held unreasonably, problems ensue. In the case of the reasonable skeptics, we can leave them alone. The facts which follow are convincing enough.

The small-sized skeptic says "You cannot really be sure about most things because it is usually just a difference of words. People use different words to mean the same things, or else they use the same words to mean different things." Anyone familiar with the history of philosophy has good reason for holding this position. Plato is a realist who believes that the only reality is the world of spiritual ideas. Machiavelli is a realist because he doesn't believe in anything except power. Realism doesn't apply to both of them in the same way and at the same time Despite our politically correct non-judgmental times, I would dare to offer the suggestion that maybe Plato or Machiavelli or both are wrong.

There is another small skeptic that can be placated quite easily. This is the character who has trouble with "red" "rouge", and "rojo". A simple distinction can clear up the problem. A red thing is a red thing: the problem of language can usually be handled by recourse to a bilingual dictionary. When we don't have a dictionary there is always sign language.

No, I am not making fun of the twelve years you spent studying proto-Assyrian; I am only trying to *distinguish between words and things*. Words mean whatever most people mean by them; problems of technical vocabulary can be resolved by appeals to technicians or technical dictionaries. Words are like buses, common carriers of the most general denotation (definition). Experience colors our words with the connotations of past experiences; these will differ for different people. (For example, Obama may denote an ex-President. Depending on the reader, it may connote many other things.)

A further distinction between word and name follows easily enough. All *names* are proper names (Declan Finn) and all *words* are less specific.(Your English teacher may have called them common nouns to get this general quality.) They may be expressible in terms of each other, but in normal usage, they are distinct.

Let's go back to your orange. We still have that problem: How do you know it really is there? Before you say, "Don't be silly!" and slam the book shut, let me tell you the story of a very devout Anglican bishop who felt the only way to protect the spiritual world against the dangers of encroaching materialism was to deny that the physical world existed. In fact, it was he, *Bishop George Berkeley*, who posed one of the classical trick questions in the history of philosophy, "Does a tree falling in a deserted forest make a sound?"

Stop and think before you answer that one. (Planting a Webcam is cheating because that is merely a mechanical extension of the human ear and eye. No recorders allowed on the terms of this puzzle)

We could get more scientific and say that there must be sound waves present when that tree falls. That really does not help: all the scientist is saying is that trees always make noise when falling. Berkeley could respond that, "The tree always makes noise when there is someone around to hear it: what is important is that the hearer must be present."

Berkeley's argument anticipates the discovery of the theory of relativity, but the universe seems more stable. Otherwise, we get stuck with some interesting conclusions. If there is no one on your block right now, there is no way you could instantaneously prove your house is still there. If there are no explorers or picture-taking satellite at the North Pole right now, then there is no North Pole: it just pops in and out of existence when somebody is looking at it. Stupid , isn't it?

Never multiply explanations beyond necessity said one of history's most complex over-simplifiers, William of *Ockham*. KISS: keep it simple, stupid. George Berkeley's presentation is too complex to be real.

Intuitio entis, the intuition of being, is the awareness that there is something out there. In infancy "out there" may be kind of murky. (It isn't until the child puts its toe in its mouth and bites that it discovers there is some difference between the toe and the toy.)

It might be impossible for the child to say what it is. (Notice how they call everything in pants "Dada", even Grandma in her pants suit?) Nevertheless, no matter how you qualify it, there is the direct knowledge that something is there. In philosopher's shorthand, *direct knowledge is referred to as intuition,* and *"that vague something" is referred to as being. The intuition of being is the necessary and reasonable, but unprovable, assertion that our senses make contact with reality more or less accurately.*

To unpack the definition a little bit: Berkeley, for all his apparently off-the-walls approach to reality, had latched on to an important point: KNOWLEDGE IS THE UNION OF THE KNOWER AND THE THING KNOWN that therefore there are limits to sense knowledge. That leaves us on the horns of a dilemma: either we can trust our senses, or we cannot. If we decide not to trust our senses, then we must live our lives as catatonics, locked into a corner, unable to trust anything, even the sense endings in our feet which tell us that we are touching the floor. If we rejected our senses and tried to live as though we expected the world to disappear at any moment, we would quickly wind up in a home for the permanently bewildered.

The other alternative is to trust our senses within limits and with reasonable, prudent skepticism: with the awareness that the flu will affect our taste buds, that the swizzle-stick in that half-drunk Black Russian only *looks* bent (if it looks straight, stop drinking), that the lukewarm tap water only feels warm because we've been shoveling snow, and so on.

For a couple of chapters, let us shelve the question, "What is reality"? I do not want to open the question of non-physical realities until the more normal experiences are put into some sort of order. (So, he's going to get back to the orange, at last, right? Right!)

If we concentrate on that poor orange, and give it our full attention, some interesting things show up. We have established that it is orange in color, with flecks of yellow, green, and brown. Touch it! Close your eyes and really touch it. Imagine that you are blind, and all your information about that orange is coming in through your sense of touch. Now, feel it!

If it resembles most oranges it should feel pocked, semi-hard, and slightly cold. *Hot/cold, rough/smooth, hard/soft: these are the stuff of which our tactile abilities are made.* This is the first sensation of the infant newly hatched.

The sound of an orange is only for those who are listening. The soft juicy squish as the sections come apart in your hand comes only if you are listening to the promise of wet liquid to come.

Once in your mouth, two things continue to happen. The touch is still there, consistency, softness, coldness. Aroma and taste are added. Taste is almost disappointing on analysis: physiologists say that *human taste buds only register four effects: sweet, sour, salt, and bitter.*

FOR THE NITPICKERS: ScienceDaily (Feb. 26, 2002) — Humans can recognize five tastes: bitter, salty, sour, sweet and umami. Of the five, however, umami is the most difficult to describe — it's the flavor associated with monosodium glutamate (MSG). Now, researchers have identified a taste receptor that responds to amino acids, including umami, and they hope to develop a more precise description of the molecular events that allow the brain to perceive the five different tastes.

With the discovery of the new receptor, scientists have now identified taste receptors for amino acids, bitter and sweet tastes. Given that many amino acids are essential components of our diet, this work may also aid understanding of how animals, including humans, regulate nutritional intake to achieve a balanced diet. Better understanding of taste receptors may permit scientists in the food industry to formulate new products that have specific tastes.

A research team led by Howard Hughes Medical Institute investigator Charles S. Zuker at the University of California, San Diego, and Nicholas J. P. Ryba of the National Institutes of Health reported the identification of an amino-acid taste receptor in an advanced online publication in Nature on February 25, 2002.

Most of what is classified as taste is the combination of taste and smell. Aroma causes such a complex of reactions in the human being that biologists and physiologists have difficulty categorizing its effects.

Sight, sound, smell, taste, and touch: that's the whole list. Or is it? Not quite! It has size, shape, and weight; here we need another distinction.

"Size, shape and weight are *objective primary qualities* as opposed to color, sound and taste, which are *subjective secondary qualities*" That was the opinion of a commonsensible *John Locke*. Even Berkeley caught Locke on that one. Shape is not objective, just multiply subjective; that is, it is the kind of thing which can be experienced by more than one sense. Shape can be known through sight and touch; distance by sight, sound echoes, touch, even smell (if you are trying to locate the dead thing in the back of the refrigerator).

The distinction needed is between *the things which can be experienced by one sense (special or proper sensibles*, like color to the eye) and those *things which can be known by more than one sense (like shape, weight, and other common sensibles)*.

Let's summarize what we have so far: the intuition of being is our only more-or-less accurate assurance that our senses make contact with reality. The objective characteristics (sensible qualities) of a thing more or less correspond with the subjective sense data which comes in to us through our senses. Our senses each have their own specific functions when it comes to color, odor, taste, touch, and sound and have overlapping ability to learn about things like shape, size, distance, etc.

If we go against the common consensus on the "real" color or taste of an object, probably the most reasonable step which we can take is to have our own apparatus checked out for color-blindness, colds interfering with our sense of taste, neurological impairment with our sense of touch, etc.

Now somebody taking a course in human anatomy should rightly object to the outmoded physiology. There is nothing sacred about the number five. Five senses were adequate for ancient biology, but are not sacred or magic numbers. Medicine in the last few centuries has added to our knowledge of the several senses: *kinesthesis- our sense of motion, equilibrium- our sense of balance, and interorganic (visceral)- internal sensations.* .

These eight senses are also a good example of what was meant earlier about philosophy giving us a framework within which we could fill in the details. Most students of mammalian anatomy could fill you in on the rods and cones of the retina, the organs of the Corti, the olfactory bulbs and taste buds, the nerve endings on the skin, in the muscles and within the body, and the semicircular canals: the physical apparatus by means of which we carry out these activities.

So far we are only considering these *subjective sense data* as they appear to us. Do not surrender the grasp on external reality that the intuition of being gives us, but *the distinctions between the objective and the subjective* can be overdone*: to say that things are distinct is not to imply that they are separable.* To draw too large a barrier between "me" and "everything else" is to overdo alienation.

There are four ways in which the concepts of objective and subjective can be combined.

1. We can try to consider the objective thing in an objective manner, try to consider external objects keeping ourselves out of them as much as possible. You usually know nothing about a science textbook's author except the name

2. We can also consider the objective thing in a subjective manner concentrating more on our reaction to them than on the thing itself. Think of the TV reporter: "Your family has died your house is burned, you're arrested.... How do you feel about that?"

3. Psychologists involved in self-analysis consider the subjective objectively when they study their own reactions, when they go more deeply into themselves in order to understand what

makes them tick, and on the deepest level to understand what subjective states are common to all humans. Psychologists or playwrights, or even the medieval Everyman performing an examination of conscience is involved in this kind of objective examination of their subjective state.

4. Finally, we can consider the subjective subjectively, a mode of behavior that is limited to the more neurotic characters, who, by concentrating on themselves in this unreal way, only make their estrangement from reality worse, what psychologist Carl Jung would call the pathological introvert.

In this and the next chapter, we are going to get inside human beings in an objective manner, to be objective about the human subject, to be objectively subjective.

Well, what does happen when these sense data are reported by our particular senses? Some grade school students and a greater number of high school graduates know about the nervous system of the human body. The electrochemical transmission by the nerves gets the sense data to the brain stem. That is where everything gets "put back together again".

It might appear picayune to say that our ear cannot smell and our eye cannot taste. But it does not require a degree in medicine to see that the orange started out whole in the outside world. Our perception of it is as a whole orange. But our senses have sub-divided it in the process of sensing it. Therefore, there must be, inside our head, an ability to take the data from our outside senses and put it back together again. The medievals called this the "sensa communis".

The *"sensa communis"* is translated as 'the common sense' . It is NOT the same thing as our colloquial "common sense", which attributes good judgment and is rare enough anyway. No, this "sensa communis" is more accurately *a coordinating sense: the physical, chemical ability of the brain to reassemble the data made available by the particular senses.* This ability to combine and distinguish sensations is *what the modern psychologist calls perception.*

Perception involves our ability to handle spatial relationships. Some athletes are born and not made, insofar as these super athletes may have been born with a greater lung capacity. Similarly, extraordinary abilities in the area of perception may also be part of basic anatomy.

Sensation and perception deal with the outside object while it is present to our senses. Both are physical and chemical abilities. They differ only as to the specificity: we perceive with 'our' senses and thus have more data available than any one sense has. Not only do we perceive with our senses, we are able to perceive our senses. Have you ever been so tired that, while walking down a corridor, you were seeing that you were seeing? As in a movie, when you are seeing through the eyes of one of the characters, sometimes we are able to stand behind our own eyeballs and see not only what we are seeing but how we are seeing it. This is the ability that photographers build upon in perceiving a striking photo before they take it. We'll see more on this intellect + perception later

While sensation and perception deal with objects right there in front of us, *imagination and memory are the internal senses which help us to handle things when they are no longer present to our external senses.*

Imagination is the physical, chemical ability of the brain to reproduce the image of an object which is no longer present to our senses. That last sentence is a transliteration of a medieval definition. Notice the transliteration, not translation. The problem is with the word "image" (*imago*). The word is too limited. You can recall the smell, taste, and even sounds associated with an object.

While "image" is a mistake of translation, it is a highly suggestive mistake. Vision is the most powerful of the senses. Reading is limited only in the numbers of words per minute which you can read, but speeding up a lecture on tape without

21

losing intelligibility is more limiting.

In a hierarchy of senses, the most limited would be taste, then touch, smell, hearing and sight. Sciences like embryology and developmental psychology would generate a similar hierarchy but in order of time rather than power. Thus perception is superior to all the external senses, and imagination the strongest power we have yet considered.

Imagination is not an ability limited to human beings. It is an ability shared by lower animals. If you have ever seen a dog or cat make noises or run in its sleep, you have seen the visible signs that it dreams. Sophisticated rapid-eye-motion measuring machines in the laboratory only confirm what common observation testifies: animals dream.

It might be reasonable to object that humans have imagination to an extent which other animals do not have. Such skill in human artists is not an act of imagination, but an act of creativity, explained below.

Imagination is mimetic but not mnemonic: it "remembers" things but in a timeless manner. It wouldn't be hard for you to conjure up the image of a long-stemmed black rose. It would be a trifle harder to remember exactly when it was that you last saw one--if, indeed, you have ever seen one at all. *That distinction, between remembering something and 'remembering when', is the difference between memory and imagination.*

Some psychologists distinguish between long-term and short-term memory. It is a distinction with which most people are familiar. Some students experience short-term amnesia when they walk out of an examination. This blankness comes from last-minute cramming and is an example of that short-term memory which fades after one to three days. Long-term vs. short-term memory is a fascinating area in psychological investigation: I have been told by a neuroscientist that dreams facilitate the passage from short to long term memory Neuroscience also confirms a medieval opinion that the younger you learn, the longer you remember and, further, that you hit your mnemonic peak at age 25.

Memory is the kind of thing one uses when giving testimony in court, while imagination performs the act of day-dreaming. The Unconscious of 20TH Century Psychology is probably housed in imagination and memory. We do not control our dreams and cannot by sheer willpower choose to remember or forget. When memories are fueled by emotions of great force, that energy can only be sublimated (have its energy burned up in the service of some goal which re-directs it) or repressed (have its energy dammed up for later explosion). They are noted here only to show how modern psychology fits within this framework. Some of the psychological notions about character must wait for analyses of habits.

Finally, we get to the most debatable of knowing powers, *the estimative sense, the knowledge portion of instinct.* In animals, there is no problem; you can watch animals that have never seen a natural enemy run away at full speed. There must be some kind of inherent or inherited knowledge within the animal. Even a newborn lamb, kept in protective custody until it is an adult, will run from its first sight of its first wolf. If it didn't have this instinct, it would not get to see its second wolf.

On the question of instincts in man, the specialists disagree. Some schools of psychology and anthropology argue very strongly for the existence of instincts in the naked ape called human. There might be some kind of archetype buried deeply within the collective unconscious of the human race or there might be some other type of mechanism at work. Different schools can even appeal to the simple one-celled planarian swimming in the water. If you teach a planaria to run a water maze, then chop it up and feed it to another planaria that new generation will learn to run the maze in even quicker time. This is a dramatic argument for chemical learning.

Sociologists and different schools of psychology emphasize the acquired knowledge which comes from our experience.

They assert that, if there were any instincts in mankind, they are amazingly weak. Even the "instincts" of self-preservation or mother-love are apparently contradicted by the suicide and the child-abuser.

With such a split of opinion, all that philosophy can do is appeal to the broadest kind of experience. It seems safest to say that, if we do have instincts, then humans overrule them quite easily. If there are instincts, then they get quite easily lost in the maze of other behavior done by the human. By 2010, scientific consensus favored a 70-30 split, favoring heredity over environment in making us basically what we are.

What makes all of this so difficult to analyze is a two-fold complication: one medical, the other philosophical. The physical, direct control over the human brain is the last frontier of scientific research. There are maps of the brain still being made which in more or less accurate detail can locate specific areas of the brain which control certain human mental abilities. I have yet to see any map locating--and proving the location of--the instinct as such.

The more philosophical problem revolves around the difference between the mind and the brain.
If I tell you that the last thing which went through a bad guy's mind was a .45 caliber bullet, there is some poor word choice involved. In ALL of the knowing powers of humans which have been examined so far, there is little or no difficulty in equating these powers of the brain with powers of the human mind. In fact, there would be no problem at all if these were the only powers of the human mind. But there is a remaining power of the mind . . . intellect.

To call us rational or reasoning animals is not quite accurate. The terms need a kind of refinement. In one sense, animals 'think'. Watch a bloodhound do its work. The animal will come to a fork in the road and, if the scent on the first fork is negative, it will proceed down the other road without stopping to check. Or again, the monkey, locked in a room with a banana dangling from the ceiling, will find ways of piling up objects until they allow the animal to climb up and get that banana, if only by accident.

Both animals seem to "reason". Maybe we are not so special? This conclusion every materialist in history preaches. It is too hasty a conclusion. Some insist the bloodhound is not acting logically so much as following a faint scent rather than no scent. Some psychologists say the monkey does not reason but achieves height by random piling of boxes.

Even the so-called ability of animals to use 'tools' fails to distinguish between the monkeys who thrown rocks and stones or pandas who use grass to encourage ants to become their lunch and humans who create permanent tools... the panda does not use a knife or spoon

There is a vast catalogue of human works in all the ages and all the places through which the human animal passed. There is no [subhuman] animal art, music, literature, or anything else which intelligence leaves behind. Ants create complex tunnels and nests, but none holds a degree in engineering... You cannot even find a foreman in an ant farm!

Beavers build exquisite dams, but no one has seen one build a split-level or a ranch model. Some birds can be identified sight unseen by the design of their nests. No animal deviates from the path of its hereditary training, except man. Every animal is exclusively programmed by heredity and immediate stimuli. Man is the only truly wild animal.

But all that we have so far may be a difference in complexity. Is man only a different degree of animal? Or is he a different kind of animal? A lot of scientists and philosophers like to gloss over the differences by speaking about consciousness and ignoring that only humans are reflective, SELF-conscious

There is in the history of thought a stubborn and contrary opinion to the materialist. Plato and Augustine, Descartes and

Leibniz, held that to be human is to be a spirit inside of a body. These are two different realities so unmixable that how they contact each other borders on magic. To be human is to be two different things. This "dualism" is almost as strange as the materialist, but with less scientific justification.

These apparent spiritualists have one important thing going for them, the nature of concepts. Concepts are not physical things. In biological theory, you can touch dreams and memories with an electronic probe in the brain. Even if phantasms, images, and memories are physical, electrical, or chemical would NOT affect our present philosophical considerations. But ideas are peculiar for their very generality.

Ideas, generalizations, concepts: whatever you call them, they are different from all other types of knowledge. Sensations, perceptions, memories, imaginings, and instincts are all particular, all revolve around concrete, particular objects. Call them potential intellect Concepts are general, nonspecific, and are not just summaries of all our past experience.

If the only chairs you experienced were the chairs in the room where you are now reading, you could still get an idea of what a chair is like. Once you had this idea, you could walk into a totally strange room and identify new objects as chairs. The concept of a dog covers all dogs, past, present, and yet to come.

Ideas bridge the gap between what we know and what we do not know. The paradox of this type of knowledge: I cannot teach you anything which you do not already know. On this premise, I cannot teach you anything. To teach you something I have to use terms and ideas which you already know. If I am only pointing out to you what you already know, then I can't be teaching you anything new, can I?

That is the paradox of ideas: because we generate them from our experience,[literally 'pull them out...abstruere...pull out...abstract them] we normally only think of them in terms of the context of our own experiences. If a teacher can expand your horizons, can get you to apply your old ideas to new experiences, then you have been taught something new in terms of something you already knew.

Ideas in themselves are something peculiar. If you analyze any physical thing, you find that it has parts. Anything that has parts eventually falls apart. *Ideas don't have parts: they are simple, discrete insights which are quite separate from all their instances.* The concept of redness is something different from every red object which you have ever seen. This is so for two reasons. If red were merely present in one object, then nothing else could be red; but many things are red; therefore, redness is not the characteristic of just one thing. Second argument: If red were limited to just the objects that you already know, then you could never apply the idea of redness to anything new; but we do recognize new objects as being red or green or blue or whatever; therefore, redness is something different from red objects.

If ideas do not have parts, then they are something simple which cannot fall apart. Since everything which is physical has parts, therefore, ideas in the sense of universals, generalizations, concepts cannot be physical.

Lest that sound too strange, consider the nature of mathematics: you have seen a wide variety of round objects, but you can never have seen a perfect circle, because such things have existed only in the human mind for three thousand years. The perfect circle was a product of the human intellect long before precision technology could draw one perfect enough to fool the naked eye. The intellect has pulled it out of experiences with circular objects. *This drawing-out or abstraction seems to purify the idea, giving it a polish, purity, and clarity which it did not have in the physical world.*

Not only are ideas simple, that is, have no parts, their very generality tells something about the human intellect's range which is infinite in comparison to the other animals. That incomprehensible math course isn't an argument for a limited intellect. Trying to learn too much in too short a period of time

27

is a physical limitation (time) not a mental one.

In finishing off this section, let me sketch a possible mechanism for the intellect's functioning.

Take all the concrete, particular knowing powers we share with animals: sensation, perception, memory, imagination, estimative sense, particular reason. These are the source of all our knowledge, no matter what form it takes. *There is nothing in the intellect that wasn't first in the senses.—except intellect itself* All knowledge begins with sense experience. *All of these knowing powers are potentially capable of becoming something intellectual. In fact, we can refer to the entire list of abilities under one name: the potential intellect.*

Next, have you ever added the same column of numbers three different times and gotten four different answers? Or beaten your head against a language for three or four years, working on just brute memory? Obviously, this is *active* intellectuality, the active struggle on the part of the human being to make sense out of things, to pull meaning out of our physical experiences.

The light dawns: suddenly you find yourself seeing the mistake you've been making in that addition problem. There even comes a point when you begin to think in the language you have studied so long and so hard. For a split second, there is that feeling of relief, understanding, enlightenment, even contentment.

The last two paragraphs describe what could be called the two sides of intellect. *The active intellect draws out of the potential intellect the concept which the passive or possible intellect rests content in understanding.*
Don't slide over that last point too quickly. The passive intellect rests content in understanding the concept. In a society which equates hectic with happy, it is worth noting that we can be occasionally made content by just knowing. We might not be able to do anything with that knowledge, but the knowledge in

and of itself seems to carry a satisfaction for the anxieties which come from not-knowing. Even to know the name of an incurable disease is better than not knowing why you're ill.

Once again: all physical things are particular, limited, specific things. The impression they make on our mind is as discrete individual things and neurology lays claim in principle to one day isolating these discrete imagos. To this point we have nothing more than a collection. Light, the light of the intellect, illuminates and dematerializes the collected experiences. Plato (centuries before Christ), Augustine (fifteen centuries ago), and today's cartoon strips all use the notion of illumination or the light bulb going on in an effort to make our materialist vocabulary express this personal, internal, act.

Each person must generate his own ideas. We pull our shared ideas out of shared experiences--that is why only your most intimate or unique experiences might be most difficult to communicate to another. *This is the balance: our ideas are ours--subjective--but are based on mutually accessible outside experience and a common knowing mechanism in all humans and therefore our ideas share in objective common truths.*

Intelligence, if we will only use it, is able to get more out of our senses than nature has given them to begin with. We can augment our senses in two ways, by extension and by intensification. We augment our senses by *extension* when the intellect generates new devices which can extend, improve, or enlarge the natural abilities of our senses. Telescopes, microscopes, and eyeglasses extend our sight as cellphones, sound amplifiers, and hearing aids extend our hearing.

Alternatively, we can improve our senses by simply paying attention to them. This *concentrated attention/intensification is the difference between observing and merely seeing, listening and merely hearing, differentiating fragrances and merely breathing, feeling and merely touching.*

An example might help. Whether you read the following

paragraph or have someone else read it to you, it should make the same point, whether of seeing/observing or hearing/listening. If you read it to yourself, READ IT ONLY ONCE. Do Not Go Back and Reread!

You are the captain of a Boeing 747 going from New York to Cuba. The most distinguished passenger in first class is Jack the Ripper, seeking asylum under the Castro regime. The most noticeable passenger in second class is a little old lady in tennis shoes, wearing a Kermit-for-President pin in her lapel, and carrying a plumber's wrench sticking out of her handbag. The stewardess is Lady Gaga playing Corporal Klinger in drag.
Question: What color are the pilot's eyes? You should know.

When it comes to imagination, the intellect can not only augment it, but also can make it fantastically creative. Yes, you can train creativity. *Creativity can be defined as the power of the intellect to take apart and reassemble into new arrangements the images stored in the imagination.*

Because creativity depends upon imagination, there will be some people who are naturally more imaginative than others. But because creativity is more than just natural powers and abilities, it can also be taught. Just like the over-achiever who outperforms his capacity because determination overcompensates for nature, so too, the most creative people may have less creativity by nature but more by training.

One of the first problems in training creativity is the roadblocks which are already inside us. "I'm not creative," is the usual whine. The irony of that statement is that it is rarely true.

Most people are immensely creative, but not in what they narrowly consider to be the creative arts. One can be a creative driver--if the police don't catch you at it. "Creative" has appeared in letters of reference meaning 'liar' Some people have a knack for arrangement and order, others for free and easy chaos: in both cases it requires some creativity to arrive at that type of environment.

Probably the greatest example of what I mean is a classmate of mine who took her degree in Pharmacy back in 'the day'. Her great creative ability was to recognize what condition people were in, and then find just the right word or tone to set them at ease. A small thing, maybe, but when was the last time you knew someone with sufficient imagination to be unfailingly tactful? Everybody is creative in certain areas: it's just a matter of finding out the specific area for an individual to master.

Personal roadblocks are not the only ones to developing a sense of creativity. Culture also plays a role. "We've always done things that way." That is the standard response from people who are afraid of change, who quite often have forgotten the original reason for doing things "that way" in the first place. What is even more frightening is the way that many people internalize that way of looking at things. They cannot see the woods for the trees because they only know one way to look at the trees: the way in which they were taught.

"But I'm different!" Really? Consider the following problems and you will see just how mechanical education has made you.

Problem 1. A man has a window above his workbench in the basement. The window is two feet high and two feet wide. It does not let in enough light. So he enlarges the area of the window. The window is now twice as large and lets in twice as much light. But it is still only two feet high and two feet wide. How can this be? (N.B. This is a two dimensional problem)

Problem 2: Connect the dots below with four straight lines. BUT NEVER REMOVE YOUR PENCIL FROM THE PAPER ONCE YOU START.(For those of you who know this one: do it in less than four continuous straight lines.)

     .   .   .

     .   .   .

     .   .   .

Problem 3. You are a secret agent assigned to break into an attaché case, photograph a paper, and escape without the enemy even knowing that you opened the case. The attaché case has a combination lock consisting not of three numbers, but of three letters of the alphabet. The only clues you have are that the letters must be in strict alphabetical order, in sequence, like ABC, BCD, etc. The only further clue is that the man setting up the combination is a complete fanatic about the Sherlock Holmes stories.

Problem 4. The last problem is only for the creatively intelligent among you: in what order are these numbers, 0, 2, 3, 6, 7, 1, 9, 4, 5, 8?

ALL THE ANSWERS ARE AT THE END OF THE CHAPTER, BUT before you go scurrying off to cheat, consider this.

To teach someone creativity requires more than just removing cultural roadblocks. (Pray to God, She will help us!) It also involves *Preparation Time, Incubation, Enlightenment, and Execution*

Preparation Time is a variable dependent upon the material involved. There are mathematical geniuses who needed very little formal training before their preparation was so complete that they discovered more than other mathematicians had ever learned. They peak before 25. Lawyers, on the other hand, must master so much law that they only hit their professional prime at 45-55 years old. Preparation to become an innovative and imaginative truck driver is not quite as long as the preparation time needed to become an innovative and imaginative Supreme Court Justice.

Incubation is what is happening when it seems that nothing is happening. You've read this silly book for four hours on end and have no idea what the author is talking about. Time for a break. In fact, taking a break is precisely the best thing to do.

The conscious circuits are overloaded; you are going to blow a mental fuse. Taking a break may be the best thing possible.

The stories of people coming up with brilliant ideas on the golf course, or while shaving, or while sleeping, are experiences called Enlightenment. The only problem with those stories is that they neglect the first two stages. Ideas just don't happen. A primitive tribesman is not going to design a new jet engine for a supersonic airplane. Experience (Preparation) and Incubation have been going on all the time.

This includes those happy accidents in the history of science. As Pasteur said, "Fortune favors the prepared mind." Millions of people have seen bread turn moldy down through the ages. It took a biologist like Alexander Fleming to become curious about this mold. It took a trained mind to get penicillin from moldy bread. It is the same with you. You have the ability to see and understand things which those younger or more stupid cannot. Hence, the discoveries we make each passing year build upon our preparation in order to see them. As comedian Nipsy Russell put it:

Seek knowledge
Go to College
Persevere until you are through
If they can make Penicillin
Out of moldy bread
They sure can make something out of you. ☺

Execution time is the rock against which some of the best ideas crash. Sexploitation paperbacks can be written by a baboon in about three days: Gone With The Wind took rather longer. It can take hours for a ten year old to render a game of Pong on his home laptop, but take hundreds of programs years to put out a single *Halo* game.

Thomas Alva Edison once said that, "Inventing is 1% inspiration and 99% perspiration." To get an idea and to hammer it into shape requires executive skills. If education is supposed

33

to do anything, it must be this: to give you the background preparation time within which to acquire a vast storehouse of ideas for you to mix and match and to give you the skills with which to execute plans based upon those ideas when indeed you do get them. Learn everything for you never know what will prove useful

Comment overheard in the school cafeteria, female student presumably referring to her boyfriend: "He has the kind of memory that remembers everything it sees. You know, wha'cha call a pornographic memory." No, that isn't what you call it (or maybe I missed the point?) In any event, memory is much like imagination in that it can be developed. There are mnemonists with total recall, but these are few and are among the freaks of nature. (I have been told that there are people with a certain type of retardation who can tell you what day of the week any event occurred; idiot savants with great mechanical abilities, but no intelligence.)

In the case of people who cannot remember all of the things they would like to, there are now whole slews of books on the market which offer to improve your memory . . . but the trick is simple.

Get as many hooks into the object as possible. I know one gentleman who remembers things in terms of the book he was reading at the time. He solemnly assures me that he recalls seeing the nomination of Eisenhower at the 1952 Republican Convention on TV because he was reading a Hopalong Cassidy comic book at the time (he was 5 1/2). One of the best reasons for believing this story is that most of us know even sillier ones.

There are people who connect names with faces by means of silly metaphors. One man tries to connect a stranger's face with the nearest looking actor or actress. Others make up weird and wonderful images to graphically reinforce the names. (How can any hungry person forget those two Supreme Court Justices, Burger or Frankfurter?)

Then there are people who play geometrical number games with phone numbers. The person who tries to remember phone numbers according to their spatial location to each other on the dial, needless to say, has trouble when handed a push button phone.

Get as many hooks into the object as possible. With concentration and practical intelligence, the ability to remember can be doubled. Intelligence, bringing imagination into play can reinforce memory just as reinforcing imagination gives us creativity.

Answers to the puzzles: I lied

CHAPTER II
MOTION, EMOTION, AND MOTIVATION

Have you ever known people who are great at theory but are incapable of action? Or somebody who knows everything but is capable of doing nothing? Or again, one who is so extremely fair-minded in seeing all sides of the question, and, therefore, comes to no personal conclusion?

In human terms knowledge is not enough. With the exception of the agent intellect forcing us to generate our own ideas, *knowledge is relatively passive*, what we require at this point is a more active element. The word "consciousness" appeared once in the last chapter not only because it also seems to be passive but also because it does not allow the precise definition of intellect, memory, etc.

If knowledge, or cognition-in-general, is some kind of stimulus working on us, *orexis* (or less precisely emotions) are our response to those stimuli. The medievals used to call orexis *"appetite"*. If I fall into the professional habit of using the word "orexis" it is because the word "appetite" has changed meaning for the average person. In fact, it is so usually reserved for food, drink, and sex, that any other use would be considered metaphoric. At least the technical "orexis" should avoid the misconstructions we get from hasty reading. [Of course an anorexic is someone with no appetite or an appetite suppressant but let's not go there]

Emotions are the things that get us moving, the motive or *motivation* for our actions. Different types of knowledge provide different kinds of stimuli for different responses. To make things simpler, let us follow the order of knowledge used in the previous chapter.

Sensation, perception, and imagination have the same sensual effects on our glands and can be considered the *same type of stimuli*. Break it down one at a time. What does the sight your lover do to your nervous system? Or the sound of an old song that was your song for someone special? Would perfume makers be in business if there weren't something attracting about their smell? [Google pheromones some time] Remember the dieter who would sell his soul for the taste of ice-cream, or the delicious shivers from the touch of a loved one.

Put all of these senses together in perception and the affect is even stronger. Remove the desired object from sight and the daydreams of imagination continue the feeling even in absentia. (Provided that the absence is not too prolonged: "Absence makes the heart go wander")
It may be cold-blooded to analyze the effects of these delights, but they are an important part of our life. In fact, for some people that is the only part of life which interests them.

These fantastic sensual stimuli which are listed above come under the heading of the *concupiscible appetites*, otherwise known as the *sensual orexis*, the broad category of *sensual motivation* and motivations. (All that technical terminology just says we do certain things because they are pleasant! But at least philosophers are no worse than the sociologists who talk of pleasure as short-term gratification, or psychologists who call these emotions libidinous.)

These "positive" emotions can be subdivided according to time:
Love is a positive attraction for pleasurable good;
Desire is love for a future good not yet possessed;
Joy (satiety) is rests content in possession of the good which we desired.
That is a highly condensed approach that deserves elaboration.

Please do not be thrown by the word love. It is not intended to lump Romeo and Juliet into some cold definition. Put the definition back into its context. Sensation, perception, and imagination are possessed by animals; therefore, we might expect animals to express desire, joy, and love. Any animal lover will testify that they do indeed express these emotions.

Even in the lowest animals, the one-celled variety, a few tests with a microscope will show that even on this level, there are reactions. Biologists will call them positive tropisms: full-fledged emotions they might not be, but they are close enough. Attraction and repulsion range over the universe from electrons to atoms to animals. Why should we expect to be exempt?

Love, desire, and joy are not the only reactions which our senses can inspire. Think for a moment about an anchovy pizza covered with hot-fudge sauce, the smell of rotting food, the feel of something cold and slimy or . . . well, that is more than enough. You get the general idea.

The reaction which most people would have to the last paragraph could be summarized in three words: hate, aversion, and sorrow.

Hate is the negative reaction to something which you view as evil;

Aversion is the turning-away from some easily-avoided thing which you view as an evil in the near future;

Sorrow is being stuck in possession of a sensual evil

(Pain is a sorrow localized in a particular organ).

The definitions, despite their ponderous verbosity, reflect the truth of the matter. Hatred is not too strong a word to describe the reaction to some of these objects. Aversion adequately describes the little kids' (and some big kids') reaction to creamed spinach or some other food, and sorrow is just about what the kid is feeling when made to eat the undesired edible.

Two more points are needed in order to appreciate the impact of these sensual movers and shakers of our frame.

First, you may have noticed use of quotation marks for the word `positive' when love, joy and desire were considered. They are truly appreciated by our society, possibly too much so: the human being seems to have difficulty keeping more than one object under consideration at the same time. Therefore, the `positive' emotions have been so exaggerated in our sensual culture that the good done by the `negative' forces of hate, aversion, and sorrow has been overlooked.

A teacher who didn't hate ignorance, a doctor who didn't hate disease, a lawyer who didn't hate injustice, would be worth nothing. What objects are *worth* loving or hating will be considered later. The present emphasis is on the subjective reactions which certain objects arouse in us. We can consider the outside world when we finish our tour of the inner world where we live. We can change externals but the basic internal equipment, by which we handle everything else, we must learn to properly use.

Second, there is a great difference between joy and sorrow, and pleasure and pain. Pleasure and pain are capable of localization, as in the warm pleasant feeling in your stomach after an exceptionally good meal, or in the toothache which is driving you crazy with pain. Joy and sorrow seem to be more in terms of the overall organism than any localized expression in a specific organ of the human body.

The world of the sensual is relatively easy to cope with. Under statistically normal circumstances we have little difficulty finding relief for our hunger, thirst, etc. Only under the irregular circumstances of, say long-distance driving, do we sometimes realize the positive joy of finding a Washroom; after a long fast, we really appreciate the taste of things.

If it is easy to get a snack or a cup of coffee, it is not so easy to get a college degree or a starting salary of $120,000 per year. [Actual starting salaries for pharmacists, physician assistants, or cyberneticists] The general characteristics of a person able to do such things might include the following: a good memory for names, faces, figures, facts; an ability to estimate people, good instincts; and an ability for quick and accurate problem solving on a here-and-now basis.

The intelligent reader is already aware that the last paragraph loads the dice in anticipation of the next topic: *the*

39

emotions which help to handle difficulty. These are the irascible appetites, or the utility motivators. In other words, when we do something not because it is necessarily pleasant, but because, for one reason or another, it is useful. It is involved in those acts where we value something not for itself but for its ability to get us something else. (E.g. we do some jobs for money, we want money to spend on things we enjoy, house, family, travel— something we want in itself. We many not love Gen Chem but it is a means to being a doctor)

The stimuli, the types of cognition which pump up these emotions, are memory, estimative sense and/or particular reason. Consider the office worker who remembers that the Christmas season is the time for office firings--the company prefers to fire certain people rather than give them a Christmas bonus. Or the student who has not studied for a particular examination but is convinced that she can read the teacher like a book, and therefore has no worries about the exam--the test is returned with an F on it. Or, finally, consider the case of the driver on Interstate 80, who sees another car jump the road divider and come straight at him at 75 miles an hour.

To balance the ledger, the difficult can also be the most satisfying. How will that clerk feel if he gets a special merit raise in addition to a Christmas bonus? Or the student who successfully cons the professor into raising her grade? Or the motorist who, with the speed and reflexes of a James Bond, swings his car out of the way of the oncoming juggernaut without so much as a scratch?

The emotions which I have been trying to engender in your nervous system are these same utility motivations or irascible appetites. To name them: Hope/fear, Daring/despair, and Anger.

Hope is the irascible appetite, utility motivator, which helps us to some hard-to-attain good which we might not be able to get. The element of difficulty is seen in our language: we might like a cigarette, but not in the same way as a good-paying job. We might desire a good meal, but unless we are eating at a hospital, prison, or dormitory, usually it is not so difficult a thing to get as to be an object of our hopes.

The phrase 'which we might not get' introduces an element of doubt which is essential to understanding all of these emotions. If at the start of a college course you were certain that you would receive an A+, then there is very little left to hope for, or to work for. Similarly, you do not hope for anything in the past: the past is fixed and final, and hoping will not change a single detail, for better or worse.

Fear is the irascible appetite which helps us to avoid some hard-to-avoid evil which we might not be able to avoid. Again, the real difference between, for example, fear and aversion, can be seen in the folk wisdom of language. We might have an aversion to creamed spinach, but really fear death, disfiguration, or dismemberment; be averse to cigar smoke, but fear being crippled. The very strength of our emotions is our help in facing the very strength of the difficulty.

You would have to escalate the situation to fully see and appreciate the pair of daring/despair. Let us take the last three seconds before that car hits yours. *Daring is the irascible appetite, the utility motivation, which drives us to take urgent (and, yes, daring) action in order to secure some imminent but very difficult good in the very near future.* In the days of the Three Musketeers, it was a soldiers' truism that "He who would save his life must lose it"; an outnumbered soldier who did not fight as though he were unafraid of death might very well soon be dead. The politician, fireman, businessman who wasn't willing to risk fame/life/fortune might well lose it anyway.

So there you are, doing automotive acrobatics with your car, all in a split second, none of which you would be able to do under normal circumstances. (Never thought you could move so fast, did you?) While all this is going on, what is going through the mind of your passenger?

Your passenger is probably bracing for the worst in the firm conviction that there is no way out of this mess. *Despair is the utility appetite which makes us resigned to a hard-to-avoid evil whose seeming inevitability in the near future is almost certain.* Since there seems to be no way out of it, you might as well prepare yourself for the worst. To put it in the context of the automobile accident, consider the words of one father handing over his car keys to his child for the first time, "If you drive 10,000 miles a year, the chances are one in three that you will have an accident. Don't worry about it; these things are bound to happen."

If you have followed the discussion so far, you will notice that all of the irascible appetites are paired off. You cannot have 100% hope, because there is no sense in hoping for a sure thing. You likewise cannot be 100% afraid, or else you just resign yourself to the sorrow to come. After this type of analysis, what sense are we to make out of Anger, the fifth item on the list, the only one without an opposite?

Not caring, being apathetic, having no feelings, feeling the force of no emotion, is not an emotion, but the absence of emotions. Apathy is not the opposite of anger, but the absence of emotion altogether.

People get angry because they care. Anger is the only two-pronged emotion which contains its own opposite inside of itself. To put it a bit more formally, *Anger is the utility orexis which seeks to secure some hard-to-attain good by attacking a difficult evil which stands between us and desired good.* In short, if you didn't care, you wouldn't get angry in the first place.

Since all of this stuff is such heavy going, let's go back a little bit and flesh out the details of this side of our emotional life with a few of the insights which philosophers gathered long before psychology existed.

Fear comes in so many forms, it is difficult to know where to begin. There are dictionaries of fears and phobias; it seems that there is nothing in the world which people do not or cannot fear. In fact, *anxiety can be defined as a vague and formless fear which has no specific object*, the kind of discomfort edginess where something is bothering you but you just can't put your finger on it. Sometimes it is just `nerves' in the sense that we are tired or exhausted and haven't the sense to slow down or rest. Sleep knits up all our cares; slowing down enough so that your frayed nervous system can re-knit that bulletproof vest of normal mental health.

Other fears have specific objects or phobias: there are people afraid of open spaces or closed spaces, high places or low places, cats, dogs, or a million other things. Among the emotions we feel, most people would not normally consider *admiration as a form of fear*. Think back for a minute to that fantastic teacher you had in grammar school. The paragon of all virtues, someone you wanted to be like when you grow up, who could do no wrong. In that sense admiration is really a temporary fear which caused you to suspend judgment about them because they were so overwhelming. Maybe one of the most unusual experiences we can have is to go back to the old school and wonder what we ever saw in that person.

Of course, there are some people who never get over their admiration for another; they permanently make themselves stupid on the topic of that person; in fact, that is precisely what the medievals called it, *stupefaction*. There are people who just will not listen to anything critical of their favorite, be it someone they know personally or some actor or politician. On that topic, they are permanently blank.

As I said earlier about hate, aversion, and sorrow, there really are no such things as negative emotions. The negatives are generated by excesses or defects in our emotional life. Aristotle's notion that all vices are the unbalancing effect of `too much, or too little' appeals to a norm of the perfect human. This notion is deeper than mere `inappropriate affect', a psycho-social norm of adjustment. Both notions will be applied extensively in the last half of the present work.

The person who keeps up hope and is able to keep up the

43

spirits of others is a subject of admiration. Even the swashbuckler of exquisite daring excites us as a desirable type of person to be. But the fearful are `neurotic', the despairing are `losers', and those who get angry are `boorish, uncivilized, or dangerous' in common estimation.

And there, dear reader, you see the reason for emphasizing the free play of the intellect or the techniques of creativity in the previous chapter. We are very much the prisoners of our culture, the programming of our local environment. It might require an exercise of the imagination to see the good contained in these negative emotions, but it is well worth the effort.

Fears can be an object of fun as seen through history: only a few hundred years ago tomatoes were thought to be poisonous! Fears may be exaggerated, silly, sick, or even pitiful, but can you imagine a person totally without fear? I do not mean a courageous hero: someone once said that a hero has fears, but he runs them, they do not run him. No, the person totally without fear is either the psychopath of the clinical psychologists or the sociopath of the sociologists or just too stupid to appreciate the danger of the situation. Despair, while not the object of fun that great comics like Charlie Chaplin make it, usually makes someone a "failure" in popular opinion. Aren't there times and circumstances when the sanest thing to do is give up? The whole world is full of people who are in their second choice occupation because the first was closed to them for some reason or another. A wholesome and healthy recognition of one's own limits is not sick, but sane. As Dirty Harry Callaghan once said "A Man's gotta known his limitations."

(It might be advisable to make a distinction between despair and depression at this point. At first glance, there seems to be only a time distinction between the philosopher's despair and the psychologist's depression. Depression is a long-term despair, well, almost. Depression has only one symptom: anhedonia, the inability to take pleasure in what you once enjoyed. These `black moods', which Lincoln, Churchill, and others experienced frequently and for long periods of time, confer a strength and stability which allows the depressed to continue functioning under the most highly stressful conditions. Hence, even depression has much that is good in it . . . provided, of course you admit the existence of other good things beyond the merely pleasurable.

On the other hand, Ernest Becker is probably correct when he describes depression as a state where everything appears urgent and useless/meaningless at the same time. His suggestion that depression and neurosis are stupid blunders caused by our inability to think our way out of our habits gives new meaning to an upcoming chapter on prudence). Figure out for yourself why I might disagree with the prescription for antidepressants and anxiolytics for everything and anything and anybody--- especially grade school children. Or medicalizing boredom by calling it ADHD.

Anger, first controlled and later explosive, is the material of so many dramas it is almost a cliché: the long suffering individual who tolerates a variety of evils and finally retaliates by explosively wiping out all malefactors to the cheers of the audience. The audience might well be cheering the successes of justice rather than mere violence; anger might only be applauded when the good it seeks to achieve is one which we share.

Note the distinction between anger and violence. Violence is a term used to mean the use of force in the outside world.

You wouldn't like me when I'm angry. observes Bruce Banner before it becomes *Hulk Smash!*

Even the saints of different religions who did violence to their own bodies were using force in an objective, visible act against a body which they were treating as an object by their fasts, sleeplessness, and mortifications. In this chapter, we are not treating violence, but only anger, the emotional reaction inside of us. Anger causes certain internal reactions, like heightened blood pressure, increase of blood supply to the feet and fists (the 'fight or flee' syndrome), and tightening of the muscles of the body. None of these symptoms might be visible externally. In fact, the most dangerous anger might be that

45

which transcends fire and is more like ice.

Anger, the most attacked emotion in our society, is probably the most slandered. In itself, anger is a good thing, capable of securing for us some difficult good which is hard to get and which in the process disposes of that intervening evil. ["I hate my life, my poverty, my working conditions, my neighbors so much that I'm going to graduate get a good job, a beautiful spouse, and a large pile of money" and I'm going to put up with all the #$%^ that stands between me and getting what I want"] The conditions under which the use of anger might be right or wrong are not at issue here; later, when we can get some criteria of right and wrong, the expression of anger can be judged.

To summarily state the reasons for this prolonged defense of anger: we should not be willing to write off one of our basic parts as evil, just because a large segment of the society thinks it evil. Nature does not do things without a reason. Even without knowing that reason, the fact is that we do not have much choice in the matter: anger is built into us. Whether we choose to act like stoics and kill our emotions; like Christians who absorb evil rather than pass it on to others; like masochists who absorb evil to enjoy suffering; or like sadists and increase evil because we like others' suffering; these are choices which we can make. Whether we convert the anger into ulcers or violence, kill it with transcendental meditation or sedate it out of existence . . . no matter what we do with it, the anger remains a part of us.

Gathering together what has been so far collected in this and the previous chapter, one can design a flow-chart which lists all of the pathways of our cognitive and affective life.

One of the major problems with this kind of chart is that it gives the optical illusion of static things.

First, these are not things: we are not talking about different organs or glands or loci in the brain; the primary emphasis is on the activities which these abilities or powers perform.

Second, intellect has been omitted from the discussion in this chapter and nothing has been said about will. These omissions are for the sake of clarity: the abilities considered so far show the relationship of our emotional lives to that of the animals. It can be most disconcerting to recognize that all the human emotions are not something distinctly human but shared by all the animal world.

This emotional life can be stated most simply: the beginning and the end of all things is love. We see something, and we find ourselves loving it, desiring it, and we will not rest content until we enjoy the possession of it. The IT doesn't matter for the moment: it can be a person or a thing; what matters is that it is the object of our affections.

Let's say it turns out to be more difficult to get than we thought at first. The new challenge quickens the blood; if it is something which is hard to get but can be gotten quickly, then daring might come into play. Frustration might increase our anger until we are willing to take drastic measures to get it. If we succeed, we can enjoy it.

The mechanism also works if we fail. Recognizing the possibilities of failure, our fears might increase and cause us to redouble our efforts. Finally, despair forces us to one last desperate gamble, we blow our stack in anger and blow the whole thing. We wind up unhappy, sorrowful, stuck with an evil: the loss of the thing we wanted. *The arc of the emotions begins with love and ends with love possessed or lost*

Our fears are the mouse seeing a cat; our despair is little different from that of a jungle beast capitulating before a stronger one in order to stay alive; our anger differs little from that of a cornered rat.

It is at this point that the anthropologist can make his most crucial mistake. There is a lot of truth in the above descriptions and analyses. But the simple clarity of seeing humans as just another ape is a clear truth which obscures the whole truth.

Intellect and Will are missing, and they are the "little difference" that makes such a big difference.

Will can be defined as the intellectual orexis, a simple definition that tells us nothing unless we stop to reflect upon the type of knowledge which causes the orexis. Man is the only animal with the sheer desire to know. Man is the only animal with an unlimited capacity to know. Time is a physical limit not an intellectual one

If our intellect can produce new things in conjunction with the imagination, then its corresponding motivation must be immense. If the Intellect is infinite, then so must be our Will. If there is no limit on our capacity to know, then there is no limit on our capacity to want.

And there you have the human dilemma: there are a million things we can have and a million things we can not have. The mind outruns the body. Because of the limited powers of the human body, the unlimited powers of the mind and `heart' are only more poignant.

Humans have a natural tendency to be absolutists: true believers, in Eric Hoffer's phrase, like the religious fanatic, the Nazi, the Communist, the Utopian are all expressions of this tendency. Even the cynic testifies to this trait in us: there would be no disillusioned idealists if there were not first an ideal.

To seek something which will satisfy the human mind and heart cannot be done just inside the human alone. The time has come to look at the outside world and see if there is anything which is capable of making us absolutely happy as we want to be. If there is not, then we had better make plans to settle for something other than happiness.

Even we must give up the search for happiness, the basic nature of the human being has been considered in its `given' form. The rest of reality must be the next item on our agenda, before we can explore human acts, interactions, and those habits which constitute our `second' nature.

CHAPTER III
THERE IS A WHOLE WORLD OUT THERE
(Matter, Form, and Soul)

In self-defense, we should start with all of the things that we have not the paper mills or lifetimes to investigate: that is just about everything in the outside world. George Washington Carver spent his entire life studying the peanut. The physicist spends his life exploring the subatomic zoo contained in just one atom. The Life and Works of Thomas More or Thomas Aquinas absorbed the lives of many scholars from the deaths of these men until the present. All that can be done in one short chapter is consider the different types of things which exist. If one of them tickles your fancy, you can spend the rest of your life filling in the details.

In the outside world, there are three types of things: the inanimate, the animate, and the intelligent. The sciences which study these three spheres are so multiple as to boggle the mind, with subspecialties increasing by the month.

The `simplest' of the three (and that not-so-simple) is the inanimate world. Ancient philosophy has given us two large tools to help us analyze the inanimate world, tools which can even be used in all other areas. These two tools are Aristotle's doctrine of the four causes and his theory of form and matter.

The theory of form and matter came about as the result of what might be called today a paper experiment (as opposed to a laboratory experiment). Begin with the following problems: what makes a statue of Napoleon a statue of Napoleon?

The question is not as simple as it looks. Consider the subsidiary questions: would it be a statue of Napoleon if it were made of white plaster? If it were made out of wood? Clay? Silly putty? Wet lasagna?

In the face of these questions, it seems that the defining characteristic of an object is its shape. It would be a statue of

Napoleon because it looks like Napoleon. But now flip the question over: could you have a statue of Napoleon made out of nothing? That question is just silly, isn't it? The statue has to be made out of something, but the raw materials are less important than the shape of the finished product.

There you have the definition of the theory of hylomorphism. It states that all physical objects are made out of the union of form (shape) and raw materials (matter), and that you cannot have the one without the other. The statue can't exist without both taken together.

You can multiply simple problems like this forever. The shape of a bow-knot remains whether you tie it with string, ribbon, wire, or cooked spaghetti, but you must tie it with something.

For all its apparent simplicity, this analysis has several traps for the unwary. Our language has changed since Aristotle was first translated into English. (His words were hyle and morphe) How often do we throw away something as a mere formality and want to get down to more important matters? Look a little more closely at any meeting for a moment and you will see the importance of this separation of form and matter.

Robert's Rules of Order provide the format (form-at) in which people can handle their business; communicate their information (in-form-ation) with a minimum of fuss and bother. Once you dispose of these rules, you cease to have a formal (form-al) meeting, and have now gone into a free-form discussion. In short, once you take away the rules which give form to the meeting, you have changed the type of meeting that it really is. In fact, once you abandon the rules you no longer have a meeting, but just a discussion group. It is not even free-form, just amorphous, shapeless… a bull session.

The notion of form and matter, called hylomorphism, is a most powerful tool for analyzing anything. In fact, the different sciences are different because they can consider the same object as their raw material and can come up with different results because they are using different forms of analysis.

The sciences which study human beings illustrate the point. The physicist studies the human body from the formal viewpoint of treating it as any other piece of matter. Therefore, among his other conclusions, he can tell you that your suicidal body will fall from the Empire State Building at the accelerating velocity of 32 feet/second2, minus air resistance.

The biologist studies the human body from the formal viewpoint of any living thing and can tell you what kinds of things will stop you from living. The cardiologist might recognize your heart on the operating table, but not be able to recognize you at all, taken as a whole.

The English Prof. studies you as you are expressed by your written leavings, the economist studies you from the trail of your money expenditures, and so on, down through the entire spectrum of the different scientiae (a Latin expression meaning something broader than just the physical or social sciences).

Homo faber, homo oeconomicus, homo erectus, homo sapiens, homo esteticus, homo socialis, even homo religiosus, are definitions of man but man under the aspect of tools or money, thought or art, society or religion. How rich and varied are the names of man and his artifacts! Or as Professor Kingsfield used to say on the TV show The Paper Chase, "You teach yourselves the law, I teach you how to think like lawyers": all of your majors are nothing more than the four year attempt to get you to think like a pharmacist, accountant, historian, and so on

In fact, hylomorphism gives us the ability to analyze anything. Two history books containing the same facts about the same country and time period may be as different as night and day because the form in which the authors express and emphasize them gives each of the facts a totally different meaning. Matter is the mask; lumps of matter make things to be individual. This lump of plastic and that lump of plastic are all that distinguishes two copies of the same CD. Only by separating (abstracting) form, withdrawing it from particular matter, can we call these "the same" record.

To analyze everything in this broad philosophical fashion yields some interesting insights. When the facts seem out of order with other things we know (technically known as a congruence theory of truth), we might have to broaden our frame, come up with a larger form in which to fit all of the details. This is one of the reasons philosophy is valuable: it is the largest frame which the unaided human mind can generate in order to order and organize all of our experiences. For this reason, many have considered philosophy the queen of the sciences of mankind   (I exclude theology for the moment because it claims to be a science of God, who is beyond our scope at the moment).

Form and matter are not something static as much as something relative.   Likewise, form and matter can be distinguished but not physically separated. Separate a form from a statue (except in our mind) and both form and matter crumple. The molecule is the chemist's form, made up of atoms. The megamolecules studied by biology are made up of smaller molecules, just as the life of the animal gives overall shape to the differing cells and organs which are the material expression of that form.

In fact, when we get to living things, the notion of form and matter is almost too simple to help in this kind of complexity. For this reason, we must use a subdivision of form and matter for living things, a relationship of body and soul.

There is no more battered and abused term in the history of thought than "soul". Its history is worth investigating to find out where all the trouble came from.

In Greek, psyche or soul was used by Plato to mean mind. Modern psychologists continue with this sense of soul when they study the human psyche. On these terms, you might expect that the only things which have souls are human beings. One would get the impression from most preachers who are willing to help us to save our souls that they share this notion of Plato's.

In Latin, *anima is the word for soul and this follows the tradition of Plato's most famous pupil, Aristotle.* It should be easy to see in anima the idea of animation, animal, and indeed any form of animate life because, for Aristotle, having a soul meant being alive.

In choosing between these two definitions of soul, we will need a clear awareness of just exactly what we are choosing between. Plato's is at first the most attractive. It asserts man's uniqueness in the universe, underlines our importance, and makes it easier to talk about the immortality of the soul. If the soul is the mind and is capable of functioning independently of the body, then there is very little problem in proving the persistence of our personal existence after the death of the body.

Unfortunately, this perspective has its problems. If the soul is so easily separated from the body, how do the two of them survive together here? It rather makes physical life for man to be some kind of a punishment and there are passages in Plato which echo this view. While the next world attracts with its view of something new and exciting---if a bit incorporeal---his account would have us give up all that is pleasant or useful in this world.

The view of Aristotle is more easily digested by the scientific society in which we live today. *Soul is life.* It is the first activity of a body which exercises the ability to live. What Aristotle is saying is something like this: A living thing carries on activities which other things do not. An animal moves itself with its legs; a rock only moves under the pressure of outside forces. An animal grows by making its food a part of itself; a crystal only `grows' by adding independent parts to itself.

Underlying all of these activities is something which keeps them all together. This is not something magical, but a reasoned scientific conclusion. Let me take two examples, one from the inanimate world and one from the animate.

Throw a log on the fire and eventually you get ashes. This is what the ancients called a substantial change: you started with a piece of wood and all you have left is a pile of ashes. Now one of two things happened: either the wood was annihilated and the ash created in its place (which would make a god a very busy fellow) or else there is something which is common to both wood and ashes.

This last conclusion is drawn by analogy to other, easier changes. *The apple goes from green to red, its accidents (appearances) have changed (accidental change), but it is still an apple.* The apple was continuously present throughout the change. The scientists reading this probably feel smugly secure in their knowledge that carbon was continuously present when the wood went to ashes. But what is important here is not the example, but the solution. Scientific reasoning has forced us to assert the existence of something we could not see, feel, smell, taste, or touch. We assumed the real existence of this hypothetical entity because it was necessary to explain what was going on. In short, we needed *the existence of something real which was only knowable rationally, not sensually*

The principle is the important thing because the problem still exists. Aristotle reasoned that *prime matter* would underlie any change from one substance to another. Today we know that carbon was the prime matter in the wood example. But today we have another variation of the same problem. E = mc2 means that matter can be converted into energy. To rephrase Aristotle's problem: is matter annihilated and energy created? Or is it more economical to assume that there is some third element, as yet unknown, which underlies these changes as carbon did in the previous example? Some physicists call it massergy, but it is Aristotle's prime matter going around under another name. Maybe you prefer protomatter? Same idea.

In the case of living things, we have to use the same type of reasoning. There must be something there which, even if we cannot see it, must be keeping the entire organism together.

Aristotle's soul is what the scientists today call homeostatic equilibrium. It is the activity of the living thing to keep all of its chemical reactions in some balanced proportion to the whole living thing, and enables it to thus fight off the pressures of the outside world which would throw it out of balance and thus kill it.

In animals of any size, this equilibrium is more complex than in simpler plants because there are more things to keep in some kind of balance. *In humans we have the most complex balancing problems, not only a homeostatic equilibrium, but also a psychosomatic equilibrium. The animal must expend effort keep all of its organs together; humans must keep a balance between psyche and soma, mind and body,* brains and buns together.

In humans, soul refers to the whole life; it is the power which keeps everything functioning, not just the mind. Psychosomatic equilibrium, for all of its technical ponderousness, reflects something which we have all experienced: the interaction between our mind and our body.

If you are coming down with a cold, your personality might change; if you do without carbohydrates, nature's tranquilizers, you can get cranky; if you eat too large a meal, you get drowsy. The relationship is not just one-way, even though all of these examples are of the body affecting the mind. It works just as well the other way. You feel depressed and you catch a cold; you are too busy to get sick, and you do not get sick; you slow down or get disgusted with your job, and along comes a convenient illness to get you a few days off. All of these experiences are fairly common. The mind-body relationship is a two-way street going on within one and the same person.

It would be unfair if I didn't mention the reason why many philosophers and theologians are uncomfortable with this kind of Aristotelianism. The problem can be said in five words: the *mortality* of the soul. No, that is not a typo: think about it for a second. If equilibrium is what keeps the parts of an ameba together, then what happens to the equilibrium (soul) of the ameba when the animal dies? Answer: it dissolves because it had no more reality than the parts out of which it was made.

It is much the same case with other animals. All of the activities of an animal are tied up with individual, physical, concrete objects. Both its knowing powers and its emotional system are tied up to specific organs and hormones. When they go, there is nothing left. Heartless as it sounds, our experience by itself gives us no reason to expect to meet Lassie in some kind of doggy heaven.

It should be clear by now why the hatred in some quarters for Aristotle's notion of soul. While soul is clearly tied up to the here-and-now existence in the physical world, there seems to be very little reason for assuming that such a soul would survive death. But there is such a reason. In fact, it is a reason mentioned and underlined in the last two chapters: intellect and will.

The human being performs several activities which transcend the limitations of the physical body. While not continual everyday experiences, they are frequent enough to testify to the fact that our intellect and will, at a certain level, function without involving the human body. Have you ever gotten so engrossed in something that you lost all track of time? Have you ever daydreamed your way past your bus stop? Have you ever been so involved in play or love that you lost all contact with the real world? If you have, then you know the kind of experience to which I am appealing. It is not so much occult as obvious; not so much mundane as transcendental, because it is a mundane, worldly everyday experience of us transcending our own limitations of time and space.

There is good reason to hold the immortality of the human soul, to think that a significant part of the human person survives the dissolution of the body. Not because the soul is some mysterious ghost inside of our bodily machines, but rather because, as in the case of an earlier theoretical and unseen entity, the atom, one can see its effects inside us and in others. If the sheer power of day-to-day living were not enough to convince us that our vitality will outlast our bodies, look at what psychologists and thanatologists tell us about the human attitude toward death. The little child has a clear and uncluttered view of reality unblocked by all of the fears and entanglements and complications of so-called adult life, and so, for the child, death is incomprehensible. When the time comes to face these fears, thanatologists like Kubler-Ross tell us that this is when humans become the calmest and the most hopeful.

Granted that the feelings and wishes of the human being may indeed be wish-fulfillment, that they may be the projections of our fears. But before they are written off so quickly and glibly with the technical terminology of psychology, remember one fact: the human Intellect and will are unlimited.

There is nothing in nature which does not have limits-- except man. There is nothing in nature whose wants are excessive, and unlimited--except man. Our knowledge can make us want things which we have never seen, and our loves have over and over again gone beyond what doctors tell us are the normal limits of the body's capacities.

All of the detailed work on the nature of ideas in Chapter I lays the foundations for this view. Ideas have a foundation in nature but they are radically different from nature. Circular objects exist, but our mind invented the perfect circle of geometry long before technology could have made one. I dislike the connotations for the word "spiritual," since it includes the charlatans of spiritualism, but what else are we to call an intellect which has the power to dematerialize the image of the physical object, purify it of its individual characteristics, and generate a perfect image of what that type of thing essentially is. The words matter little: *not-physical, immaterial, spiritual, all approximate the experience.*

The `immaterial' is a concept which is derived from the notion of matter. History shows up two such concepts: Aristotle's which dominated nineteen centuries (400 B. C. to

1500 A. D.) and this chapter, and the concept of modern physics. We have seen the dematerialization of form from matter in the human mind. The object studied in physics is the mass or matter which occupies the space-time continuum. Even by that definition, we can call any being `immaterial' which is not a temporal-spatial measurable continuum. The thoughts and decisions contained in my mind elude that continuum: the body acts in space and time, consciousness and the contents of consciousness are timeless, just as the concepts of truth and beauty are timeless.

The equilibrium of the amoeba ceased to exist when the parts ceased functioning. The equilibrium of a human must persist on some kind of minimum power when the body of this special animal dies. We can only speculate on human persistence after death. Much of what we `know' is really our beliefs about religion or spiritualism. The most that philosophy can reasonably outline are the reasoned facts.

After death, the body gets ecologically recycled as worm-food. The soul of a human being would have difficulty doing anything or learning anything new, since its normal avenues of knowledge are buried six feet under. It would only be capable of acts of intellect and will, of thinking and loving. Philosophically we come very close to the ancient Greeks, who spoke of `shades' living half-lives in the underworld after death and burial. Whether there are other paths open to us after death is something which philosophy cannot evaluate. The best that philosophy can do here is to critique any religion which offers us information in this area to see how well the religion's revelation squares with our own experience in this world.

Before we consider anything else, let's catch our breaths with something a little more mundane and mechanical. It is quite a leap to build from subatomic particles to living beyond the grave. *Aristotle's doctrine of the four causes* should help us to get back to the ground, and ground the flights of philosophical ecstasy for a little while. Until death we remain material beings. We may be embodied spirits or spiritualized matter, the nomenclature is merely one of emphasis. In either case, Man, the great amphibian, still has one foot in each of two worlds.

According to Aristotle, part of being wise consists in knowing the right questions to ask. In fact, all of the questions we ask can be broken down into four groups: How do you make it? Why did you make it? What's it made of? What is it?

If the last two questions ring a bell, it is because we have looked at them before. (If they do not ring a bell, re-read the beginning of this chapter.) *This final cause* is the final goal, the end-in-view which we had in starting the project. In human beings, this is the first thing to establish. Man works by jumping ahead to the end of the process, then going back to gather the materials and perfect the mechanism until the formal product equals the finished dream, end, or goal.

One of the nice things about this type of analysis is that, like hylomorphism, the four causes are a tool which can be used to analyze anything. To use some wide-ranging examples, consider murder mysteries or medical research on cancer.

Murder mysteries break down into subcategories along lines suggested by the doctrine of the four causes. Police procedurals (how-dun-its) emphasize the efficient cause; suspense stories revolve around whether the final goal will be achieved or not; detection stories revolve around the way in which the detective gathers his clues (material cause) into one pattern (formal cause) which reveals the killer.

Medical research on cancer seeks to isolate the cause of cancer (final goal); discover the mechanism by which cancer spreads/can be controlled (efficient cause); discover a vaccine to counteract it (material cause); and do this with the certainty of the scientific method (formal cause).

As might be apparent from the four questions, we are dealing with the analysis of something made by intelligence. It almost looks as if we could only analyze the things of man with this type of tool. And yet, three of the four questions, requests for mechanism, parts, and arrangement, are equally the stuff of which the natural sciences are made. It is when we arrive at the fourth question, the one about purpose in nature, that we are in strange-sounding territory. Unless we want to get into areas like Nature personified, a Creator God, or visitors from outer space, we are going to have difficulty in saying that "nature acts for this purpose", or that "nature intends that effect." There are real problems talking about the mind of the cosmos, unless we mean one of three things: chance, pantheism, or creation.

If the universe is built by chance, then, given infinite time and infinite arrangements of elements, the stability is rather wondrous to behold. I must admit that when one starts calculating the chances of our world existing in its present ecological interconnectedness, I find myself being hypnotized by the poetry of the numbers involved. Such notions of chance go quite contrary to my experience. Now eminent statisticians tell me that if I throw my final exam papers down the stairs often enough, they will fall into alphabetical order. This might be true, but the overwhelming odds favor an intelligent alphabetizer.

The pantheist or the panpsychist who talks about the mind of the universe is at least on better ground. There are signs of thought and planning in the world of living things. My problem with this view is slightly different: is the whole universe one vast intellect? If the whole universe thinks, then I do not understand the unintelligence of my pet rock, which just sits there and does nothing. This is a confusion between the artist and the work, making the novelist a character in one of his novels; two different kinds of things are being mixed: the size of the universe and the quality of thought. Which is more awesome, the size of the universe or the fact that a well-trained astronomer can get the universe inside his head? Which counts for more: quantity or quality?

As to whether or not there is a Creator-God is a question which requires a good deal of spade work before we can answer the question: is there a God? and the subject of a later chapter.

One of the major preliminaries to such an investigation is the need for building a frame large enough to hold even the idea of a God. That is the task of Chapter IV.

CHAPTER IV:
AND NOW A WORD FROM OUR CREATOR

Materialism (not meaning what ethicians call greed but in the more general, ontological, philosophical sense ("that's all there is"): is it verified by our own facts and experiences? About 95% yes: the overwhelming number of our words describe our experiences of physical things. In mathematics and theology we get to experience something real that is not physical; only when we perform an act of love which goes counter to our emotions do we experience something real but not glandular.

Five percent of our words reflect something transcendental, something which carries us intellectually (but quite physically) into consciousness of a different type of object. That 5% is the portion which contains a hint of an explanation, a rumor of angels. Playing a game or a musical instrument, making love or writing a book, anything that takes away our usual sense of "clock-time', doing anything which puts us into a psychic top cruising speed indicates are suggestive examples.

Appealing to experience is a dangerous gambit because non-verbalized experience is most ambiguous. The artist cannot explain what makes his insight better than that of others. The lover cannot always properly interpret the ambiguity of the beloved's gestures and reactions. The gamesman cannot explain to us mortals what it is like to beat the World Chess Champion, the Superbowl Quarterback, or the political incumbent.

Without deserting the realm of experience (for that gives color to the black and white of reasoning), look at the way theoretical entities work in science. Long before anyone proved that atoms were there, they had to be there: it was the only way to explain whole varieties of phenomena otherwise inexplicable.

What follows falls under the same type of logic. In a strictly scientific logical system, God has the same logical status as a subatomic particle. Without the existence of either, whole types of phenomena do not have any explanation. This god-theory is no less scientific than the atom-theory of the 1700's, or the search for all the pairs of quarks. Or 'dark matter'

Now note the limits of what reality is. Modern Man routinely argues for the existence of the 'physical' characteristics of decidedly non-physical phenomena in the ordinary sense of that abused word. The existence of radio, television, and laser rays is accepted as part of physics because the physicist knows the mechanism that makes these wave particles do their own thing. If researchers discover that telepathic communication works on a similar model, then some occult phenomena become a part of physics.

The current difference between radio waves and ESP is merely *the difference between the natural and the preternatural*: maybe something different from our limited notion of what the physical is but hardly supernatural. In fact, to go a step further, if it can be shown that God exists, then IT too would become something `natural'. An orchid that could talk would be *supernatural in the strict sense: something impossibly beyond the nature of the flower as flower.*

In dealing with the preternatural, only our sense of `natural' would have to broaden to take into account the new awareness of a wider reality, for example if we found the gene which controls death. Now that the 19th Century concept of matter as something mechanical and determinate (deterministic) has become the 20th Century concept of indeterminacy, probabilistic models, and quantum mechanics, matter gets lost in a maze of mathematical matrices, dematerialized into what you may not be able to see, hear, feel, taste, or touch but still under the term "energy."

Some mental limbering-up exercises are in order. See if you can make up a list of characteristics which could apply to everything. By everything, to get a sufficient panorama, include as sample beings the following: god(s), angels, George Washington the President, Lassie the dog, limburger cheese, Kermit the Frog, the square root of minus 1, your pet rock, and the New York Mets. Now, close the book, and see if you can come up with five such characteristics.

Back so soon? The list produced by the Middle Ages for what they called *the transcendentals of being* has the following five characteristics on it: *essence, existence, unity (unum), desirability (bonum), and intelligibility (verum)*.Plato called them the one, the true, and the beautiful

[While I doubt that "everything IS beautiful in its own way", Plato does give me an excuse to direct the reader to the seven massive volumes of Has Urs von Balthasar *The Glory of the Lord*[1], wherein he seeks to recast most sterile theological discussions into an aesthetic appreciation of the summum bonum, the greatest good, God as the highest beauty [**beauty being truth in its most attractive form**] and therefore the most desirable]

There is a little trick to solving the riddle above: the analogy of being.

Be Warned: Protestant theologian Karl Barth called the analogy of being the very invention of the Antichrist himself![2] However, Protestant Dean Norman L Geisler[3]is not so pessimistic.

Analogy may have first been taught to you in English class or in preparation for college entrance exams, or diagnostic testing. In any event, you recognize that the sequence 1, 2, ?, 4, 5,! has as its next element the number 7. Analogy is best seen by contrast with the notions of univocity and equivocity.

When a word is univocal, or unequivocal, it says one and only one thing. With the rare exceptions, most words have more than one meaning, as can be seen in any large dictionary.

1Ignatius Press, San Francisco,
2Kirchlich Dogmatik, Introduction(1932) quoted by SL Jaki in The Keys of the Kingdom, Franciscan Herald Press, Chicago,1986,p136
3in Thomas Aquinas: an Evangelical Appraisal, [Grand Rapids, MI, Baker,1991]

However, words are coined, especially technical vocabulary, when we want to be completely clear, univocal as to our meaning, as with a word like 'syzygy'.

When a word is equivocal, it means two differing things which have no apparent connection one with the other. Thus 'execute' means to carry out someone's orders or to kill them off. Or 'bear' as in the child, home from hymn-practice, who wants to meet Gladly, the cross-eyed Bear (said child having misheard the hymn, "Gladly, the cross I'd bear"). *Analogy is halfway between the other two: it refers to the application of one idea to two different things that are partly the same and partly different.*

Consider the word "foot": the foot of a human and the foot of a mountain are two rather different things as any shoemaker can tell you. Nevertheless, *there is a similarity, and even a strict proportionality (hence the technical term analogy of proportionality)* between the foot of the mountain and the foot of the man. Each foot stands in the same relation to the rest of it: at the bottom. Head of man, head waters of a river; field mouse and Apple's computer mouse; reading a will and reading someone's face; the good car and the good spouse (Good God!) are all analogous uses of good Similarly "Health" is the primary analogate which permits us to speak of healthy foods and vitamins (causes) or healthy blood or urine samples (effects).This is the *analogy of attribution.* [4]

Now take one of these transcendentals of being. *Unitas, unity: everything that is has its own unity and self-identity as this particular individual.* The cheese and the rock have a physical unity; Mickey Mouse has an imaginary unity; George Washington and Lassie have biological unity or biological identity; even the NY Mets have a group unity or identity based on the unity of their intention to work together as a team (sometimes). God and angels have, at least, a conceptual unity.

---

4. G. Klubertanz, St. Thomas on Analogy (Chicago: Loyola UP,1960; Ralph Mc Inerny, The Logic of Analogy (Nijhoff, the Hague, 1961); Battista Mondin The Principle of Analogy in Protestant and Catholic Theology, Nijhoff, the Hague,1963)

Verum, intelligibility, or to spell out the idea: everything that is, is true. That is, everything is capable of giving us information. One of the paradoxes of the "real" world of the physical is that unintelligent beings are intelligible . Even the most inert gas still retains something to teach the chemist. That Man learns from the more complex forms of life, human and otherwise is not so surprising as is that rock. It might indicate the soundness of Aristotle's "defect": his anthropomorphism.

An inanimate thing made out of wood and chemicals can give us information, especially insofar as that describes a book, which after all is a physical object. We expect the book to communicate because we expect it to be our medium of communication with its author.

Likewise with a painting: we expect it to tell us something about the painter's own reaction to the subject. But the materialist insists inconsistently that, when we read the book of nature, its author is not only anonymous but non-existent! Einstein knew better: "The eternal mystery of the world is its comprehensibility"[5]

Bonum, desirability: everything that is, is good. Say, now, that is a bit much to swallow. Stupidity, ignorance, disease, war, famine, pestilence, and plague are good!? Well, not quite. The notion of transcendental goodness is rather hard to swallow. Clarifying first the notions of good and evil will improve the situation.

St. Augustine taught that evil does not exist. Augustine was no fool: he wasn't one who believes that sickness is only in your head, that you can think your way to better health. Rather, he realized that evil is not the normal or structural heart of reality. He saw that *all things are good in themselves but, when some of the goodness is destroyed, they turn into a crippled good called evil.* Examples are obviously needed at this point.

Among goods we can recognize personal goods, social

---

5 The New Yorker 3/17/73

goods and ontological goodness. *Strength, speed, smarts are personal goods; peace, order, justice are social goods, and this structural goodness, the notion that everything that is, is good is called transcendental goodness.*

(Incidentally, the three-way distinction is one way to untangle the laughter which usually follows the presentation *of Leibniz 's doctrine that "this is the best of all possible worlds"* His statement is hopelessly false in the area of social goods, ambiguous in the area of personal goods (given our misuse of them) and true in the transcendental sense as we shall see below. Parenthetically, while we are still inside these parentheses, this illustrates that every system of philosophy is more richly appreciated when seen against the background of problems it can solve.)

It is the general consensus of the western world that rape is not a good thing but that sex is indeed a good thing. How can a sex act (good) become a rape act (evil)? Not because of the act, but rather because of what is not present that should be: all of the gentleness, affection, eroticism, fertility and fidelity which are part of a human sexuality considered in its fullest, taken at its best.

Take any example you care to: murder with a knife (are you going to say that all mankind is totally evil or that knives should be made illegal or, worse yet, dull?); grand theft (does that make money evil in itself?); even the most powerful symbol of evil, Satan (is existence bad? or angelic intellect and power evil?). The problem in all of the cases can be better appreciated when considered in conjunction with the nature of free choice which will be considered in chapter six. For the moment, notice that the choice of evil is the choice to destroy, to choose a lesser good over a greater, or to concentrate on that which is missing.

All *physical* evils can be explained as a lack of something which should be there. (Cf., chapter on law below to appreciate the notion of 'oughtness'.) The damage done to the front end of a car by falling into a three-foot deep pothole at sixty miles an hour is nothing to laugh at. It is quite dangerous and quite damaging, but what has caused the damage was something that wasn't there that should have been.

In the case of moral or ethical evils, the choosing agent has opted to destroy some of the natural good which is contained in the object in its natural state. Sugar is good in itself but evil for the diabetic, salt is good in itself but bad in excess. Everything that is, is good: why the permission exists for people to do evil is a question unanswerable and even unaskable unless we demonstrate God exists and gives permission for us to do evil... Otherwise the problem belongs to the atheist to solve the problem [for her]of explaining why goodness exists.

A proper appreciation of the relation between good and evil requires that we recognize four types of opposites:
1. Contradictories ("A or not A" or 0,1 binary logic),
2. Contraries ("Some are, some aren't"),
3. Relatives (you are parent to your child but child to your parent), and, finally,
4. Privatives. In any pair of privative opposites, one item is the primary partner (light, eyesight, health) and the other only exists by absence, defect, or privation (darkness, blindness, illness). In a perfect world, we might never even imagine blindness or illness. The first term is the norm, the second is the defect. To define light as the absence of darkness as if both were equal (As Carl Jung held) would only be true if darkness cast shadows of light or, likewise, if health were just one item lost among many diseases, instead of being the norm against which all diseases are measured as light or grave (pun intended).

EVIL, WHETHER PHYSICAL, MORAL, OR SOCIAL IS A PRIVATIVE

The last two transcendentals of being, are essence and existence. Essence is simply stated: everything that is, is a certain kind of thing. We may not know what at first but, despite John Dewey's attempt to discredit the search for essences, people still ask, "What is it?"

Existence is quite a bit more difficult to handle.

"There is at the back of all our lives an abyss of light, more blinding and unfathomable than any abyss of darkness; and it is the abyss of actuality, of existence, of the fact that things truly are, and that we ourselves are incredibly and sometimes incredulously real. It is the fundamental fact of being, as against not being; It is unthinkable and yet we can not unthink it, though we may sometimes be unthinking about it..."[6]

Here the power, flexibility, and accuracy of analogy helps in clarifying the reality. Existence is at the core of reality. If something is real, then it exists. It does no good to equate the real as simply the It may make the reader feel better to learn that Augustine himself said "I was thirty before I realized that real and body were not the same"]

Something cannot be and not be at the same time and in the same respect: that is Aristotle's definition of the Principle of Contradiction and it is just as modern as the Scheffer stroke (/) system of binary logic (0,1). X cannot exist and not exist. The problem of talking about nothing is that we tend to treat nothing, nothingness, non-existence as if it were a something.

This tendency to reify nothingness shows up most vividly in **William Hughes Mearns** (1875–1965), poem:
Yesterday upon the stair
I met a man who wasn't there
He wasn't there again today
Oh, how I wish he'd go away
When I came home last night at three
The man was waiting there for me
But when I looked around the hall
I couldn't see him there at all!
Go away, go away, don't you come back any more!

6GK Chesterton. *Chaucer*(1932) in CW vol. xviii p172(San Francisco, Ignatius Press, 1991)

Go away, go away, and please don't slam the door
Last night I saw upon the stair
A little man who wasn't there
He wasn't there again today
Oh, how I wish he'd go away
"Antigonish" (1899)

Rocks, the square root of minus one, nightmares, team spirit, and even fictional characters are real, are existents--even if only in the sense that they are not-nothing. Yet they are different in their analogous modes of existence. Real existents can be intramental or extramental. Mathematical concepts, imaginaries, like green Martians--even nightmares and hallucinations--are conceptual entities, beings of reason who possess mental existence. Few would deny the reality of physical entities. *Even the whole question of God's existence is more precisely whether God is only an imaginary existent or exists in a real, extramental, non-physical form.*

Look at the world around you. Things are constantly coming into existence or ceasing to exist. Volcanoes throw up new islands, and rain and earthquakes wear them away. People are conceived and die. In fact, there is nothing inherently impossible in thinking of a time when the entire universe might cease to exist. This is what is called the awareness of the contingency of existence. In its starkest personal form: out of every 100 college freshmen, 1 will be dead before the graduation date.

In logic, if A implies B, then B is dependent upon A, A is necessary for B, B is contingent upon A. This relationship of contingency and necessity lies at the heart of our existence and at the argument for the existence of God. Schelling calls it the ultimate question: Why is there something rather than nothing? Yet, like Milton Munitz,[7] Schelling calls it a despairing question[8] and Bertrand Russell called it a 'brute fact'[9] about which no

---

7*The Mystery of Existence*
8*Werke* Schroter ed.,Munich,1954, vol. 6 pp. 7 & 242]
9 In H.J. Hicks, ed. *The existence of God* Macmillan.1964 pp. 174-175

questions may be asked-- a rather unreasonable position for a philosopher.

Kant[10] argued that the universe was an inconsistent notion, in an argument which his firmest follower recognized as invalid[11]

If our most shocking awareness is the discovery of our own contingency, then what are we contingent upon? We are not contingent or dependent upon our parents: they had a role in our starting, and if they didn't starve us or otherwise kill us, they have also helped us to survive. However, in the strictest sense, neither they nor any other thing on earth accounts for our continued existence from one instant to the next.

If everything in the universe is contingent on everything else, what does the universe depend upon for its continued existence as a whole? Atomic phenomena depend upon the existence of atoms, and the existence of the contingent universe depend upon some kind of Necessary Being.

In the 1950s and 60s, "Steady state" physicists argued that hydrogen atoms were emerging from nothing all over the universe (a direct violation of the laws of conservation). Why should scientists and philosophers act so unscientifically? Because a Uni-verse, a unified cosmos, re-creates the cosmological argument for the existence of God on the basis of the scientists own data! Science requires that the laws of science operate uniformly all across the cosmos: the universe is consistent. Kurt Godel in the 1930s proved that any counting system (and the universe is a system of things which can be counted) cannot be consistent and complete at the same time.[12] The Universe is consistent, therefore, it cannot be complete. This "'incompleteness", this scientific requirement that there be something outside the series of a completely different nature, makes the universe a contingency which requires a Necessary Being: Source of Existence and contingency.

10*Critique of Pure Reason*, NK Smith trans, Macmillan 1929,p,449]
11 NK Smith, *A commentary on Kant's Critique of Pure Reason*, Macmillan, 1923, 2nd ed. 1923 p 519]
12Ernst Nagel and JR Newman: *Godel's Proof.* NYU Press 1958

The problem with understanding this relationship is to sufficiently broaden one's mind not only to envision the frame of the universe, but also to imagine something standing outside and underneath it, keeping it in existence. Of course, the spatial description has its own limitations: one of the paradoxes for existence is that This Being is Atlas holding up the universe, This Thing is something totally beyond our imagination and experience, in fact, IT is so utterly different from us that even to think about it is a trifle frightening, like a sci-fi alien or the God of Job or Isaiah. Christian scriptures suggest that it can be a terrible thing to fall into the hands of a living God.

And yet, at the very instant we realize how transcendent IT is, we are face to face with the fact that IT is the preserver and conserver of my existence: in that case IT is so immanent that IT is "more intimate to me than I am to myself". From the Greek notion of being God-possessed (literally, en-thu-siastic), through Augustine (quoted above) to Francis Thompson's poem about flying from himself in order to escape "The Hound of Heaven" and even to Carl Jung's internal archetype of God in our minds: all an awareness of God-within-us (immanence). So God is not just within us (extreme immanence or pantheism) or just outside of us (extreme transcendence as in the 18th Century Deism). As the formula says: "God is in us but not shut in; outside us but not shut out".

This text has had a reluctance to call IT 'God' is based upon two things: objectively, one must find out something more about this Being before we call IT by a too-familiar name, and subjectively, we must also consider the reasons why the very existence of this Being is viewed as a threat by those who would prefer IT did not exist.

First, some further characteristics of this Necessary Being which has brought the universe into existence. The ability of a thing to act is in inverse proportion to the raw materials it is working with. It is harder to make a house if you have to begin by making your own brick, rather than by buying them premade. In fact, the more basic your raw materials, the greater your power must be if you are going to bring it to fulfillment. Now, since everything that exists is dependent on this thing for its existence, they must have started from a condition of pure non-existence, a potential zero. Therefore, the powers of this thing must be infinite.

We now have an Infinite Necessary Being with an infinite capacity to act (omnipotence). Since such denotes absolute power over existence, God cannot delegate such power to another[13] Whatever words used from here on must be strictly by analogy or else be negative terms. These negative terms, which Aquinas called negative theology, are based on the premise that, if you make a long enough list of what something is not, you eventually get an idea, by elimination, of what the thing is. "In God we cannot say what he is" [14]

For example, the notion of infinite is really a negative idea: it is saying that this Being has no limits. Once we establish that this Being is infinite, several consequences follow from it almost immediately. "Infinite" literally means no limits: we are talking about something which cannot be limited by space or time. If this thing is infinite with respect to space, then it cannot have a body because all bodily things are limited: furthermore, since it cannot have a body, it must be non-physical, immaterial, or spiritual and is omnipresent in virtue of the fact that it can have no physical location.

This being is infinite with respect to time. Therefore, it is eternal, a negative term meaning that it has no limits with respect to time. On one hand "Eternity is in the Now"[15] from Man's terrestrial point-of-view; on the other hand, everlasting 'today-ness'.[16] the 'enduring present'[17] the Eternal Now is the whole time canvass from the point-of-view of the God who is outside

---

13 Su Th. I,Q45, a,5]

14[St. John Damascene, De fide orthodoxa, I,4.PG 94,797]

15. Heidegger. *Nietszche* v,i,p311f

16hodiernus, Augustine, Confessions, XI,13

17Bergson, La Pensee et le Mouvant,Paris,1950, p170

the time sequence. As we go back to the notion of analogy, please realize how limited our terms indeed are.

To use a more secular example, consider these lines from the poet Byron:

She walks in Beauty as the night
of starry skies and cloudless climes
And all that's best of dark and light
Meet in her aspect and her eyes.

And what has Byron told you about the lady? Literally nothing, but that nothing is highly suggestive. You have been told something but what precisely eludes the power of words.

Because we are limited by the power of words. there is the temptation to lapse into a sort of mystical silence (That of which Man cannot speak, let him therefore be silent- Wittgenstein). But if intellect has any worth at all, then we have to investigate as though our very selves depended upon IT as indeed it might.

When a book exists, what is its relationship to its author? In the case of The Complete Works of Willam Faulkner, we can read a book and discover something about the author from the nature of the work itself. The book is not the author, but, as the book is a product of the author's mind, we can find traces of the author's mentality in the final product.

Historically, there have been theologian-philosophers like Augustine and Bonaventura who even found vestiges of the Trinity in natural occurrences like the shamrock of St. Patrick. But since any concept like the Trinity is based upon theology's analysis of a believed revelation , it rather falls outside the scope of philosophy. Likewise, terms like substance and accidents may help us precisely locate the miracle of the Eucharist in the doctrine of transubstantiation but the analysis does not explain the miracle which the believer accepts.

The contingent created universe is orderly. Order denotes intelligence. IT as both infinite and intelligent can be properly called omniscient. (Again, a negative term which at first glance appears a positive: it simply asserts that there is no limit to this Being's knowledge.)

Combining the omniscience of this Being with the intelligibility of the universe, we find a partial solution to the paradoxes of the intelligibility of the Unintelligent. For you and me, true knowledge means conforming our minds to the object. Our knowledge is correct if and only if our ideas conform to the thing in itself. In this case, as in the case of Aristotle's artist, we are dealing with the creative intelligence in which the product is expected to conform to the intended specifications of the producer. Hence, the objects in creation are expected to conform to the mind of their Maker. Dorothy L Sayers has made a whole book, *THE MIND OF THE MAKER* approaching the mind of God from her mind as a maker

Since this Being, has acted to bring the universe into existence, therefore, this being must have the capacity to act. The nearest ability we know to this power we call will. Since this being is infinite, its will can be called omnipotent (no limit on ITS power of action).

Now again, we come up against one of the paradoxes of reality; the notion of goodness. If desirability is a characteristic of an object which has no desires of its own, we are in the normal course of things allowed to assume that it was packaged with an eye to making it more desirable: that is what advertising and marketing are all about. Again, on analogy of Aristotle's artist, we find ourselves living in a world which is incredibly desirable, in which intelligibility and delight abound in every object. There is good reason to argue as before: Where we react to the desirability of an object, the object is conforming to the desirability built into it by the original manufacturer. Therefore, not only is this being a source of all intelligibility in the universe but the Source of all goodness as well.

This explains why G. E. Moore in <u>Principia Ethica</u> said that the good is undefinable. Sensual goods, economic goods, spiritual goods, useful cars, good food, good men and women (Good God!): the variety is overwhelming without the principle of analogy. Only analogy makes this variety intelligible. When C. L. Stevenson said "good' means "I like it", he is correct but only because we react to objective goodness. Evil as a wounded good (Privative) explains why we even desire evil-- because it still has some residual good content.

Likewise, A. MacIntyre in his <u>History of Ethics</u> complains that "God is good by definition is a circular and therefore false argument. He would be correct only if a circular argument were a contradiction. Plato said "The One, The True, The Beautiful" were the marks of The Highest Being (the summum bonum or highest good) and it took over a thousand years to recognize that good does not always equal beautiful. Plotinus, Aquinas, and others would answer MacIntyre by pointing to the circle which is in truth formed by the fact that everything emanated from God and ultimately everything returns to its Creator. ITS will must be good because it is the source of all the good we experience, the primary analogate. As will be seen later, IT is the only possible source of our happiness, the complete satisfaction of our infinite wants

.

If you stop and reflect on the last few paragraphs, you can see something taking shape: IT almost looks human, IT has an intellect and a will, but no body. We cannot call IT human, but from the facts established so far, it is not stretching the language too far to call IT a person, if all nature is the image of ITS personality.) Beware: all philosophy reaches is God The Being or God as God but never to God as Father[18]

The universe appears orderly. In fact, it is so orderly that most of our needs can be taken care of without insuperable difficulties. It is horrible that people today starve because of politics, not Providence. This Providence is best appreciated by its etymology: providere, to see ahead. It is from this

---

18Su.Th. Ia,1,6,7

providential aspect of nature that the metaphor of a paternalistic god has come into usage. ("Progress" is the atheist's poor substitute: true in science, progress is false not only in the humanities but also in Man. Are You or I morally better than King David? or Bhudda?)

Leave aside the notion of god and concentrate on the notion of father-like. It is the source of one of the more tragi-comic word games of recent times: do you call God mother or father? He or She or IT? This most pathetic discussion really has no place here because it seeks to change political consciousness by shaking up the usual understanding of words in order to effect relations between the human sexes. No word changes on the part of the human race will influence the existence of this Being. Our words are highly limited as to their accuracy to begin with: It will not do all that much damage to change a few pronouns. It is highly legitimate to use either gender about IT: IT carries on activities which by analogy might be called father-like or mother-like. I would have to know each person's family history before I could know which gender to use to make 'providence' speak to them most effectively.

If I seem a trifle unserious about this problem, it is because it does not touch upon the nature of this Being. Even "nature" is a misleading word, easily confusing us with Nature. This is a natural being who is Creator of Nature, and Who can be known by means of our natural, unaided, reason. The better word is "essence" because we want to know what kind of a being this is. Since it was earlier established that IT does not have a body, IT cannot have genitalia! Secondly, it is more important to get a clear idea about this Being than to cloud the topic with sexual politics. Therefore, whatever words get across the idea that this Being cares, are perfectly valid. It is the reality that is important.

The argument from contingency and necessity on is based the most powerful argument in the traditional arsenal. Arguments from order in the universe get bogged down in complex discussions of chance; arguments from cause and effect get lost in arguments about ancient physics, and its notions of cause and effect. Almost all of the traditional arguments get bogged down in complexities which only obscure the points at issue.

The little child knows better than to be thus confused; when it colors the grass purple or the sky brown, the child pays tribute to the awareness that things do not have to be the way they are. All this argument asks you to consider the fact that these things do not have to be at all.

To put the choice in the starkest terms: there is nothing in our lives that is permanent. We get too attached to certain things and then are deeply disappointed when they die or disintegrate. If we go by the testimony of only our physical experiences, we are alone in a physical universe which is totally beyond our comprehension: we cannot unpack even the smallest atom and totally understand how the pieces fit together.

The argument from contingency and necessity is the choice of reason or unreason in the universe. If we are committed to using our heads, and that, for humans, constitute our only hope, then we cannot say that the universe is blind, perverse, and unreasonable. To say that an orderly process of evolution has produced a reasoning human is one thing; to say that this reasoning animal finds the universe meaningless, purposeless, and absurd is the kind of grim joke that only a suicidal existentialist could believe.

To say that we are contingent but are contingent upon Nothing (no-thing), is to contradict ourselves. Some may have to re-learn how to use the emotional side of our nature, but we do not have to cut off our heads to be in better contact with the freer flowing of our hearts.

To ask the question gives the answer: if we seek to explain what happens in our physical world, then we are intellectually bound to continue the quest beyond the limits of the galaxy or to the limits of our own existence.

Afterword : Some Famous Arguments

Some claim any argument is good enough to deny the existence of God or to slander the Catholic Church (like using any stick to beat a wild dog, 'any stigma to beat a dogma'). Modern atheism and current bigotry support 'Anti-Catholicism is a permissible form of anti-Semitism.' [For those Roman Catholics in America who believe their financial respectability has made their beliefs acceptable, listen to Thomas Hobbes: "Whether whatsoever comes to pass proceed from necessity. or some things from chance, has been a question disputed amongst the old philosophers long before the incarnation of our Savior... But the third way of bringing things to pass... namely freewill, is a thing was never mentioned amongst them, nor by the Christians in the beginning of Christianity...But for some ages past, the doctors of the Roman Church have exempted from this dominion of God's will the will of man; and brought in a doctrine, that...will is free, and determined... by the power of the will itself" ["The Question concerning Liberty, Necessity and Chance" English Works, London 1841, Vol. 5,p.1] Those committed to fair argument must accept the strongest of the atheist's arguments and must disown the weakest arguments in God's favor

St. Augustine's argument from universal assent--that everyone everywhere has always believed in God's existence--is no more valuable than psychoanalyst Jung saying man has an archetype of God in his head or sociological surveys which find Ph.D.'s in the natural sciences accepting the existence of God. What truth there is in Augustine will be considered later under the TAO, Kharma, lex aeterna in the chapter on law. Universal assent fails because Human choices or Group beliefs can exist quite independent of objective truth, like bigoted beliefs about other races or ethnic groups, or the bizarre beliefs of local weirdoes: sincerely believed and objectively false are not contradictory. It is our task to see Man in the full context of reality and it makes quite a difference if God were only a being in our mind instead of a Being Source of Reality

Blasé Pascal's Wager like its replay in William Barrett's

Lilies of the Field starts from the fact that we must die. Even if you claim no certainty about the next world, the choices are clearly two: Heaven-Hell, and eternity of Pain or Joy...OR....Nothing. Minimal religiosity requires 2 hours a week: one hour in church on Sunday and a cumulative second hour composed of morning and evening prayers each day.

Will you wager 2 hours out of 168 per week? If you lose, If there is Nothing after death, then you lose little; but if you win, if there is Eternal joy waiting for you, the payoff is out of proportion to any merely human lottery. And you must bet because you must die. Or in the words of the atheist Mexican shopkeeper in Barrett's novel, who is helping some nuns to build a chapel in the American Southwest, "Senor, If I am right and the Sisters are wrong, I have done something which makes me feel good. On the other hand, If the Sisters are right and I am wrong,.... then this is fire insurance." The Wager fails because sensualists will sleep-in on Sunday in the belief that 'a bird in the hand is worth two in the bush', that two hours I am "certain" of are worth more than "pie in the sky by and by."

The third and most famous failure is the Ontological Argument credited to both St. Anselm and Rene Descartes. Imagine the Greatest Conceivable Being. By definition this conception must include all the greatest perfections to an infinite degree. Existence is just such a conception. Existence must be solely in the mind or correspond to something in reality (sole in mente aut in re). It is obviously better to have a real $100 in your pocket than and imaginary $100. This Greatest Conceivable Being must possess real existence because without real existence a Greater Being could be imagines, a real one. Therefore the Greatest Conceivable Being, God, must exist. Anselm claims that God is the unique being whose existence is built into His essence. The ontological argument fails because we gather the notion of real existence from the experience of real things. We can attribute real existence to Mickey Mouse if we are children and we will be wrong. We can attribute real existence to that train coming at us through the wall and we will be wrong because we are hallucinating. Connecting the Concept of Real Existence with the Concept of the Greatest Conceivable Being adds up to a Combined Concept but not to an extramental reality. You must start with an outside reality to come to a real conclusion, this never gets outside the mind.

The five ways or quinque viae that Aquinas used to show the existence of God have enjoyed a resurgence in recent popular culture due to the books of Mortimer Adler and Robert Jastrow.

The first way begins with the history of experience. We realize that we are born into the middle of things and that 'everything has to start somewhere' in terms of everything that mean there must exist an Unmoved Mover who starts the process of change. Astrophysicist Robert Jastrow (in *God and the Astronomers)* uses the empirical principles of physics itself to show God the Creator.

In summary, he cites the "Big Bang" theory for the origin of the cosmos. Astrophysics, using background radiation, traces back all physical objects to one very dense pinhead lump of matter which exploded outward to make our still-expanding Universe. This implies that something existed, a primeval lump about which we know nothing. We do not know what it was like, what it came from or what caused it to explode.

We have just reinvented the argument for God the Prime Mover, the Starter of the Process. No philosopher who recognizes the integrity of philosophy as an independent discipline will be totally dependent upon the latest theories in Science or Theology or whatever the dominant discipline but Jastrow's conclusions are frank: science, forced by its own theory and experience to recognize the existence of something which it cannot know by its own scientific methods must join the philosophers and theologians who got to this Something long before them.

Stephen Hawking [19]tries to turn time and space inside out and obfuscates Jastrow's argument and thus justifies philosophy's independence of the latest scientific theories. Much more on the

---

19*A Brief History of Time*, Bantam Books 1988, Cf. also "Master of the universe" Newsweek 1/13/88 pp56-65]

point is Stanley L. Jaki's 1989 work[20]which underlines the fact that, the more particular facts we know about the universe, going back to the first 200 seconds of the Universe's existence, the more the Universe could have been something else, another way of saying contingent, something which could have been otherwise, based upon the free will of the Creator

THE SECOND WAY: If the Prime Mover is an argument from the start of time, then God as First Cause or Uncaused Cause is an argument which uses 'start' in a different sense. David Hume denied the sequence of 'cause then effect' because he thought it was confusion of "B comes after A, therefore A caused B". This logical fallacy of post hoc ergo propter hoc, 'after this therefore because of this', is a good practical maxim but cannot be raised to the level of a principle in the proofs for two reasons: as was seen in the first Way, every horizontal linear sequence of causes must start somewhere because we see the middle of the sequence in our daily lives. Either there is a first cause--no matter how long the sequence--or else nothing gets started. A world of effects with no starting cause cannot happen. In This Second Way, there is a whole set of vertical causes, hierarchically arranged which work simultaneously to bring about an effect. For example, pen, ink, paper (material cause), muscles and nerves (biological cause), intellect and will (psychic cause) all conspire to bring your love letters into existence. To ask what causes man to be able to think may be a request for formal, final, material, or efficient cause--or Ultimate Cause. And this some call God.

The third `way' is the argument used in the body of this chapter, an argument Aquinas derived from Maimonides, which Mortimer Adler expands on in his book New Ways to Think About God.

The fourth way is the argument from the degrees of perfection. We live in a world of good-better-best. We extrapolate degrees of cold from experiment and discover that, if

---

20*God and the Cosmologists*,Regnery Gateway, Washington, 1989.p39,45

we could ever get to -273.16C or -459.69F, all molecular motion might cease at this Absolute Zero. Likewise if we extrapolate from good-better-best, we should arrive at Absolute Best, and this some call God.

The fourth way is the argument from the degrees of perfection. Fact: order and organization exist in Nature in great sophistication. Fact: in the human sphere, things in numerical, alphabetical, library, or any other kind of order, are the result of an intelligent placing and sorting. Evolution no more answers the question than saying that I sorted by hand or computer: it answers the means (efficient) cause, not the formal cause. Chance answers nothing: to say that our ecology fell together as one change out of 1,000,000,000, etc. for fifty more zeros casts a doubt so small as to be insignificant.

Realize that in the expression 'X to 1' odds '1' is a mathematical convention not necessarily express a real single chance. If one doubt undermines a whole principle, realize that this is an existing order, a point which brings us back to way three and the reason why scientists are theists. "When I behold the sun and moon, the work of Your hands, what is man that You should be mindful of him, or the son of man that You should care for him?" You have made him a little less than the angels, placing the world beneath his feet." The argument from order runs from the Age of King David (8th Psalm) to Subatomic Particle Research Laboratories.

Why don't these `proofs' always work? Because one proves some THING to some BODY.

If you have a hang-up on God, all I can ask of you is a temporary suspension of your disbelief until you see the sketch of an improved life. I am not willing to assume that you and I are so far apart in our views: concerning certain opinions about God, I, too, am an atheist. Even the prophets of Israel delighted in the fact that they were iconoclasts towards false icons, atheists toward false gods.

You must also exercise a certain amount of honesty with yourself. Don't say you disbelieve in God, when what you really mean is "if God exists, He will louse up my sex life." Do not assume that the existence of a deity necessarily implies that your hobbies are evil. It was the god of the heretical Manichees who said sex was evil, not the god of the philosophers.

If I deal a little light-heartedly with the deity, the explanation is fairly easy to see: if God loves me and wants me to be perfect, then it is something which is perfectly compatible with the humanistic desire to want to be the best human being I can be. If this deity wants to help, who am I to argue with It?

Modern atheism, a creature of the last three centuries, is in one sense a total fraud: man never can deny the existence of An Absolute. Everyone has something which counts as an Ultimate Concern. Therefore all atheists are idolaters. It even shows in the language: the god almighty dollar, the cult of youth or beauty or success, or anything else we worship with our whole mind, heart, soul, and strength. It is also a tribute to American illogic that 10% of all U.S. atheists even report praying daily[21]

"Thus we have refuted the philosophers on their own terms". This quote from Aquinas, written during the only angry episode of his University career, is worthy of calm reflection. Let us consider the foundations of modern atheism.

The modern atheist draws from modern science, the psychoanalytic theories of Freud and Jung, and the problem of evil posed by Nietszche. (who was not the first to say that "God is dead"[22]
Modern science in its physics, biology, and history seems to provide. The principle of the conversation of matter and energy states that matter and energy cannot be created or destroyed. Since physics works, we don't seem to need a creator.

If physics has abolished the Creator, then Evolution has disposed of Adam and Eve. If Copernicus showed that man is

---

21Poloma and Gallup survey, as in Newsweek 1/6/92, p 43
22Hegel "Glauben und Wissen" (1802) Werke, Frankfurt,1970 V.2, p.432

not the cosmological center of the solar system, it seems that man is just another monkey according to Darwin.

Modern Science has also inspired Auguste Comte to frame his famous theory of the History of Progress. History shows, he says, that we have progressed from mythological societies dominated by religion to rational societies where philosophy is king. The last and highest stage is the technological society which modern science has made possible. Some of the followers of John Dewey would go one step further and suggest that the job of philosophy should be to advance science and battle the reactionary forces of religion. In this scenario, the condemnation of Socrates for atheism, of Maimonides for heresy or Galileo for contradicting Joshua 10:14(How could Joshua make the sun stand still if the sun were the center of the solar system?), or even the Boston ministers of the 1800's (who fought childbirth anesthetics because "scriptures say you shall bring forth your children in pain and suffering.")--all 'exemplify' religion's evils.

So why do people still believe? Sigmund Freud, the father of psychoanalysis, completed the work of Copernicus and Darwin in "putting man in his proper place". Freud calls religion a "universal, obsessive compulsive neurosis". God is a result of "projection": where as little children we could look up to our parents for help and protection, as fearful adults we use Our Father as our linus blanket. All of this is rooted in the Oedipus complex, the refusal of a child to share his mother with the child's father--Freud explicitly spells out the infantile tantrums in terms of Oedipus, the child abandoned who grew up to kill his father and marry his mother. In short, "sex is destiny" and our psyche is rooted in our biology.

Carl G. Jung is the perfect "second" to Freud. History abounds with such seconds: Joshua after Moses, Peter after Jesus, Elias after Francis--consolidators rather than innovators. Jung made psychoanalysis respectable, softened Freud's deterministic biologism, proved that it wasn't just a "Jewish science"--and even substituted a moderate agnosticism for Freud's militant atheism. The results are not necessarily any better for religion. In Jung's analysis, he finds an archetype of God, buried in our hereditary subconscious. It is a God, buried in our hereditary subconscious. It is a God with four faces, three male, one female--the Jungian basis for belief given to Father, Son, Holy Spirit, and Virgin Mary.

Finally, there is Philosophy's Argument from Evil. If God is omnipotent and omniscient, why does he permit Evil? Or, as Frederick Nietazche put it, "If God is good, he is not God; if god is God, he is not good".

Leibniz argued that this was the best of all possible worlds--and pessimists ever since have been afraid that he was correct. Nicholas Rescher maintains that this can be supported by seeing this world as a maximal blend of order and variety. But we can still ask, why God didn't make the universe a better place. Absent an answer, God must be a wimp or a sadist . . . or non-existent.

The great merit in these arguments for atheism is that they are all true. As Aristotle said, it is virtually impossible to say something totally false. Every one of them is partially true; furthermore each one of them is almost totally true--in its own context. But as James Clerk Maxwell has observed, " One of the severest tests of a scientific mind is to discern the limits of the legitimate applications of acientific methods"[23]To explain:

The law of conservation is the first law of physics. Not the first law of the physical world, but the first law of the discipline which studies the physical world. What good would physics be if matter or energy could be created or destroyed? If things could pop in and out of existence like an old re-run of some magic show? The present author, for the sake of argument, will not have recourse to a notion of miracle, or even to Jastrow's words on the big bang which started our system of physics. God would be rather stupid if he had to miraculously violate His own laws of nature on a frequent basis--that would show an amazing lack of foresight (AKA Providence).

23." in Scientific papers, WD Niven,ed. Cambridge UP 1890,v.2 p759

As Thomas Aquinas realized: even if matter were eternal (making conservation possible), matter would still be eternally dependent upon God as its source for continued existence. The quality of physical existence has never changed: even if it were eternal, it would still remain eternally contingent. "Thus we have refuted the philosophers on their own terms"[24]

We have not substituted Jastrow's physics for theirs, or sought exemptions for miracles but have sought to preserve the truth of conservation where it is true (in physics) by pointing out where it is falsely over-extended (into philosophy).

Physicists who are atheists or agnostic by preference and who lack the ability to separate their antecedent philosophical commitments (or their psychological predispositions) from their scientific data are having a bad time living with the anthropic principle[25]. Carter would not approve of my definition of his ter]: the universe was made for man. Start with the first 10,000,000,000th of a second (10-10) in which ten billion antiprotons were balanced against ten billion plus one protons[26] or the drop in explosion temperature from (10 to the 26th power or 100,000,000,000,000,000,000,000,000 degrees Kelvin to a few thousand degrees in the first 200 seconds [27]or the explosion that would have been an implosion if gravity had been one part in 1040 stronger [28]or "why the sky has to appear blue... why mountains on earth cannot be higher than the Himalayas" [29] This is Pascal's probabilism with a 1990's vengeance: if the universe was not made for man by a purposeful designer and creator then

24Aquinas, De unitate intellectu contra Averroists
25[fn Brandon Carter, "Large Number Coincidences and the Anthropic Principle in Cosmology" in MS Longair(ed) Confrontation of Cosmological Theories with Observational Data. Dordrecht, Reidel, 1974, p 291-8
26Jaki,"The Creator's Coming",Homiletic and Pastoral Review, Dec 1984, pp10ff
27Cosmologists p47
28[fn SL JAKI THE PURPOSE OF IT ALL, RegneryGateway, Wash.,D.C.,1990, p.101]
29Ibid p.51; VF Weisskopf "Of atoms, Mountains and Stars: a Study in Quantitative Physics" Science 187 (1975)pp605-612

the wildest opinion is the believer in chance not God. Atheist and Physicist Fred Hoyle says it best: " A commonsense interpretation of the facts suggests that a superintellect has monkeyed with physics, as well as che,mistry and biology, and that there are no blind forces worth speaking about in nature" [30]

Evolution: so much irrelevancy clusters around the topic! That Darwin was (maybe) a theist is not evidence. Pope Pius XII taught as Roman Catholic doctrine, monogenism, the derivation of the family of man from one set of parents, is also not evidence. The missing link IS evidence. The concept of a missing link is a hopelessly muddled part of evolutionary theory: if the missing link shows the art, language,[No, Virginia, I do NOT believe that apes or dolphins use those arbitrary conventional signs called words. Panting and groaning, yes ;speech, no.][31] tools, or other material effects of intellect, it is Man; if not, it is ape. Like 0/1 binary logic, it is/can be only one or the other.

Everything in evolution other than the human soul is compatible with the existence of God. Furthermore to say that God used the mechanism of evolution to invest matter with a relatively autonomous principle of dynamic development is a tribute to that foresight mentioned earlier, performing large scale actions on the basis of a few built-in

The missing link is required by evolution to explain the gap between monkey and man. The missing link will remain missing, must remain missing, because for it to be real would make a contradiction-in-terms actually exist. Intellect is either Potential or Actual, in computer logic either 0 or 1; if the missing link has an actual intellect then it is human--if not, then it's a monkey. The reduction from potency to act, from monkey to man, is the work of a separate Creative act, the work of an instant rather than generations.

Arthur C. Clarke comes close to this when his 2001 monolith intervenes to make a monkey truly think (just as another intervention would be needed at the end to make man into a disembodied Star-Child). The gap is present in all

---

30[Quoted in Jaki.Purpose. p103
31For further details see SL Jaki Speaking of Apes NY: Plenum,1980]

anthropology: man paints and does not just paint better than a great ape, man constructs tools and not just better tools than a chimpanzee, and so on through all the works of man. It is the terms of the evolutionists which are defective at just the crucial point which would support atheism. The current term "punctuation" is the evolutionist's recognition that evolution "jumps" and no intervening forms can be found. Lancelot G Hogben in his very funny book, <u>Science is a Sacred Cow,</u> suggested that science has a few links but most of the chain is missing!

Auguste Comte's history would be more interesting if he told the whole history of progress. Socrates was put to death for atheism by a democracy annoyed because some of his students were tyrants in a previous administration--he died for his political, not his religious, sins. Religions have had their inglorious moments: but whether or not Maimonides or Spinoza were excommunicates are membership judgments made by the local Jewish communities (not all that different from the American Jewish community which in 1990 similarly excommunicated Rep. Barney Frank) One political act which might or might not violate a religion's general principles is as useless a basis for judgment as using one jury's poor verdict to wipe out trial-by-jury as a legal principle.

The case of Galileo is an example of the Cardinal who was a better scientist than Galileo. That the Copernican theory of heliocentrism was developed by Nikolaus Kopernik, Cardinal-Archbishop of Cracow, Poland, is an irony of history. That impetus was not discovered by Newton (1670) but in 1340 by Nicholas Buridan (acting on a physical implication of a Catholic Church Council doctrine called creation in time) is one of the better kept disreputable secrets of the historians of science.

Cardinal Robert Bellarmine, S.J. pointed out to Galileo that heliocentrism was a theory and should be taught as a theory, not as a fact. And even Galileo knew that Sts Jerome and Augustine taught that not every word of the Bible need be taken literally [32]The first-hand direct observation of heliocentrism was only

32SL Jaki "Galileo's rehabilitation" Fidelity, 5/4(1986)pp 37-8 done on the 1960's space flights: Galileo's fame is based on doing the right thing for the wrong reason. Any drive to canonize St. Galileo merely points up the ignorance of current churchmen: T. S. Kuhn (a supporter of Galileo) has amply shown in The Structure of Scientific Revolutions how Galileo's skills were more political than scientific. Conveniently ignored is Galileo's equation of human knowledge of geometry with the Creator's [33]

Religions have mangled their message but Comte's historical perspective requires us to record how religion has fostered progress.

First, when even St. Jerome thought the fall of Rome meant the end of the world, it was Augustine, Bishop of Hippo in North Africa, who formulated the task of the Christian as raising up an Earthly City worthy of the Heavenly City. Six hundred years later, the Church created the University: lectures, degrees, professors, students, the whole "modern" system. The church created hospitals and infirmaries. Condemn churchmen for many sins but not for education, health care, and other things which make progress possible.

Grant Dr. Freud the clinical value of psychotherapy in ministering to a mind diseased. Grant the fact that psychiatry is a help to those religious lunatics which were the special worry for confessors and other directors of souls. While a million such facts never add up to one principle, let us assume Freud's principles are correct. Even if everyone in Freudian terms is neurotic, even he never suggested that all neuroses were based in religion. His preference was to explain everything in terms of sex, but his notion of projection is a two-edged sword: an atheist is merely projecting nothingness onto the next world precisely because the atheist does not want there to be a next world. Our wants by themselves do not create reality: the earth remains round whether we want it to be round or flat. To quote Dennis Gabor, "Have you ever known a healthy and happy psychoanalyst[34]

33Dialogue concerning the Two Chief World Systems Stillman Drake ed, UCal Berkeley, 1962., pp102-4]
34 " The Mature Society pp51-2

Father Andrew Greeley contends that Judaism and Christianity are the only two religions capable of absorbing Freud's insights. The believers in Yahweh are very sexy people: the major holidays center on birth and reproduction, "Increase and multiply," "I am the life," the spring fertility rites center on the first fruits of spring, even Easter comes from Oestra, the rabbit goddess who lays eggs, who also is remembered in estrogen, the sex hormone. Even the Easter Vigil liturgy, where holy water was blessed by inserting the Easter candle in an act of symbolic intercourse, was deliberately stolen from an ancient Roman fertility cult. Christianity is a sexy religion.

Dr. Jung's discovery of an idea of God built into our collective unconsciousness--let us assume that it is true. The God who invested matter with the ability to form an expanding universe and to evolve into higher forms of life would have no problem with building into the human the desire for an Absolute which only he could fulfill. Augustine and Dante knew this and even Plato and Aristotle suspected it. The desire for God isn't new but it may be true.

The problem of evil forces many insights. Some would settle for calling it the least evil of all the alternatives. Of course God could intervene each and every time we misused gravity to suicide off a building or used the expansion of gas laws to shoot someone--it would repeal the laws of cause and effect, result in chaos, a greater evil, and ask God to exercise Her power at the expense of Her intelligence. That God permits creatures to ask freely, to have a measure of self-government requires us to distinguish between Divine Foreknowledge (Predestination in the sense of knowing our future destination) and a Predestinarianism which denies any meaningful human freedom.

Gabriel Marcel made a distinction between a problem and a mystery. A problem is a puzzle you take down off the shelf, solve, then put back on the shelf. A mystery is a problem that we are too intimately involved with to separate ourselves from. Hence Marcel's quote that "Life is a mystery to be lived, not a problem to be solved." St. Paul had the same problem: the evil I would avoid I do, the good I want to do I never get around to.

A God who restrains Herself so we can be free, a sense of human freedom which requires that we be able to do evil (even if we don't actually do it), and Augustine's recognition that evil is a defective good--all of these are required to get a grasp of the implications of the problem of evil.

Despite Jacques Maritain's explication in <u>Existence and the Existent,</u> the problem of evil finds its fullest answer in theology, not philosophy. Stoic philosophers, confusing self-mastery with self sufficiency, were unsuccessful in solving the problem by learning to grin and bear it. Epicureans failed to mitigate evil by chasing pleasure. Yahweh told Job that the problem was beyond human powers to understand. Jesus promised that the good would suffer, that evil would win, but that our Good Fridays would not be ultimate defeats because Easter Sundays were promised. But that is faith not reason.

CHAPTER V
TYING IT ALL TOGETHER

Even the most insane of human beings acts for a purpose. We might not agree that their purposes are the best, but there is still some reason for their actions. In fact, we often notice purposes which are stacked up in some kind of hierarchical fashion in which one goal is subsidiary to another and to still yet another. In fact, if we look for the final goal of a person's life, we would probably get lost in all of the intervening goals. The pessimist would insist that most people do not have a purpose to their lives because they do not think that far ahead.

The optimist, who believes that everything is involved in some kind of process, varies the theme. He is grateful that humans do not have a goal. If humans had a goal, what would they do when they reached it? In the poignant words of song, "is that all there is?"

The intelligent pleasure seeker has a response that goes something like this: It is estimated that I will live 78.5 years. Since death is the only fact of life that is inevitable, and since after death there is nothing, I propose to live my life as pleasantly as possible, doing what I like so long as it does not hurt other people". Thus speaks the happy hedonist.

You must admit that the argument has its merits. Let the natural human follow all of the inclinations he wishes. The concupiscible appetites are not the only goal of his life: anything which gives him joy is an acceptable thing to do. Why, this Epicurean might even choose to sit at home and read a good book rather than attend another boring orgy.

Of course, we all know at least one person who is made of sterner stuff. In ancient days, she would have been called a Stoic; today, psychologists call her an obsessive-compulsive neurotic workaholic. Her responses are equally cogent: "I want to live my life in such a way that, when I am dying and going over my life, I want to be able to say that I never refused to help anybody, that

I always did my job and then some, and that I left the world a better place because I did my duty." She might sound like a drudge, but she keeps the machinery of society sound and functioning. It would be hard to enjoy much if there were not armies, fire and police departments, business and health professionals of all sorts who were willing to work their lives away in order to make us safe and comfortable.

What should I do with my life? The pleasure-seeker, whether hedonist or epicurean, seems to be following a law of diminishing returns: the more he enjoys something, the more he does it; the more he does it, the less pleasure it gives him; the less pleasure it gives him, he either must go deeper into it or find something constantly new and novel.

The duty-bound, whose rules of life are deontological, may be noble but dull. She seems to have no ability to enjoy rest or relaxation. The pleasure-seeker seems to be too dependent on his toys for what looks like a basically selfish quest, and the stoic seems too frighteningly self- sufficient, too close to the hedonist: both are rather caught up in being able to say that they did it their way. There has got to be something else.

We saw that, in the animals, the beginning and end of all their actions was love. What are the different kinds of things which we love? What are the different types of love relationships which we enter into with other people? I am going to prepare a list. Why don't you close the book and try to do the same?
****

Welcome back. What follows owes much to Martin D'Arcy's <u>The Mind and Heart of Love</u> and C.S.Lewis's <u>The Four Loves</u>. Before we begin to compare lists, consider the following question: why do we talk about `love' in relationship to all these things? What do you mean by love, if love enters as a factor in all these relationships? Or, is there one type on your list which is LOVE, some types which are love and others which are like?

Every item on your list can be or has been a love-object for somebody; in fact, the love-object which is the bright spot in their day, the thing that makes their whole existence. If I seem to exaggerate this notion of life, think for a minute about some of its synonyms: caring, valuing.

We are creatures who inherently tend to value things, some things more than others. In fact, the careless or uncaring individual tends to rankle even if we cannot identify why he annoys us. In an earlier chapter, you saw the problems of a colorblind person, and we have a variation of the same problem here. To explain color to a blind man or to explain intellectuality to your pet rock can be a frustrating experience, because, if they have not had the experience it would be rather hard to explain it to them. Some things are primary facts of experience.

Like the mother telling the child to keep its hand out of the fire, there are some things which cannot be explained, they must be experience. Sensation, emotion, love are all facts of primary experience. How do you explain love to someone who never experienced anybody caring about them, or who is incapable of relaxing long enough to enjoy the pleasures of giving themselves to something outside of themselves? Frankly, philosophy cannot help here, for we're now in the realm of the counselors, clergy, and psychologists. All we can do is hope for their recovery and move on to those who have experienced love.

Love: to will good to another and see that it be done. The definition very neatly grasps all three of the essential elements of the relationship. It is an act of will, not intellect; it underlines all of those times when we have loved not wisely but too well. It is the act of loving another, but...... can't you love yourself?.

Yes and no. The thinkers of the 17th and 18th Centuries became quite entangled in the problem of love of self versus the love of others, or as they called it, the problem of altruism versus egoism. Their whole discussion seems quite useless because they were trying to separate what could not be separated. No matter how selfish you act, it will involve going outside yourself to do something good to another: the man with his backyard vineyard may only be laboring to get himself better wine, but he is going outside himself. The narcissistic seductress whose only object is self-satisfaction, will also go out of her way to take steps to secure whatever partner or object will give her the most pleasure.

On the other side of the coin, the "totally altruistic" person is also getting some kind of gratification or return for his efforts: the satisfaction of a job well done, the pleasure of having kept his promises, the gratification of living up to the goal he set for himself as a totally unselfish person: there is always something. In religious terms, even the greatest saints who loved their God did not reject the thought of a heaven of eternal happiness as the reward of their labors. Religion is suggestive here: can you love your neighbor more than yourself? Whether you are saving his soul or helping his physical needs, for what purpose are you doing it? You might be sacrificing something that you might enjoy, like rest, or food, or time to yourself, but even so, isn't there something that you are promised to receive at the end of the process? The ratio of altruism to egoism can be 99 to 1 but it cannot be 100%

For these and a wide variety of other reasons, the argument between the altruist and the egoist is a side issue, since neither can be purely one thing or the other. Better to spend time considering the list of loves.

The following list represents the broad categories of different types of loves: the sub-human, parents, friends, mate(s), god. In fact, this is about the order in which most of us experience the different relationships unless we get permanently fixed on one and never go on to experience the others. Let us take them one at a time.

The love of things subhuman brings us to one problem that must be disposed of immediately: the one-sidedness of the relationship. Whether we are talking about the person who loves food, drink, scenery, plants, or animals, it seems that none of these things can reciprocate the love. How can you love something that can't love you back?

This might be the least of all love relationships that we can enter into, but be very careful not to denigrate it lower than it is. Reciprocity is a very elusive idea. The drunk or the glutton enjoys the warm glow which ingestion brings them; the naturalist enjoys the sense of awe before a rugged cliff; the plant lady or the man with a hundred cats all feel that the objects of their affection reward their attention. Furthermore, even if the lover did not feel loved in return, that does not affect their love. They might well be glad not to have a human lover who would make demands as only another human can: the autonomy of another human is an undesirable and complicating factor for them.

Before we reject this type of love as hopelessly defective, it is important to note two things: the lover still loves even if that love is not reciprocated. There are too many cases of John loves Helen, but Helen does not love John, for us to ignore them: her non-reciprocation of his love does not make his love cease to be love. It just makes his love rather hopeless.

Second, there is a covert mixture of loves which must be uncovered, clearly spelled out, and kept separate, at least intellectually. The lover of plants and animals may be exercising a frustrated parental love because they have no children to take care of. We are in a murky and complicated area. The emotions are too strong and sometimes conceal the root cause of the affection involved.

In the case of parental love, switch the perspective. What does it mean to say that a parent loves a child? Every person's family history enters into the picture at this point. The human animal is rather a queer bird: it seems to be unable to push the chicks out of the family nest without dropping them on their heads, to use poet John Ciardi's phrase. And that very experience might go quickly to the heart of the matter.

It seems that "mother love" is very tightly wrapped up in taking care of someone who is, to use the taxman's phrase, a dependent. For so long as the dependent is content to be dependent and passive, for so long as they accept the idea that "mother/father knows best", for that length of time there is no problem.

It is when the dependent starts acting independently that the problems start. The tug-of-war begins over what age is the right age at which to let the child exercise certain functions by itself. It would take one wiser than Solomon to judge these cases on their individual merits. In fact, inequality is one of the unique strengths of the family structure: it is geared especially for those quirks and eccentricities which we call individual personality.

The misunderstanding flourishes on both sides. Remember those famous family arguments? You know, the ones that usually start over taking out the garbage (let's face it, more family fights start over taking out the garbage than over who loves whom). One word leads to another; our remarkable memory for words which carry intonations from previous fights escalates the conflict, until mommy delivers the final crushing argument, "Look at all the things your father and I have done for you!" Mother love has become smother love.

Sociology sheds a curious light not only on parent-child relationships, but also the controversy over abortion, in a report on battered-children . Parents who plan when and how many children to have, have a larger emotional investment in the child conforming to some perfect archetype which the parents have in mind. The child who does not conform to this blueprint is most likely to be the target of increased wrath.

What makes two people become friends? If we know how it comes into being (efficient cause), it might tell us something about the nature of the relationship itself. Well, usually two people in the course of initial conversations start searching around for common ground. In the words of the proverb, "Birds of a feather flock together".

But don't "opposites attract"? How can both proverbs be

true? At moments like this, even the most abstract concepts of metaphysics can be put to good use. In that most abstract of sciences, there is a distinction between potency and act which reconciles the two proverbs, and illustrates the earlier observation of these different lives. The shy person might envy the bolder friend, envies her ability to say and do things. The bolder one might equally admire the ability the shy friend has in keeping her mouth shut while the bolder one is busily chewing on her shoe from putting her foot in her mouth. Each admires what the other actually has, and wishes she could actualize the potential within herself.

The search for common ground is the keynote of friendship. Plato said that friends have all things in common. In fact, he went so far as to hold that friendship is the finest kind of love that there is. It is a pairing of equals held together by strong common bonds.

His insight is not only valid, it holds for groups of friends which choose to strengthen their unity
by formalizing it: brotherhoods, sisterhoods, lodges, clubs, fraternities, sororities, all express this union of friends.

When you take friends in groups of three or four, added dimensions come out which were not at first apparent in the two person example. Jim may be depressed; Henry is the only one who can recognize the symptoms, but he can't do anything about it; Paul doesn't see changes in personality, but he can cheer Jim if someone points out the need.

Thus friends interact in increasing relationships as the number of the group increases. Subtract one member because of outside factors and you have lost not only that one person, but all of the characteristics of the others which he and he alone was able to pull out of them.

If friendships are so great, why has every society of friends been persecuted? Every few years, there is a push to make fraternities and sororities illegal; ancient groups like the

Pythagoreans or the early Christians were persecuted primarily for belonging to a secret society; the peaceable Quakers were hounded; and only about 80 years ago the state of Washington tried to have Catholic schools closed and require everybody to go to public schools. Why?

It comes down to one word: clique. If friends become stronger and stronger, if they bind themselves together with more and more things in common, their friendship has become immeasurably the strongest thing in their lives. The ancient story of Damon and Pythias, where one was willing to be the hostage in place of the other, "Greater love than this no man hath, than that he lay down his life for his friends".

This is precisely the trap: as we strengthen the bonds among us, the distinction between US and THEM, between Insider and Outsider becomes more marked. They couldn't understand our in-jokes, the references We make among Ourselves. The temptation becomes nearly overwhelming.

Now, it may be reasonably objected that this does not happen to all societies of friends. It may be objected that I am exaggerating the power of this type of cliquishness. All I can do is suggest that, if your friendships do not exclude others, is it that some other love has made you more outgoing or that your love of your friends is not that strong to begin with? In either case, it is not an objection to the analysis given here.

If Pythagoreans and Quakers seem too remote from your experience then consider the British writer EM Forester(1879-1970) who expressed the following treason in the name of friendship. "If I had to choose between betraying my country and betraying my friend, I hope I should have the guts to betray my country."7/16/38

Love for one's mate is the primary love in our society today. Therefore, it will be the most difficult to analyze because of the layers of memory which hide it. Let me begin by underlining what is not considered under this heading. Marriage is not here because it will be considered in the chapter on law. Nor will we consider the gender of that mate: issues of bisexuality and the like will be considered under the virtue of temperance which includes the field of sexual activity.

There is another distinction which we need here. If it is possible to have sex without love as the "liberated" claim, does the converse hold? Is it possible to have love without sex? Of course, it is. Even the periodic celibacy of the married shows that.

What about the case of unrequited love? There are people who have chosen to remain not only single, but celibate and even virginal because they were not willing to settle for second best. The one grand love of their lives was sufficient even in memory, even in non-consummation, to keep them kindly and loving and human for the rest of their lives.

This is not the statistically normal circumstance, but it is necessary as an introduction to the nature of this love especially. Romantic idolatry so clouds our perspective: its dream of two people totally and absolutely in love with each other, where each gives 100% of "self" to the other, that it is only with the greatest difficulty that the romantic soul can be convinced that this is not the case. The case of unrequited love arises so frequently that we are on safer ground by inquiring what it means for one person to love another in this kind of relationship without reciprocity.

What do you want to do for the person whom you love? Eros and Venus play their parts here, to be sure; the erotic and venereal elements cannot be underplayed. Psychology dates its founding from Freud's alleged observation that sex was the basis for everything; the least interaction between people can have most delightful sexual overtones and are decidedly pleasant, but is that the same thing as love? No.

Underlying most of the great works of romantic literature, there is a dark current with grim, if not tragic, undertones. It is the notion of sacrifice, but it has a paradoxical psychology : the lover wants only one thing, to make the beloved happy. Songs abound with titles like "I'd do anything for you Dear," or "Make someone happy"; they are valid indicators of the paradox. With this passion, the lover is convinced that personal happiness is bound up forever with the task of making the beloved smile, of making the beloved happy. In that context, the sacrifice is not sacrifice but something done willingly; the sacrifice still has overtones of doing without, but without any negative connotations because the lover feels that the effects on this beloved, increasing his/her happiness, is all that is needed in the world to immeasurably increase the lover's own happiness.

The cliché says 'love is blind'. This is one half-truth which is just as important for the half which is right as for the half which is wrong. To the extent that love is blind, to the extent that an act of the will need have very little intelligence about it, we are talking about the strongest and most powerful type of love which most people experience. The welding of two pieces of metal under the force of red hot intensity is the only thing in nature comparable to the intensity of this experience. For better or worse, the lover remains inextricably caught up in the love of the beloved no matter what happens. At its strongest, purest, finest, at its most intense, this is the form of love overshadows all the others. For this the alcoholic will give up his bottle, the glutton will grow thin with fasting, the perpetual baby will develop into maturity with amazing speed. For this, they will leave mother and father . . . .

Even in the cold light of morning, even in the most clear-eyed and hard-headed of people, the ability to see something else does not matter. The faithful wife of the politician might loath campaigning and be planning the murder of her husband's mistress, but she will still go campaigning. Kill her husband? Maybe. Divorce him? Don't be silly. She is not blind but bound, and it will be till death do us part.

In either case, this love is, for all its intensity, something not under the control of the lover. He can`t help himself. There is nothing to do about it. Therefore, direction and expression of this love is totally under the command of the beloved. Even so cynical a song as "Fifty ways to leave your lover" underlines the point that the lover is not freed until after realizing the possibility of forming another love relationship.

It is precisely the fact that the greatest forces of your life are not under your control that makes it so dangerous. Is it wise to entrust such total control over yourself to another fallible human who might be no better or worse than you but just as frailly human? It doesn't matter if your spouse is a politician or a burglar (for the sake of argument I distinguish between the two): if you want them to be happy at their job, you inevitably find yourself aiding and abetting them in their efforts. It makes quite a difference whether you marry Joan of Arc or Jezebel, St. Thomas More or Jack the Ripper, but it doesn't change the fact that you love. This is the reason why all societies have made a god or the tribe a third party to marriage contracts: to protect both parties from each other by introducing the third party as referee.

Going through our little list has become quite a depressing chore: it seems that the very strength of each love has been the source of its own weakness. Its very success contained the seeds of its own failure. Of course, there are combinations of the loves which I have not touched upon, but on the whole they only flesh-out the outline. For example, your love for your brothers and sisters I neglected because your love for them is something quite different from the fact that they are your relatives. If you can make your sibling or your mate into your friend, fine. All you've done is add to the relationship: I don't think you have altered the essential outlines. (Of course, you could kill your brother, but that hardly comes under the notion of love--unless you'd love to kill him. In which case, see the section on love of the subhuman a few pages back). As to "brother love" see "sibling rivalry", see also "Cain and Abel".

In the face of all these failures, it is rather difficult to present a decent case for a love relationship between you and God. First, a little intellectual judo, is in order. What does it mean to say that God loves you?

First, forget the cute Sunday school notion that God was lonely. On the previous analysis, this is an awesome, powerful, entirely perfect and self-sufficient Being, who can do quite well without us, thank you. On Christian terms, God is a three person corporation called the Trinity.

To reach out for something implies a lack in yourself. You want something because you want for something; you lack something and this outside desideratum will somehow make up for your lack. Because we considered the other loves at their best, we have not bought the right to ignore the weak, pathetic, crippled uses to which some people put these loves. There are people who use love as a weapon for the expression of a set of neurotic needs. They are probably the most flagrant examples of *need-love* which can be conjured up; it is this flagrancy that leaves them open for recognition and help. What about the rest of us?

I have spent very little time on the beloved's reaction to some of these love relationships because such reactions are not representative of love at its best either. If truth be told, how did you feel when someone you couldn't care less about put themselves totally in your hands? Discomfort at first? But when you discovered you couldn't rid yourself of the affection and attention, wasn't there the first glimmer of the abuse of power? Wasn't the temptation there to make them jump through hoops, just because you knew you could make them jump through hoops? If the tyranny of absolute love corrupts the lover into doing as the beloved wishes, the effects on the beloved of having this power put at their control is not much more attractive.

The whole purpose of this digression is to underline the difference between gift-love and need-love. The medievals said that goodness tends to diffuse itself. Restoration poets talk of the sharing that halves our sorrows and doubles our joys. Ever gotten a piece of news which was so good you could not wait to tell the whole immediate world?

It is precisely this overflowing from a super abundance that marks *gift-love*. If anything, it makes some humans even more uncomfortable to realize that God loves them without us giving IT any good reason to love us. What's in me to love? Nothing that God didn't put there first!

So we are back to square one: why does God love us? All religions have a deity who is to some extent involved with us. This Being's Will has chosen to make us, provides for us: that implies some kind of love.

The answer to the question is only a little less startling than the question itself. In loving us, God wants to make us perfect, per-ficio, bring us to completion, make us the best that we can be. The claim on the very face of it can have no defects; in its very statement it professes to be the most perfect and truest type of love. If it is that good, we must give IT some tasks and answer some objections before we go much further.

The most common objection raised against the love of God is that of the Cold War `kill a Commie for Christ' variety. It is an objection raised in the holy city of Jerusalem as supporters of Allah fight supporters of Yahweh; in Belfast, where Papist Christians kill Protestant Christians.

The prior loves were subject to extensive analysis of their defects, but each was considered as the best expression of that kind of love. The objection loses its force because this is no worse than the other loves in the ways in which it can be perverted. Second, in the words of an old cartoon, "The opinions expressed are not necessarily those of the Sponsor." The condemnation of Belfast by the majority of Protestant and Catholic clergy is an example of what I mean.

A second, better, test of the claims of a perfect divine love is to set it to work correcting the defects of the other loves.

In the case of the person who only loves the subhuman, there are a variety of cases where the love of the subhuman was combined with a love of God to yield a not unattractive curative of its defects. Unfortunately, most of the illustrative examples come from the history of religion. Before I begin to use any of them it is necessary to underline their limited role in philosophy. It is not necessary for you to believe what the various holy men of history have believed in order to appreciate the soundness and sanity of their actions or the healthy way in which they kept their various loves orderly. Surely, they are worthy of both admiration and imitation, but matters of faith remain beyond the limits of reason.

With that disclaimer out of the way, consider a Francis of Assisi with his love of plants and animals, a Thomas More who relished his food when seasoned with a fair number of fasts, or a Matt Talbot who found God a more powerful love than his thirst for a bottle. There are many others like this who do not have the problems of the dog owners who think dogs are more people than people, or the fanatical plant lady who talks to her plants because she refuses to talk to her neighbors.

Books for parents on how to raise children assert the respect that one must have for the individual free will of the child. This is a uniquely Western phenomenon which can be traced back to the belief that God was once a man. If there were not the example of Mary and Joseph respecting the freedom and personal development of Jesus, it is highly doubtful whether the cult of the individual could have come into existence. The book, The Discovery of the Individual puts the date for the society discovery of the dignity of the individual person at 1100 A.D. Only recently did the notion arrive in the Orient; one need only compare the role of offspring in a patriarchate to see the difference.

The only societies of friends which have managed to have strong internal cohesiveness, without cliquishness and with a strong outward thrust are precisely those organizations which hold that the group's love of God is more important than the group's love of itself. The list is long: the Society of Friends (Quakers), the Society of Jesus (Jesuits), the Order of Friars Minor (Franciscans), and the Order of Preachers (Dominicans) are but a few examples. History even provides a negative verification of this truth: in the late Middle Ages, when some religious orders concentrated more on their own group than on the love of God, the cliquishness and inter-order warfare was brutal. Without their foundation in a love of God, they were no better than any other clique, and in some cases, much worse.

The love of a mate has been hedged in by all societies in all times and all places. The rite of marriage exists in all societies. There is a natural awareness that it takes three to get married; whether the third partner be the code of the society (which frequently claims to speak for God) or the code of the cult (which always claims to speak for God), the effect is the same: thou shalt not abuse the other's love which has been placed in your hands

In all cases, the other loves never stand so straight as when they bend in submission to the love of God. The wise men of the Middle Ages had a wide variety of ways of expressing this truth. St. Augustine: "You have made us for yourself, O Lord. Our hearts are restless until they rest in You." Dante: "In His Will is Our Peace."

It is the burden of poor weak philosophy that, from page one to this page, we have gotten no further than the first questions asked of little children by the 1885 catechism written by the Catholic Bishops assembled in Baltimore. Their question and answer to the purpose and meaning of life takes up all philosophy has said so far and answers it in a nondenominational form which most of Earth's inhabitants would accept.

Q. Who made you?
A. God made me.
Q. Why did God make you?
A. God made me to know, love, and serve Him in this world and to be happy with Him in the next.

If that is too painfully unsophisticated, we can find the same solace in one of this century's wise men, Carl Jung, addressing the Zurich Medical Society in 1935 on the "Principles of

Practical Psychotherapy":

> "Therefore, when certain doctors resort to the mythological ideas of some religion or another, they are doing something historically justified . . . . If [patient] can find the meaning of his life and the cure for his disquiet and disunity within the framework of an existing credo . . . . that should be enough for the doctor."

What a great contrast to Animal Rights groups: animal happiness is a manmade projection which vividly contrasts with the more factual conclusion of John Stuart Mill who recognized that brute animals "pass their existence in tormenting and devouring other animals". Thus animals can be "divided into devourers and devoured, and a prey to a thousand ills from which they are denied the faculties necessary for protecting themselves." [35]

It is one of the annoying habits of philosophers that they must take the peak emotions and insights and analyze them back down into the mundane world. I regretfully find myself doing just that right now because an insistent question naggingly mars the whole discussion of God. Why is there a rejection of the entire notion of a deity?

You are a highly intelligent reader, who has the time to study, the ability to think, and the imagination to broaden your mind beyond the day-to-day trivia in which we usually hide ourselves. If it weren't for the existence of a revealed religion, very few people would come to any knowledge of God at all because of a lack of time, education and/or intelligence

Aquinas thought that it was very democratic for God to reveal something about himself through the life and work of Moses and Jesus. But whether you believe in these revelations or not, most people have been exposed to them through some kind of religious education--and that is the start of the problem. Many

---

35 Three Essays on Religion, London,Longmans, 1875,p58

people drop out of any religious formation as children. They thereafter write it off as something childish that they have outgrown, a phenomenon referred to by sociologists as "adolescent atheism". Usually they return to religion after marriage and parenthood "for the sake of the children", thus perpetuating the cycle into the next generation.

Furthermore, it is difficult to reconcile objective reality with the subjective condition of our knowledge. The intellect filters all our knowledge: how we intellectually perceive things will influence our reaction to it. In the line of argument followed so far, we have found a Being who is infinitely good and infinitely intelligible. It is capable of satisfying both the unlimited powers of our intellect and the infinite desires of our will. They fit together like a lock and key. That is a description of the objective situation, but our subjective experience might be quite different. First, imagine an avant-garde teacher who is trying to explain sexuality to a first grade class and has too late discovered that he has been talking over their heads for the last hour. It is now the question and answer session: a rather talkative child, whose greatest experience to date has been the thrill of a chocolate bar (with almonds) asks:

Child: Is sex something like eating chocolate?
Teacher: Um . . . Ah . . . Well, not quite.
Child: If it is something that you do, can you eat chocolate while doing it? I can eat chocolate and play baseball at the same time.
Teacher: Um . . . Ah . . . Well, it isn't usually done. No, you really shouldn't eat chocolate at the same time.

And, of course, the first grader goes away with the firm conviction that sex is something horrible because it means doing without chocolate. Leave him alone; in a few years he'll learn better.

Aren't we very much like that child? There are very few of us who casually talk of having profoundly earth-shattering mystical experiences, of making direct contact with a deity. The people who have had those experiences and who have written about them are far better teachers than the one we just listened in on. The mystical writers frequently use sexual analogies to describe the elusive experience where you are totally conscious of yourself and yet are in total union with the other. There is a very good case here for selling the delights of God the way we sell chocolate . . . or sex.

But it usually is not done that way. The Infinite Goody is viewed as if through a wrong-way telescope, and the resulting image is so minimally desirable that it is a wonder that people take delight in God at all.

Quite a different thing happens when we see and want things of a more tangible variety. Remember the Christmas when you just had to have that toy, that you would be happy for the rest of your life, that you would be the most perfect forever after, if only you got that one special thing? What happened on Christmas Day? You got it! Joy! Ecstasy! For an hour or two you play with it until it either breaks or you become bored and start playing with the wrapping paper.

Bored? But it was the very thing you wanted!

Examples in this area can be multiplied endlessly. The drunk, on the wagon, who would sell his soul for a shot of Chivas Regal, or a can of beer. The dieter who can taste the ice cream of gluttonies past and would bite the lock off the refrigerator door to get some. And let us not forget the reformed lecher, who, after a few months of chastity, would . . . well, you get the idea.

They indulge.

After the first glow of satisfaction wears off, after the nervous excitation of anticipation is satisfied, what happens? Disappointment, self-criticism, and even despair is immense; the guilt is fantastic. Why?

Because in the case of any good which we can experience physically, we are able to think about it, and think about it, and think about it. We concentrate upon all of its good points, ignore all of its defects and blow it up out of all sense of proportion until we have made a very finite and limited good into some imaginary infinite good which will satisfy all of our wants. We have placed a magnifying glass on the object of our desires; the warped vision warps our minds and ultimately our wills.

Let us suppose for the sake of argument that a person existed who could be described as a good person, a virtuous barbarian. Let us further suppose that this person always saw reality as it really was. With this clear-eyed vision, this intellect functioning like a piece of plain glass, would the notion of God be irresistible? Would finite goods be recognized as finite, and the Infinite Good as Being Infinitely Desirable? I rather doubt it.

Even the virtuous barbarian suffers from two of the basic limitations inherent in our human condition. The first limit is inherent in the nature of the intellect. As mathematicians are fond of pointing out, there are infinities and there are infinities. Our mind cannot, in our present sensual condition, comprehend, that is, fully understand all of the implications of what God is. This is the one topic which is beyond our grasp. We can know, but we cannot know fully. It might be theoretically possible to keep the image of this Being before our minds day and night, awake and asleep; we might well become better people for exercising that kind of mental discipline. But, how easily distracted most of us are! The least flash of sound can pull us away from the deepest and most engrossing thinking.

The second limit on the virtuous barbarian is an expansion of the first. If soul is the life principle of the entire body, then we are much like a gun made out of plastic trying to fire real bullets. The power of our intellect and will far outstrips our physical capacities, and yet, at the same time, the raw material which makes up us is just as liable to go off and do its own thing if it is not kept under some kind of regular control.

This experience of our divided self has driven philosophers to suggest that there are two souls in man (one animal and one rational); that there are three souls in man (animal, vegetable, and rational); or even (back to Plato again) that the soul and body operate on different wavelengths because they are different kinds of things. Theologians point to the phenomenon as the best example they have of Original Sin. Even if you do not believe in Original Sin, the experience of our being unable or unwilling to control ourselves is all too depressingly common to require much elaboration.

Is there any hope for making ourselves better? There is reason to think so, reasons which will occupy the last half of this book. Before we embark on the task of improving the human race by improving ourselves, there are a few warnings which have to be kept in mind.

If you have a hang-up on God, all I can ask of you is a temporary suspension of your disbelief until you see the sketch of an improved life. I am not willing to assume that you and I are so far apart in our views: concerning certain opinions about God, I, too, am an atheist. Even the prophets of Israel delighted in the fact that they were iconoclasts towards false icons, atheists toward false gods.

You must also exercise a certain amount of honesty with yourself. Don't say you disbelieve in God, when what you really mean is "if God exists, He will louse up my sex life." Do not assume that the existence of a deity necessarily implies that your hobbies are evil. It was the god of the heretical Manichees who said sex was evil, not the god of the philosophers.

If I deal a little light-heartedly with the deity, the explanation is fairly easy to see: if God loves me and wants me to be perfect, then it is something which is perfectly compatible with the humanistic desire to want to be the best human being I can be. If this deity wants to help, who am I to argue with It?

CHAPTER VI:
OTHER WAYS TO DO ANTHROPOLOGY

Every age does things its own way. That is a reflection of the infinite fertility of the human mind. In Auguste Comte's simplistic outline of the March of Progress, these were the ages of Faith, then Reason, then Science. One might add Renaissance belles-lettres or modern geopolitics to the list of things which influence the thinking of philosophers

It is in our concrete, here-and-now, historical reality that timeless truths can be discovered. This paradoxical creature immersed in matter breathes pure spirit. This paradox forces us to separate and evaluate those elements into their time-conditioned limiting elements as opposed to their eternal truths. That is why we still read *the 'biblical books' of the ancient Greeks, the Iliad (because life is a battle) and the Odyssey (because life is a journey)* or all those other eternal classics.

The Jewish Scriptures have given us `nefesh', a type of soul, but Sadducees and Pharisees were still arguing its immortality at the time of Jesus. St. Paul and the Christian Scriptures seem to have found nefesh too earthy, too biological, for their more spiritualized concerns. *Body can be soma or sarx* (as in somatic or sarcophagus) depending on its power for good or evil. Mind, psyche, is less valued than the new element, the pneuma or spirit given us by Christ. Plato's ascending values given to body, spirit(as in a spirited football game),psyche becomes *Paul's "Body, soul, and spirit."*

Greek religion gave us Homer's gods and Orphic religiosity. Homer's heroes like Ulysses have their *nous (intellect)* but it is overwhelmed periodically by *thymos, the drives and feelings* which burst the bounds of reason and sanity. Nietzsche for all his madness knew that Apollo's Reason periodically yielded to Dionysian revelry and ecstasy. *Orphic religion was dualism: man is not one but two things. Psyche is the root of biological and psychological life but the body is a tomb.* Eternal life was there but lost in Zeus like a book of matches in a bonfire or a drop of water in the ocean; personal immortality was not on their agenda, collective immortality, beginning with panpsychism, the theory that there was "mind in Everything" arguably begins with the Greeks.

Greek philosophy is replete with opinions. *Thales*, who thought all change could be explained by changes in *water*, and *Anaximenes*, who thought the basic element was *air*, generated part of that quartet (earth, air, fire, and water) which were to dominate medicine from a doctrine of four humors to Carl Jung's psychoanalytic notion of quaternity.

More to the point were *Anaximander's insistence on Apeiron, the unlimited*, in man; *Heraclitus's logos*, the word; and the *Pythagorean emphasis on arythmos*, the number, the perfect harmony of man within all his parts. We still say 'I've got your number' as if we had grasped an essential element. Ludwig Wittgenstein only a generation ago reminded us that the task of philosophy is to protect us against the enchantment of words. And man still partakes of the infinite.

Plato's influence drove Alfred North Whitehead to say that the whole history of philosophy was nothing more than a series of footnotes to Plato. As the first dramatist of the life of the mind, he gave us memorable metaphors for his dualistic man (a sailor steering a ship, a rider on a horse) with the three piece soul (sensual, courageous, intellectual).

His pupil *Aristotle knew we were autokinetos*, selfmoving; that life was primary and all its activities secondary; that the *nous poietikos*, active thought, was the magic in man that turned things into concepts and words.

The intellectuals of early Christianity knew that God created an immortal soul, no matter how crippled it might be by original sin. But that was a matter of faith even if it was drawn from the biologism of Aristotle the physician's son and *the cosmic unity of Stoicism in the pre-Christian Rome of Seneca and Cicero*. It was a faith which made no sense to the Hebrews for whom a God-man was a blasphemy or to the Greeks who found the need for a Redeemer degrading the dignity of that divine self-mastery which a Stoic offered as a goal for virtuous behavior.

Those first four centuries came close to slandering matter in order to glorify spirit. Clement of Alexandria saw the body as a tomb for the soul and St. Augustine thought that God must illuminate our mind before we could achieve authentic intellectual knowledge (hence references to *Augustinian illuminationism*.) Once again, the amazement at what our mind can achieve was so awesome as to be attributed to divinity. Plato thought the World of Ideas was a really real spiritual world, more real than this ever-changing world of matter. *St. Augustine merely put the World of Ideas into the Mind of God,* almost as if not realizing that *God is not exalted at the expense of man but that the exaltation of man is a glorification of God.*

With the fall of Rome, Art, Literature, Philosophy, Theology and all those High Culture fruits of peace and stability disappeared while Western Europe scrambled for survival. It took Rome over 400 years (400-800A.D.) to baptize and civilize its invaders. Christopher Dawson, commenting on the relative success of Rome in domesticating its Vandals, contrasted it to poor Byzantium who had to administer baptism, communion, and confirmation all at once, sprinkling its blessing on each wave of invaders as they ebbed and flowed around Constantine's city of Constantinople.

Fortunately, Providentially, that high culture did not disappear. Rome fell in the same years that *Benedict started the monasteries* which were to preserve the culture's seed corn. And within the century came Mohammed.

The creed which came out of the Arabian desert with its terrible simplicity (`There is no God but Allah and Mohammed is His prophet') concentrated on the `Islam', the submission, of our egos to His Will. When combined with the promise of Paradise for those who die in jihad (means spreading the faith not just 'holy war' as the newspapers say), it is no wonder that the

Moslem faith ran from India, through North Africa and Spain, and into France within 200 years. The battle of Tours (732 AD.), like Thermopylae before and Lepanto afterward, are the only reason westerners do not speak Persian or worship from the Koran.

The philosophy developed by this culture traveled where the troops could not. Overwhelmingly it was the work of three men: Ibn Sina (Avicenna), Al Ghazali (Al-Gazel), and Ibn Ruschd (Averroes).

Avicenna was Islam's Genius. A specialist on law, secular and theological, author of a medical text used in Europe for 500 years, and sometimes credited with the discovery of coffee, gathered together anthropological data for his view of man. We use fine arts not just technology, *we have an artificial system of conventional signs* A language not only infinitely more sophisticated than brute animal sounds but a different kind of thing from the way natural sounds are interconnected: Groan is to pain as smoke is to fire. We are solitary substances who use language, make plans, and need morality.

To Avicenna we owe the philosophical development of arguments for the spirituality (immateriality) and immortality of the soul. Thus: our reflection, self-knowledge, self-consciousness, must be something other than a bodily organ. If mine were brain, how could we fully know our own mind without fully knowing our own brain? But we have known our own minds for centuries and still yet today do not fully know the brain.(His argument for immortality from self-consciousness will be deferred until its modern version can be explored in the last part of this chapter).

Al-Gazel, theologian rather than philosopher, enters into our discussions because of his *fideism and occasionalism. Fideism insists that faith takes such priority over reason that reason must yield when contradicted by faith in the revelation.* The persistence of religion, the existence of unsecular man, homo religiosus, points up the power which fideists like Augustine (4th

Century), Gazel (10th Century), Blaise Pascal (17th Century), exercise on the mind of man. Even in the 'secularized' countries of the West, it is still possible to find fideistic fundamentalists who equate sophistication with sinfulness and simple-mindedness with sanctity. Only the Rabbis, Dominicans, and the Jesuits can boast of a long tradition of full strong support for faith and reason, knowledge and holiness.

Occasionalism, the seeing of all creation as eternally dependent upon the infinite whim of God, is a view of reality, a Weltanschauung or World View, which glorifies the Power of God (omnipotence) at the expense of the Mind of God (omniscience). As a reminder of the root uncertainty, the radical contingency which flavors human existence, his view is a valuable reminder of our fragility, even if its partial truth is expressed excessively-- since a fickle god is a stupid god.

If Aristotle was The Philosopher to both East and West, the perfect representative of Reason before Revelation, the noble pagan, then *Ibn Ruschd, Averroes, was the Commentator on Aristotle. His World Soul agent intellect and theory of double truth are most important errors about man.*

People who remember the Ptolemaic geocentric conception of the Universe with Earth at center frequently do not realize that this terrestrial sphere was also the lowest one of all, at the bottom of the celestial ice-cream cone. Ptolemy's cosmology and Plotinus's notion that this is the lowest point down from the heavens was combined into the notion of the world-soul agent-intellect.

Why bother with such a strange doctrine? First, because *history is to philosophers as laboratories are to scientists*: it is the place to check out our theories against other alternatives. Second, because it shows how far reasonable people will go to explain our 'divine' capacity to arrive at universal truths, generalized concepts, from a world of changeable, individual, lumps of matter. *Averroes thought that our potential intellect served up our experiences to this World Soul, which performed the functions of the agent intellect, abstracted the idea from the matter, and returned it pre-digested to our passive intellect for its understanding. This resembles Augustine's theory of divine illumination , and later, Hegel's 19th century version which was called the Zeitgeist or the Spirit of the Age.*

Averroes' Theory of Double Truth was even more influential. Rather than harmonize faith and reason like Aquinas or Avicenna, or subordinate reason to faith like Augustine or Al-Gazel, Averroes severed the two in an irrevocable fashion. *If faith contradicts reason, then the believer must reject the truths of reason and the scientist-philosopher must reject the truths of faith.* And the religious philosopher or believing scientist must cut his mind in two. Psychoanalysis has shown that such a divided mind is a rich source of neuroses and exceptionally draining of psychological energy but the deleterious impact of this theory goes much deeper.

By denying faith any power to interpenetrate the world of reason, Averroes has 'freed' nations, politics, and modern science from its usual source of all ethics or morality. The government which assassinates its opponents in the national interest, the pragmatic Machiavellian whose goals justify any means, and the "value-free" sciences which have given us biochemical weapons, genetic redesign for humans, and the totalitarian state are the fruits of Averroes' Double Truth Theory. This is not the independence of science but the justification for all that is madly dehumanizing in the tradition from Dr. Faust to Dr. Frankenstein to Dr. Strangelove.

Some of the developments which have flowed from Averroes' Double Truth include: Dante's De Monarchia, Machiavelli's The Prince, the 1648 European political settlements where citizens had to take up their king's religion (Eius religio, cujus religio),the "Glorious Revolution" of 1688 where an English king was deposed so that the money class could find another who could be forced to share his people's religion, culminating in the 1789 separation of state and official church in America and the vandalism of the churches of France. Only if religion is pure evil can such developments be considered good.

The irony is that *the theory of double truth even makes God schizophrenic. How else can the God who gave us reason contradict the God who revealed himself to us? If the god of the philosophers isn't the god of the theologians, then there are two gods, neither of who can properly be called God.* The stronger irony is that the theory is unnecessary: given one sane God (see Chapter V), it is a better--i.e., more efficient, more elegant, more reasonable--hypothesis to assume that the human interpreters of science or scripture make erroneous assumptions which collide. Anyway, which science contradicts which religion? Apart from Kali, Thugee, and other crackpot faiths, are the 19th century's mechanistic (deterministic) physical theories or the 20th century's probabilistic (indeterministic) physical theories or 21st century's expression of matter as pure energy (something immaterial) and better candidates for the Truth-of-the- Month- Club?

Ultimately this is not about God or Knowledge but Man. It is perfectly kosher to divide up bodies of knowledge, to create specializations and divide our labors to the benefit of our society. To set homo religious (Man the religious creature) at war with homo economicus(Man as maker and spender of money), or politicus (the political animal), or socialis (the social critter) as a matter of principle is not to divide up our knowledge of man but to drive a wedge between different peoples. *Erring belief is no more a reason to condemn all belief in itself, than erring scientists are a good reason to condemn all science in itself.* In Following Aquinas we seek a philosophy for the whole person..... at best Averroes gives us a divided self.

It should come as no surprise that 1300-1600 AD is not a period marked by philosophical giants. The Black Death, the literary interest of the Renaissance in rediscovered classical writings, and the savagery of nationalistic wars fought under guise of Wars of Religion or religious schism all militated against the development of systematic philosophic writing.

The emphasis on "I" the ego or consciousness of the human

subject sounds a new note in the history of thought. *The subjective turn began in medieval nominalism,* a philosophy which confuses concepts with words and then reduces both to mere vocalized sounds. By denying the reality of mental entities like immaterial; ideas, concepts or generalizations, the nominalist reduced everything to power and interpersonal relations. Once concepts lost their force, it became easier to place all the emphasis on the idiosyncratic private faith of the knowing subject. Thus Martin Luther summarizes a whole trend of the 14th and 15th Centuries when he asserts his three 'solas'. Sola fide, sola gratia, sola Scriptura: man is saved by faith alone, faith is given by grace alone, grace is known by Scripture alone

"I am saved because I believe that I am saved" is an invitation to delusion rather than an accurate objective statement of where any individual stands relative to their fate in the next world. More accurate and more modestly true are the words of the 17 year old general whose armies liberated France during this period: "If I am not in the state of grace, I pray God to put me there; If I am in the state of grace, I pray God to keep me there"-- St. Joan of Arc.

The multiplication of personal beliefs would ultimately drive some societies to privatize beliefs and de-socialize religion in order to keep civil peace. More immediately it created the Cartesian concept of Man.

René Descartes was the genius who invented analytic geometry and thus for the first time united algebra with geometry. Descartes started "by only accepting as true those ideas *which I clearly and distinctly see* as true". From this base of pure subjectivism he concluded "that my essence consists solely in being a body which thinks". This is not just a revived Platonism with "mind-body" replacing "soul-body". *The Cartesian body is res extensa, an extended thing, ultimately an object for mechanical analysis* (hence Gilbert Ryle's 1950 wisecrack that Cartesian man's mind was nothing but the ghost in the machine). This is a new principle for dividing up the world.

The ancients divided form and soul, nonliving and living; which had the effect of biologizing man, setting him squarely in the animal world, marked off only as a rational animal. *The modern theory divides the conscious from the non-conscious blurring us in with lower animals also possessing consciousness* (I will leave the term unconscious for Freud and the comatose).

Locke, Berkeley, and Hume are part of Descartes' World, despite their apparently 'objective' name as 17th Century British Empiricists. John Locke defines the person as *"a thinking, intelligent thing which can think of itself as itself in diverse times and places"*. While that will deny personhood to amnesiacs, paramnesiacs, the senile, and all members of the human species from conception through age three, nevertheless it is clearly definition a la Descartes.

George Berkeley and The Problem of Other Minds arises from so over-emphasizing my consciousness that I must acknowledge something before it exists. *"Esse est percipe et percipere": to be is to be perceived or to perceive.* If one rejects the existence of *Bereley's Universal Perceiver (God)* on the grounds that She cannot be perceived , all that is left is *solipsism, the internally self-consistent doctrine that only my mind exists-- everything else must be a product of my conscious/subconscious mind projected outward. (That "I" enter into all my judgments is indubitable; Aquinas recognized knowledge is the union of the knower and the known. That I 'create' it seems denied by the intractability of things, their refusal to obey me.)*

David Hume not only denies the existence of other minds but dares us to identify in that attic of the mind, amidst all the dreams, memories, and other impressions, one idea which is simply "me". *If Hume were correct,* that *there is no "me" but merely a location where other things collide,* then James Joyce's stream of consciousness (Mindlessness) and Sigmund Freud's denial that "I" am the personal subject of my activities (merely a combination of internal and external forces) are generating true philosophies of man. But *Hume is wrong. There is no idea in the attic "I am", the assertion of my personal, substantial, existence, "I" as opposed to the things I possess, "I" even as distinguished by the mental contents which are "mine" in yet another sense.*

I shall pass over in silence Joyce's drama of mental life because it is an exercise of imagination not reason. Freud's truth is as partial as that of his successors: selective attention is paid to part of our psychic life, different parts give rise to different emphases, and result in the differing psychological theories of Freud, Jung, Adler, Horney, Sullivan, James and Skinner. A philosophical anthropology could be constructed from the synthesis of all the various philosophies of man held overtly or covertly by differing psychological schools. But that is beyond the task of the present work.

Much more to our point are the works of Martin Heidegger and Max Scheler.

Heidegger grew out of the 19th Century European traditions from *Kant--who asserted the existence of other things but said they could never be known in themselves--*and *Hegel whose Idealism was a glorification of the mind at the expense of the objective.* Heidegger faced the questions of "the meaningless of human existence" as raised by Dostoievski and Nietzsche. In <u>Sein und Seit</u> (Being and Time), he makes "the meaning of being' the essential problem of philosophy. Concrete, historical Man is now constructing himself (Dasein) and is open to being (Sein) in the forms in which being is given to us--limited beings (Seiende). We are beings-in-the-World (In-der-Welt-sein) who find objects (Seiende) around us which are useful (beings-at-hand, Zuhandesein). They serve for something (etwas-um-zu) and we construct from them the base and apex, the Pyramid of uses which make up a human culture (um-zu-Pyramide).

In this world of the concrete, and the historical, human consciousness finds others present with us (mit-sein) for whom we have empathy (Fursorge). These existents, be they things we control (besorgt) or humans we sympathize with (fursorgt), still cannot overcome our sense of homelessness, alienation, a sense of always being a stranger in a strange land, a foreigner estranged from his surroundings.

We tell our stories "in media res": we begin in the middle, pick up the past in flashback, and then went to find out how the story ends. This represents the deep structure of our consciousness. We were thrown (geworfenheit) into a pre-existing net of relatives and objects. "The world before me" seems curiously unreal; no child understands "before you were born"; even teenagers can barely imagine their parents as having once been teenagers, much less engaging in the biological activities which resulted in the teenager's existence.

The here-and-now is not much better. We submerge ourselves in things and come up feeling empty. We fill our nights and days and still have a sense of emptiness. Blaise Pascal in the 1600's noticed that all the problems of the human race stem from the inability of man to sit quietly in a silent room for five minutes. And we all know people who cannot go off to study without radio, TV, Ipod, or cellphones making noise. Why? Because we are afraid.

The harder we try to lose ourselves, the more forceful the reaction, the stronger the sense of nothingness. The other name for nothingness is death. Man is a being-toward-death (ein sein-sum-Todt)--not some future death but the real awareness here and now of nothingness, death as an ever present possibility. It colors our whole life, this "tension-towards-death". We die alone; even two people dying in each others presence must die separate deaths. Each is as full a personality as will ever be accomplished which is why Heidegger speaks of death as "bestowing on man his ultimate personality".

The believer might wish to respond that we are homeless because our "kingdom is not of this world" or that death is our second transition from one kind of life to another (the first being from fetus to infant). This first topic is a matter of faith, the second is susceptible to reason and the burden of the balance of this chapter.

Max Scheler in his works on value raised the question of the human spirit. In part a disciple of Augustine, Scheler valued human love higher than human knowledge. The distance between ape and Einstein is large but he thought it could merely be one of degree not any difference in the kind of practical intelligence. Scheler prefers to leave this issue to the ethologists (Lorenz, Tinbergen, etc.) and concentrate on reflective self-consciousness. "I" becomes "me" by opposition to all that is "not me". I can turn myself into another thing precisely as I drift along with the current, "go with the flow". My spirit manifests itself through asceticism: "I" becomes "me" by saying "no" especially to my own drives. Self-mastery increases self

Scheler is suggestive, interesting, and is possibly correct but not on a basic enough level. "I" am always aware of my "self". This center of self- consciousness persists whether I am rich or poor in possessions. It persists even if I lose an arm or a kidney. I'm still "me" whether whole or amputated. This "me" eats and breathes (Aristotle's vegetative soul); this me is an acting person with some acts which are physical and expressed through my body (Aristotle's brute soul) and other acts which are mental-- thought, prayer, choosing--not requiring body actions (Aristotle's intellectual soul). And yet "I" persist as one "me" throughout all these activities (one soul, the unity of the person as one being).

"I" am a substance, a freestanding something: that is part of my own self-consciousness. Reflection shows me that I am a composite, am made up of parts, and yet the parts all have one center, my soul or self. That this self is separable shows up most clearly in what I know and what I want. We have seen knowledge as an act of dematerialization, an act which in the universalized concept strips away the matter from the particular thing, matter which makes the thing an individualized something. If thought means taking away matter, then thinking matter is a contradiction in terms and 'immaterial' (spiritual) must be a necessary and essential characteristic of thought. And therefore of the "I" who do my own thinking.

What I want is everything. Individual things attract but do not fill up my wants. I want to be happy, absolutely and permanently happy. This is neither greed nor egomania but part of the universal structure of the human will. It is impossible for a human NOT to want to be happy.

So here "I" am with an inexhaustible thirst for knowledge and an infinite desire for happiness living in a world of finite things. Finally, "I" exist. This personal existence is primarily predicated of "me" and only secondarily of the body through which I express by 'self'. If 'I' were nothing but a form of an animal body, then the form disintegrates with the body. But 'I' am aware of 'me' doing mental acts without body acts ---longing, choosing, thinking --and there is nothing contradictory in the concept of "disembodied consciousness" which would make it unsuitable as an object for our analysis.

"I" exist on both the physical and mental levels with so little fuss that it requires concentrated attention to appreciate the gap between the embodied consciousness which drives this nail into this wood using this hammer and the disembodied consciousness which turns its gaze to eternal truths of mathematics or beauty or cosmic unity without ever moving a muscle. The Great Amphibian-Man-lives in matter and spirit as the little amphibian frog Kermit lives in water and air.

To sum up, in the words of Maurice Merleau-Ponty, "Man is a being-in-the-world, with-others, for a project."

CHAPTER VII
ETHICS, ACTIONS AND HABITS

Terms like ethics and morals take their origins in words which have social implications. Ethos and mores reflect the notion of tribal customs. In a less reflective world, to do right was often the same things as to conform. In a pluralistic society, we can choose even between societies and subcultures. More important we can decide for ourselves every issue of right and wrong that is presented to us. In the ultimate analysis, only humans can be responsible for the effects of their own decisions, for better or worse

.

The basic principle of ethics is that humans are rational animals. The only thing which separates us from the rest of the animal world is our capacity to think. Therefore, *any deliberately irrational act on our part takes away that which is distinctively human about us and is therefore dehumanizing, immoral and unethical.* The implications of this definition will be unpacked in the course of the next few chapters. For the moment, let us concentrate upon the characteristics of a normal human act and all of the things which can interfere with its optimal functioning.

There are *three acts of the intellect; apprehension, judgment and reasoning.* In the act of apprehension, we understand, we see something even if we do not fully comprehend it. For our purposes it will suffice to note that

Apprehension is the intellectual awareness of an object.

In the act of judgment, we connect two ideas together, and because of the linking we can talk about the truth or falsity of the combined statement.

In the act of reasoning, we string collections of statements together in order to logically spell out the implications of the collected statements.

In the course of performing a basic human act, we can use reasoning to fit apprehension and judgment into their proper positions along the way.

Let us begin with the story of COLLEGE: it is a complicated story, spelled out in some detail in order to make it easier to analyze into its separate parts.

What do I want to do for a living when I grow up?
Is it something which requires college?
Which Major?
Which College?
How do I get in?
What does it take to graduate or enter the job market?
.

Analysis: there are two different types of activity going on The first involves knowledge, getting or acting on it. The second involves choosing, selecting, desiring and deciding.

To chart the progress would look something like the chart on the next page.

THE TWELVE STEPS IN A HUMAN ACT

INTELLECT			WILL	
PART ONE GOAL OR END				
1. Apprehension	This career grabbed my attention	**2.Velliety**	A Volition or wish but not strong enough to move to action.	
3. Judgment of a goal;	I really can become this profession	**4.Intention**	I WILL become this type of professional	
PART TWO: MEANS				
5. Counsel	This profession requires college	**6.Consent**	These colleges meet my wants for location, major, size, cost, growth, reputation and personal interest	
7.Conation: judgment of means	Of 300 schools, I really want	**8 Selection**	This college looks best	
PART THREE: EXECUTION				
9.Last Practical Judgment	I will need transcripts, rec-ommendations, checks	**10. Command**	Dammit, DO IT	
11.Supervision of execution	Essay reads well , no typos	**12. Enjoyment**	I am relieved the app got submitted	

A few comments are needed to follow the chart. First, the behavior described falls into three parts: ends, means, action. In less active behavior, most of part one and part two can be done inside the head, only in part three do many of our ideas take on the form of external physical action.

Actually, the most important part of a human action both ethically and psychologically is contained in the first part: INTENTION It is here that our wishes get changed into reality; all of the other parts are comparatively speaking only window dressing.

A person's intentions make a person to be a certain kind of person. How many of you know people who aren't really good, they just haven't been sufficiently tempted? It can safely be said that some of the most surprising human actions brew inside a person for a long time before they finally take on visible form in the outside world.

Distinguishing every one of these steps is important because there is an insight to be garnered about the nature of the human apparatus in action. So long as we can keep our day-dreams separate from reality, the wish stage of the thinking process can be one of the healthiest safety-valves we can have.

This desirability of dreaming is seen clearly in the case of the mystery writer who has killed off his boss, his wife, and a variety of his friends any number of times in the fiction which he produces. Because he puts his dreams to such constructive use, he remains on excellent terms with his publisher, is married to the same woman for the last thirty years, and enjoys a wide variety of friends who are waiting to see which of them will be bumped off next. I wonder how many students, employees, and others have dreamed of killing their teacher/supervisor.

It is the intellectual act of judging a goal which usually keeps the wish from becoming the intention in the case mentioned above.

As the opening to the tv show *Castle* points out: There are two types of people who think about ways to commit murder: psychopaths and mystery writers. The difference between the writer and the killer rests in the elements of sufficient reflection in the intellect and full consent of the will. Even if the deed is never done, we are talking about a person who has made himself into a killer to himself. If that gets repeated often enough, look out when he finally gets a quick and easy opportunity. The newspapers regularly print stories of the nice, quiet person who one day flips out and walks through the office killing everybody in sight, or the nice family type who one day slaughters the entire family.

The intention is the subjective basis of all ethics. If a

person deliberately chooses to act irrationally, then he has chosen to debase himself and has diminished his humanity. The effects of such acts are cumulative. Note that here irrationally is not used as a synonym for crazy but indicates that we chose to act contrary to what we knew to be better.

To argue that with intention you arrive at the fullness of a human act might seem to select a point rather early on in the process of action. But such an early point is inherent in the nature of human endeavors, is psychologically sound, and indeed is essential if we do fully understand the role of the human being with respect to the rest of reality.

If a person sets her head and her heart on a particular goal, we are already in a position to judge whether it is a goal which is good for man or not. There are laws of psychic equilibrium just as much as there are physical, biological, and chemical laws, which we can violate only at our own peril.

If we accidentally fall out of a window, the fact that we didn't intend to commit suicide will not make the final splat any softer. The fact that we are jittery and on-edge because of too many Red Bulls will have its inevitable effect on the chemistry of our nervous system. The fact that we are eating more and moving less will make us fat, even if we do not consciously intend to commit gluttony. Hence the infamous Freshman 15, the average 15 pounds added by dormitory frosh.

The choice of a lesser good when we could choose something better is as much a minor fault as that extra oreo cookie is to the dieter. Nothing major, perhaps, but it all adds up.

Psychologically, it is a valid truism that where your treasure is, there also will be your heart. A good deal of moral philosophy rests somewhere between modern psychology and religion. Both get inside the human head. Philosophy is able to make a value judgment on the authority of reason where the psychologist prefers not to pass moral judgment on his patient and the theologian passes judgment on the basis of some

130

revealed authority.

One of the implications of the last few paragraphs is that we are really not fee when it comes to our intentions. If the choice is between being the best human we can be and diminishing our human capacities, then there really is no real choice. We can be good or we can be cripples. There is no third alternative. We will see this in more detail in the later chapter on law.

It is **in the acts of consent and election that the real notion of free will comes into its fullest.** The human intellect follows its own laws of natural causation. We want to know things and we want to know that they are true. Nothing makes the average person more uncomfortable than to think that a friend has lied to him or is holding back part of the truth. One of the most unsettling experiences in life is to think that all your beliefs and actions might have been founded on a lie or a misconception.

Just as the intellect is geared naturally to truth the human will is inexorably geared to want something because it is good. As we saw earlier in discussing the notion that "everything that is, is good", the person who chooses to do something evil, does it because there is something good in the action. Notice I did not say he thinks there is something good in the action. There really is something *objectively* good in the most evil and depraved action which a person can perform. The horror of a sane person comes from the realization that the evildoer has become so obsessed with their little good that they have blocked out everything else.

The killer of a blackmailer seeks relief from danger to his wallet and his reputation. People have a right to their own money and their good name, don't they? In fact, there is no evil act that does not have some good at the root of it. This grim optimism is borne out by analysis in every case but such ontological or structural goodness doesn't make all our acts ethically good.

The notions of ethics come into play when we analyze the choices available to the person. This is where consent and election come into play. A person who is not aware of any alternative is a person acting under necessity. Sometimes the psychological and social limitations on our environment might force us to do an evil because we think we have no alternative. To take an extreme example, a person taught from birth to hate his neighbor for his race, creed, or color might not be doing anything subjectively wrong, because he doesn't know any better.

To understand the point of the example, it is necessary to make a distinction between objective evil and subjective responsibility. An action might be wrong or undesirable and yet we do not intentionally make ourselves the worse by doing it. Two of the broadest examples are the distinction between a human act and the act performed by a human, and the notion of the modifiers of human responsibility.

By a human act, I mean one done consciously, with sufficient reflection and full consent of the will. By the act of a human, I mean an action which is unconscious or contrary to conscious intention, which in the strict sense of the word is involuntary. Thus, in most cities it is illegal to smoke while riding in mass transit: this is a human act which the state assumes was under your control and you chose to do it anyway. On the other hand, consider the plight of the drunk who is rather unsteadily making his way home, gets on a bus, and proceeds to throw up all over the place. He has made a far greater mess and health hazard than the smoker, but it is more than likely that he will not even get a ticket because it is generally recognized that the action was beyond his control.

We are not just a Platonic soul using a mechanical body. Our existence is all of one piece and all the parts interact with each other to form an immensely intricate pattern of complexes. It is the interaction of the other parts of the human which interfere with any kind of clear and rational decision. The modifiers of human behavior are many and varied, but some of the more obvious ones come from antecedent emotion and ignorance.

By *antecedent emotion* is meant any emotion which exists before the decision itself. The experimenting adolescent carried away by lust is less responsible than the cold-blooded seducer. The bankteller opening a safe at gun point is hardly an accomplice. It is important to underline the antecedent nature of the emotion.

A person who is psyching up to do something cannot plead the extenuation of great emotionalism because he is now into the realm of consequent emotion, emotion following upon the decision to do the action. The bankteller who acts from a motive of fear is in quite a different category from the burglar who is with fear on his latest escapade. The thief carries the greater responsibility because his conscious energies are overruling his sane and health desire to get the hell out of there.

This notion of modifiers of responsibility is an old story in the law courts. The different degrees of murder and manslaughter are predicated upon the sanity and emotionalism of the killer at the time of the killing.

If the courts add to our appreciation of the emotional modifiers of responsibility, then psychology and sociology have added to our awareness of just how much we are programmed by our society and the individuals who mold our little psyches. Thus, in the earlier case of the blameless bigot, we have a good example of the limited responsibility because of ignorance. The modern social sciences have considerably limited the area of free will.

Free will itself is a bit of a misnomer. Our will is just as inherently geared to desire something good as our body is geared to falling at 32ft/sec2. It is far more accurate to talk about *free choice of the will*. Reference to the chart at this point will show that *free choice of the will is applied only to the notions of consent and election*. In terms of our overall life, the distinction holds: while our goal is fixed at being the fullest human we can be, there are a wide range of options open to us as to the means we choose to channel, focus and intensify our labors. It is most unlikely that we can be doctor-lawyer-clergy-man-novelist all at the same time. In this area all that we can do is seek the best advice possible as to our abilities, examine our own inclinations, and make the best (s)election from the whole list of choices.

By separating free choice from intention and limiting it to an area of means, we avoid the problems of the workaholic who has made his job, his means of earning a living, into an end in itself, the be-all and end-all of his existence.

To summarize the last few pages is to make the startling discovery that the vilest deed may be done by someone totally blameless and that the kindest act, when done for nefarious motives, might make its doer an exceptionally evil character.

Habits. The word usually connotes something dead, dry, lifeless, a semi-mechanical, almost unconscious part of human behavior. *A habit is a pattern of behavior, formed by repeated human acts, of something we are free to do or not to do, which inclines us to do that thing with greater ease and facility, liberating our higher faculties to do other things.* About the only way to start is with habit formation. A habit is a pattern of behavior formed by repeated acts: do it over and over again until you get it right. Once you get it right, do it over and over again, and suddenly you find yourself doing it without even thinking about it.

Once habits are linked up to human acts, there is a clear distinction between nature and "second nature". In terms of the distinction, the involuntary acts of the autonomic nervous system are a regular part of the natural order. Deep breathing exercises are something we are free to do or not to do, which will increase the capacity of our respiratory system. Thus the difference introduced in the first chapter between seeing and observing, hearing and listening.

If we were to analyze habit in terms of the doctrine of the four causes, we find that we are lacking a part of the definition.

Habit: a pattern of behavior (formal cause), formed by repeated acts (efficient cause) of something we are free to do or not to do (material cause).

But for what purpose? Why? If you are an expert pianist, it wasn't something you just "lucked into". If you can drive a car safely, shoot a bow and arrow expertly, tend a garden and keep everything alive: these are only rarely the accidents of native genius, most often they are the fruit of hard work. The purpose can be simply (and preconception-shatteringly) stated: because habits incline us to do a thing with greater ease and facility, they liberate our higher faculties for other things. The great power of Habits is their liberating quality, not our mechanical enslavement to them. To concentrate on the chains and overlook the liberation is like concentrating on the hole to the exclusion of the doughnut around it.

The person who has all of the mechanics of safe driving down cold is the only type of driver who can momentarily enjoy the scenery in safety. The touch-typist who knows the keyboard without looking is now free to concentrate on the shorthand transcription of the notebook or the creative imaginings of the writer. The person who has learned to ski on snow or water can do everything so gracefully and expertly that he can enjoy the wind whistling past at sixty, the scenery, and the smooth turns, without fear of breaking his neck.

Even some of the harder to break habits left over from childhood, like nail-biting, originally started because it was a way to get rid of broken nails or relieve anxieties.

The ease and facility is such a nuanced thing that it has slid past some of the keenest philosophical minds. It causes paradoxes of easy virtue and diminished pleasure. It explains why a difficult task which someone did because it was difficult becomes easier with repetition. It explains why there seems to be a law of diminishing returns concerning anything we do just for the fun of it: the original concentration which we brought to the pleasure dims with repetition. The drinker doesn't get happier with increased dosage, just drunker. The saint does not find the practice of asceticism getting harder by the minute, but easier. Such is the adaptability of man, the one animal in nature with the most flexible plasticity.

Two last questions: if you have a habit you want to break, how do you get rid of it? The first place to begin answering the question is to underline something which may have slid past you in the course of the definition. The habit only inclines us, it does not determine our behavior. On a scale of one to one hundred we would start off at zero when we have no habit at all; even with habits well developed, we never react such a perfect 100% that we are purely and totally a creature of habit.

How important it is to repeat that point over and over again to people who are constantly in despair of ever breaking any of their habits. To make people aware of the fact that they did not acquire a habit in a day and that they shan't get rid of it in a day, is a cliché which people never feel the full impact of until they begin trying to break a habit.

If the habit is deeply entrenched, begin by setting your mind to be gentle and patient with yourself. This is the kind of intellectual judo better suited to the human mind than a frontal assault on entrenched habits.

The best suggestion would be to run the definition backward. If the habit is now a minimally conscious one, rearrange things so that every time you do it, you force it back to consciousness. For example, if you want to quit smoking gradually, you might want to carry your cigarettes in the most inconvenient place possible so that you have to become aware each time you want one. Of course, the easiest way to break a habit is to substitute another one for it: chew on pencils, unlit cigars, etc. (Just make certain that the cure is not worse than the disease: people who took up licorice in lieu of cigarettes wound up eating so much a day that cardiac arrhythmia set in!)

If you have a habit pretty well developed, how do you

deepen or improve it? The key, as Robert Montgomery said when he was giving President Eisenhower lessons in articulate enunciation, "OVERDO, in order NOT to under-do." It is the same with any other type of habit. If you would perfect the playing of an instrument that you practice an hour a day, then practice two hours.

In view of the analysis so far, with its unexpected mixture of description and value judgment, it should come as no surprise that the definition of virtue and vice should be defined descriptively. *A virtue is merely a good habit, that is, one which advances us toward the goal of human life* sketched in previous chapters. *A vice is merely a bad habit, that is, one which takes us further away from happiness, fulfillment, and love.*

As might be expected from the previous discussions on habit, we should expect to be a little gentler with vice and a little harsher with evil acts, than is the usual reverse. It is the reverse psychology which is humane for the human animal. An occasional drunk you might be able to shock out of a habit, so that they will go back on the wagon; a deeply habituated alcoholic must be treated far gentler, be prepared and cautioned to expect regressions and learn to break his habit more with serenity and gentleness than with any harshness and a self-defeating frontal assault.

While all virtues are the product of intelligence, we must not expect all the virtues or vices to reside in the intellect. Some of them have specialized functions in conjunction with specific powers of the human organism. In what remains of this book, we must exercise extreme selectivity or else we will get delightfully lost in all of the specialized habits which the human animal can acquire: everything from picking out the correct notes on the piano to picking a pocket, preparing a soufflé to preparing an X-rated movie.

To outline the remaining chapters; in chapter eight we will consider the intellectual virtues; in chapter nine, the virtue of justice; in chapter ten, the potential parts of justice; in chapter eleven, courage; in chapter twelve, temperance. Prudence, Justice, Fortitude, and Temperance: the cardinal or hinge virtues, on which rest the hope of opening the door to a fully actualized human being.

CHAPTER VIII:
THE INTELLECTUAL VIRTUES

There are some things we want to know because they are necessary for action and there are other things about which we are just plain curious, an intellectual itch that needs scratching. When we talk of habits of the mind which have their focus primarily in the mind, and which are good habits, they can be referred to as the intellectual virtues. When the intellectual virtues are geared toward the practical, they are known as the practical intellectual virtues; when they are directed toward knowledge for its own sake, they are known as the speculative intellectual virtues.

The speculative intellectual virtues have nothing to do with speculation in the common sense of the term where it is used to mean guessing. theoria in Greek or speculativa in Latin both aim at knowledge for its own sake, wanting to know the truth of things. It is impossible in a fully "together" human being to separate all the functions which work well together. (If physics ever does come up with a Theory of Everything, also known as the Grand Unification Theory, it may have put itself out of business by learning all there is to know in its own field. It will be interesting to contrast that with the claim of Aristotle that matter is infinitely aka indefinitely divisible)

The speculative intellectual virtues are three: understanding, "scientia", and wisdom. Understanding is a habit developed by the power of understanding [36]It is a habit because the more you understand, the more you are able to understand. It is a habit because understanding can be developed, like any other habit, by concentrating on its development and extending its range. For example, with practice, you can not only learn to use the card-catalog in the library, but, with greater familiarity, can even learn to anticipate its little quirks.

"Scientia" refers to any organized body of knowledge with a clear set of first principles and working axioms. "A science has

---

36cf the passive intellect in ch 1

its unity by treating of one class of subject matter" [37] I have used the Latin word to avoid getting it confused with our much narrower sense of modern science. On these terms, there can be a science of auto mechanics, of fairy tales, or of detective stories. A little later we shall have occasion to make a rather lengthy digression about the relationship between the philosophy and the specialized scientiae which make up, for example, the college curriculum. The difference between understanding and scientia can be seen if we continue the example of the library card-catalog. While we might understand how to use it, we call the person who knows the principle of cataloging a library scientist. They know why a specific book has a specific number, down to its last decimal point, and why it is located in that part of the library, and how its contents stand in relationship to the rest of the collection of books in the library.

Wisdom is the peak of the speculative intellectual virtues, and the hardest one to nail down with just a definition. You can define *wisdom as the speculative intellectual virtue which comprehends an entire field in terms of one most basic insight*. In other words: the greater the intellectual virtue [virtus as power] the simpler.

This wise simplicity is the heart of the matter, and yet, if improperly understood, can miss the mark entirely. Socrates distinguished between four types of knowers.

The first class comprises those who do not know and do not know that they do not know: since they have no sense of their own ignorance, they can be amazingly bold in presenting their own ideas.

The second class comprises those who do not know and know that they do not know: since they have a glimmer of their limitations, they tend to be a little bit more hesitant about their certainty.

Those in the third class know but do not know that they know: like the student who has studied imperfectly for an examination they know the answers but are hesitant about asserting them.

---

37 Posterior Analytics I,28,87a38

Finally, the fourth class consists of those who know and know that they know: they are certain about their certainty.

If you clearly follow the different groups, you can see how the fourth group and the first group can be easily confused. This confusion between groups one and four is the root cause of the confusion between a wise simplicity and a foolish oversimplification. Those who fall into the middle two groups can appreciate the kyklos of paedia, the circle of humanities, which we now call encyclopedia knowledge. If knowledge is a circle, then as the circle of personal knowledge grows, so does the vast edge of the circle where our knowledge makes contact with the field about which we know very little. In short, the more we know, the more we know how much there is that we still do not know.

To get back to the simpler example of the library card-catalog, which we understand and about which the library scientist has a scientific knowledge: in relationship to the card-catalog, who would possess the role of wise man? What very simple, very basic insight underlies the whole structure on which the classification system and all those millions of cards is based? You will hate yourself when you know the answer. Your reaction will be, "that's obvious", or, "he's so wise because he thought of something as simple-minded as that?" Putting numbers on books.

Just as those who know what they know can be confused with those who don't know what they don't know, so too wisdom in the modern world of the 19th and 20th Centuries has given way to its dark side shadow, ideology. Where wisdom assimilates all into its basic insight, ideology seeks to twist reality until it fits its 'perfect' system of ideas. Consider for example the bigot who thinks welfare is a codeword for black, when the majority of public assistant recipients are white, or the liberal ideologue who equates minority with poverty, ignoring the fact that college educated, intact black families made 86% of their white counterparts (NR8/17/92) or that the US Census 1990, shows 2/3rds of Afroamericans are now middle class or upper-middle class professionals!([38] Ideological blindness has been the curse of the 20th Century and in the case of Hitler, Stalin, and Mao more deadly than the worst religious wars

The practical intellectual virtues are immeasurably simpler to understand. Practical science is knowledge directed to doing and making, morality and art respectively.[39] They are only two: art and prudence, but neither means quite what you think.

Art is the practical intellectual virtue which enables us to do or make something with great ease and facility. The pre-requisites for this virtue are a certain physical ability and a certain frame of mind. But the notion of art is far broader than it appears. Re-read the definition. It does not just refer to the so-called fine arts of art and music, play and dance; it also includes more than the mechanical arts of the craftsman or mechanic.]

Art in this definition is broad enough to include the art of taking tests, the art of cooking, the art of medicine, the art of child-rearing, and literally millions of things which we do each day. Because we are talking about a practical art, it includes any disciplined activity in which we do or make something. That is why the terms of ancient Greek philosophers is so useful. The active intellect (nous poietikos) or practice or know-how (techne) still show up in English as that practical art which ranges from poetry through technology. Very practical tasks, indeed!

Prudence is the cardinal virtue of the intellect, it is the basis for all of ethics, and it is the one virtue which is the necessary pre-requisite for all of the others. Without defining it for the moment, let us call it the virtue of reality.
Think about that last phrase for a second. How many times and in how many ways do we alter the data of reality to suit our own purposes? How many times do we react so hastily to a situation, get so quickly excited at someone's statements that we do not really hear what they said after our emotions started

---

38analysis by Chicago's Junius Wilson.
39[ST I-II,57,4

running. How many times have we played with the playback mechanism of Memory, replaying a disturbing incident, until we have edited it and colored it to put a more favorable light on it, so that we don't appear to have been as foolish as we really were? How many times have we been unwilling to learn from others because we already knew it all? Ben Franklin is always half-quoted in this context, and the full line deserves citation, "Experience is the best teacher . . . for a fool will learn from no other."

As the questions might imply, solteria (objectivity), memoria (an honest memory), and docilitias (a willingness to learn) are the pre-requisites for any kind of prudence.

The honest memory implied by memoria presumes the willingness to view our errors in an uncompromising honesty. But, painful as that is, the alternative is worse: condemning yourself to repeating the same stupid or harmful behavior over and over--simply because you chose to ignore the reality the first time. In such a case, the courage and truthfulness of an honest memory can have a liberating power: it can free us from our worse self.

Docilitas is not the docility of the apple-polisher nor some slave of a student whose one thought is to "hear, obey, and pass". Rather it is an eagerness to learn, a desire to extend ourselves outward and take into ourselves new knowledge. Thus docilitas may be the characteristic of the research professor who realizes that the prof is still a student, still has so much to learn, and, above all, still wants to learn more.

Solteria can best be seen by its opposite. Envision a cafeteria table, six people having coffee, and A starts to say something which B, C, and D disagree with. These three have stopped listening after the first paragraph. They are so busy framing their reply that they are no longer open to the rest of the argument being presented. Solteria is the act (or habit) of leaving yourself "in neutral" until you have taken in all the information presented. A variety of solteria is found in courses which teach people how to listen since premature reaction is a great foe of listening. Even "advocacy journalists" who disdain "objectivity" must get the quotes right and the better journalists make certain that even the positions they opposed are presented accurately. Thus memoria, solteria, and docilitas are essential to gaining prudence. The stupidity of the neurotic who impedes his own progress and traps himself in unproductive behavior is just one of the prices one pays for lacking prudence.

Since prudence is the cardinal intellectual virtue and since it is a practical virtue, we must not expect theoretical certainty concerning prudential judgments. This is one of the more disconcerting things for people to become aware of; they confuse the clear, orderly methods of the sciences and wish that all human thought could follow that pattern. Life is not as neat as a geometry book. There are people who get more upset about their mistakes than about some of the evils that they do.

The honest man has only got his honesty for his protection. If we can say that we did the best with what we had, that we acted in the best possible way under the circumstances as known to us at the time, then there is nothing more to be said or done, except possibly to learn from any mistakes for the next time.

One of the best ways to come to an understanding of prudence is by comparison and contrast. Aristotle held the doctrine of the Golden Mean, or, as the medievals put it, "Virtue stands in the middle, between too much and too little." Most people, on first hearing the expression, think that it means some type of automatic compromise, but that is a trifle simpleminded. As Martin Luther once pointed out "The history of the human race is that of a drunk falling off a horse. After falling off on the right side, he then proceeds to remedy his mistake by falling off the left side."

For the first example, consider a good habit which is not one of the specifically moral virtues. Take the example of the professional musical performer who has over-rehearsed: the performance is dull, dry, lifeless, the mechanical elements have

144

taken over and thus there is no creative interpretation. The performer who hasn't rehearsed enough also gives no creative interpretation because there is too much time spent on getting the notes and phrasing right. The perfect combination of sufficient rehearsal and interpretive analysis is the one which is located between these two.

In the case of prudence, virtus stat in media. If prudence is the rough and ready ability to make a decision with whatever speed is suitable to the occasion then it is possible to be under-prudent or over-prudent, neither of which would be a good thing. Thus, when people deride prudence as being the stodgy characteristic of the banker or the insurance company, they are not talking about prudence but over-prudence.

What are some of the things which distort a person's grasp on reality? It might seem presumptive for philosophy to go near the domain of the psychologist, but before psychology existed, Aquinas offered the following analysis: When someone is imprudent or impetuous, unable to make a decision, the root usually lies in the sensual appetites. The over-affection for certain objects which give pleasure makes them indecisive: resulting in the dithering or impetuosity of a person who "would rather not think about it."

The psychoanalysts even agree that the glittery and erratic, brilliant and brittle behavior some stars is rooted in their over-affection for the sexual. Philosophically, I think we could expect to find the "I'd-rather-not-think-about-it" syndrome in any addict of concupiscence, anyone who made sensual satisfaction the primary love of their life: the drunk the aesthete, the glutton, the gourmet, and the gourmand are not different in imprudence from the nympho and other sexual maniacs.

Well, what about the person who is overcautious, over-careful, who must analyze sixteen different ways, looks around for a seventeenth, and then repeats the process all over again? Before we jump right into why they are that way do not forget that the Urban American obsession with speed may distort our view here. In nothing said so far is there the least hint that

Aristotle or Aquinas shares the New York disease of "hectic equals happy".

To alter the words of Winston Churchill, when it is not necessary to act, then it may be necessary not to act. Go back to that banker slandered in the last paragraphs: would you really feel happier about your money if you knew that the officer in charge of your account was a gambler, a drunk and a lecher. The prudence in this case might well be more than is demanded of other vocations. (While banks do not like to lose money on bad loans, they will criticize an officer who has too few bad loans, on the theory that he is so overcautious that he probably is turning away customers.)

Despite this defense of the prudent professions, there are people who study a subject all out of proportion to the need for action. In fact, there are people who have missed priceless opportunities because "I have to think about it." Why?

Here, too, the suggestion of Aquinas is psychologically sound. As the imprudence of the one was rooted in the sensual motivation, so the over-prudence of the other is rooted in the irascible or utility appetites. This phenomenon of thought-induced inaction often indicates someone who is wrapped up in typical utility objects like money, power, fame, reputation, security. They would rather have the self-contained security of the stoic than venture forth on any action which might imperil that which they treasure. It is useless to point out to them that all of their objects-of-interest are means, tools, things to be used. The analysis provides a good vehicle for understanding the sensualists of the sexual revolution as well as the overcautious children of the depression.

Because prudence deals with keeping our heads screwed on straight, it differs from the activities of the artist. Because it is a practical endeavor, it differs from the speculative, and even serves as a corrective to the speculative. Using the division of the five intellectual virtues, you can see the root cause of both the mad scientist and the cultured torturer. The scientist, becoming obsessed with the sheer desire to know, loses contact with reality until all humanity, all ethics, and finally all sanity flee in the face of his obsession.

The scandal and shock which some people felt on meeting a cultured Nazi in the 1930's or a civilized dictator in the 1990's can also be explained using the analysis so far. There is nothing incompatible about being and understanding, so even a wise person can still possess the intellectual cunning which is the over-prudent perversion of those who lust for power. The folklore of mad scientists, evil geniuses, and dark angels, for all its fictional extravagances, is firmly rooted in the observable characteristics of real people. (And remember the broad definition of sciences offered above: Economist Richard Posner in Sex and Reason[40] trying to measure the comparative costs of masturbation, mutual masturbation, and marriage surely qualifies as a mad scientist for the 90s!

It is time we took a good close look at those special sciences mentioned earlier. While I propose to give only a brief overview of the terrain, it is of the utmost importance that philosophy be seen and appreciated as the thing which keeps the diverse strains of all the other disciplines knit into one mental fabric. If the average person first meets philosophy in the classroom, then it is incumbent upon philosophers to justify their activity in relationship to what is going on in the other classrooms. Philosophy stands as the integrating force for all of the separate sciences and as the critic of the presupposition of the basic concepts and methods of each discipline considered singly.

A three level pyramid represents the degrees of abstraction or abstractness of the objects studied. The lowest level, the level of nature, is the broadest, lowest, and the most filled with different words, terms, and ideas.

Since we are incarnated intellects, most of our vocabulary will deal with the things of the physical world. Take the example of a medical technologist examining a sample of blood for a complete series of tests. The first operations are on the purely

---

40(Harvard UP, 1992)

physical level: look at the blood under a microscope. Just looking can give information about certain diseases: sickle-cell anemia can be seen. Certain blood diseases distort the color or shape of the blood cells.

The next operation is a trifle more abstract: a red blood cell count. How many red blood cells are there per cubic centimeter? In this case you are no longer interested in the physical characteristics of the cell, you have abstracted from, forgotten about chosen to ignore, the color, shape, etc. This is the type of operation which is essential to the nature of mathematics.

This is the second level of abstraction, which has caused more grief to the history of thought than any other. Because things like geometry, mathematics, and logic are second order entities, they are more a product of the mind and have less of a clear contact with the physical world from which they were pulled. This has driven philosophers to speculate about the existence of a world of ideas, where mathematicals were just as much objects as trees and rocks (Plato); it has led others to rightly link mathematics and geometry (the analytical geometry of Descartes); it has also encouraged many to believe that ideas are something wholly produced from the basic structure of the intellect without reference to reality (Kant).

The twentieth century added a new twist to the problem by the highly learned reduction of algebra and mathematics to the realm of logic (Whitehead, Russell, etc.). Let's see if a clear understanding of the mechanics can be articulated.

When an infant sees something "out there", it might not know what the thing is, but it knows, with all the clarity of the uncluttered mind, that it IS. The child has already latched on to the first half of the *principle of contradiction: Something cannot be and not be at the same time and in the same respect.* From this basic principle you can not only generate an entire system of logic, but you can also articulate a full theory of mathematics in the process. Because the basis in reality is so slender and the elaboration by the mind is so complex, it is quite easy to forget, ignore, or overlook the role which knowledge from the outside world played in starting the process.

It is impossible in the space of this slender volume to explicate in detail the mechanism in child psychology by which it comes to be a logical and rational human. Space also forbids any detailed articulation of the steps involved in going from the principle of contradiction to the realm of calculus. For the first, the works of Piaget are a good starting place; for the second, the works of Tarski, Carnap, Whitehead, or Russell should be consulted. Needless to say, because the mind bears the major burden of the development, there are a potentially infinite number of arithmetical or geometrical systems which can be generated. This forms the basis for multi-dimensional geometries and some of the more advanced work in the mathematical sciences.

There is a vague, shaded border-land overlapping the world of nature and the world of math. The term "the mixed sciences" refers to the scientific revolution of the Renaissance when people started expressing physical realities in terms of mathematical formulae. Many a physics and chemistry student, lost in a pile of equations, has wondered quite rightly whether they were studying the physical world or doing math homework. They actually were doing both.

To analyze nature with mathematical tools is to use the notion of form and matter to express physical realities in a mathematical format. The mathematics increases our power of analysis if only we are careful of the traps in the tools. In a brute empiricism of purely descriptive nature, the description is closely fitted to the experience being described. In mathematicized science, we introduce problems of "fit". How well does the nature of the terrain conform to the geometry of the road map, or vice versa? How accurate is Newton's physics in the world of quotidian experience? How accurate Einstein in the world of speed-of-light travel?

Is the loss of concrete reality sufficiently compensated for by the new knowledge gathered by quasi-mathematical analyses? It must be decided in each case. Evaluating Einstein because he has given us atomic energy is different from evaluating genocide based on overpopulation statistics. The efficiency of scientific slaughter in the Gulag Archipelago is a good example of the mad scientist loose in the modern world. The tools confer power. Power is morally neutral. Only the direction and use of that power for specific purposes can be evaluated in an ethical context.

The world of metaphysics is more abstract yet. We cannot reach it so much by separation, ignoring facets of objects, so much as by a simple direct insight. We do tend to "blink at the most evident things like bats in the sunshine"[41] but minimal knowledge of the highest things is more desirable than a thorough grasp of the top 20 pop charts [42] If the physical world is inhabited by changeable beings, and the mathematic world is occupied with mostly intellectual beings-of-reason, then the world of metaphysics has a far smaller population. It seeks to discover the characteristics of unqualified being, being-as-being. You were doing metaphysics in chapter three when you were searching for the "characteristics common to everything".

Metaphysics has three subdivisions: epistemology, ontology, and rational theology. *Epistemology is the branch of metaphysics which is primarily aimed at defending the powers of the mind, searching out the limits of our knowledge, and broadly outlining the mechanism by which we know things.* We saw epistemology at work in chapter one, when we studied the cognitive life of man. In chapter three we saw some of the limitations of knowledge. Even in economics one can see the free-market as the epistemological claim that no one knows everything ... and therefore centralized state planning communist, socialist, or dirigism in any form is the attempt by the state to do what it cannot know how to do because no one possesses all of the world's creativie or entrepreneurial insight

41Aristotle.Meta,II,1,993b10]
42pace Aristotle, De Partibus Animalium I,5,644b31

Ontology, which studies being-as-being with a specific intensity, includes what we saw when we considered the transcendentals of being: essence, and existence, unum, bonum, and verum.

Rational theology is the science which develops ways of analyzing being for the purpose of proving or disproving the existence of God. Theodicy has been used as a synonym for this type of investigation. Rational theology seeks out the characteristics of this God, once it can be shown to exist. [43]

The philosopher's use of the term rational theology is not intended to imply that all others are irrational theologians. There are probably more irrational philosophical theologians seeking to disprove the existence of their own subject matter than there are religious nuts.

Rather, Rational Theology seeks to understand God to the extent that reason can make contact with this Being. Revealed theology claims that we do not have to make contact with It: It has made contact with us. To appreciate the difference involved requires explaining the difference between reason and faith.

Faith is accepting something as true on the authority of another. In this broad sense, it includes history, the evening news, and other disciplines where we accept the fact on the authority of the person telling us the facts. The best we can do is compare authorities and, if they agree, it is more reasonable to assume that they are telling of real events rather than to assume that they are engaged in a conspiracy .

In the area of religious faith, the truths of a religion are accepted because one believes that it is a truth, based on the authority of God.[44] One first of all believes somebody, and then, secondarily, some thing. If our teachers and clergy and parents are credible, then we tend to accept what they tell us.

Note the two different uses of reason in this context: You

43fn Aristotle Metaphysics VI,1, 1026a19.1,2,983a10
44 ST I,1,8,ad2

may have reasons for believing your friend, but there is no way you could reasonably know what they know unless you accept their narration as truthful. Thus, there is quite a difference between being anticlerical and being atheistic: history is filled with prophets who did not have too high an opinion of the established guardians of religion. (To twist the distinction another way: Jews and Christians have frequently gotten into trouble for being atheists as regards their neighbors' idols or false gods.)

What is essential in this act of faith is the belief in the experience of Moses or Christ or Mohammed. If God speaks to or through them, or in the case of the Christians, if Jesus is God, then we would be crazy not to listen. The role of philosophy in this context was spelled out by A. Hilary Armstrong when he commented, "If Christ says, `I am the Truth', philosophers have the right, duty, and obligation to ask, `May I see your credentials, please?'"

The role of philosophy in assessing the reasonableness of the primary act of faith is taken over by theology once we do make that act of faith. All of the philosophical analyses in the world will not make a person a believer; the most reason can do is preserve us from the more unreasonable forms of religious experience like mass-murder cults.

This interplay between Rational Theology and Revealed Theology is based on a premise essential to philosophy and held by some religions: namely, If God is the Source of All Truth, then the God of the philosophers is the same as the God of the theologians. If the God of Scripture is the God who gave us our minds, (and how could they be two?) then there can be no contradiction between philosophy and theology. If such contradictions appear, either we have misread and misunderstood Scripture or we have reasoned our way to an unwarranted confusion. Rational Theology can only reach are the "preambles of faith" [45]which according to Judaism and Roman Catholicism are also revealed: "For the rational truth about God would have

---

45 preambula fidei CG I,5

appeared only to a few, and even so after a long time and mixed with many mistakes"[46]

The Unity of Truth cannot be exaggerated. One of the most pernicious ideas of the later Middle Ages was a doctrine of double truth which sought to split man's head down the middle: on the one side, rational man would know certain things were true by reason and experience, while on the other side, religious man would believe a totally different set of truths. Rationally, faith was false; Fideistically, reason was a liar. Who needs this kind of schizophrenia?

Before you deride it, consider how many people base their lives on a double-truth philosophy. The person who sows his wild oats on Saturday night, then goes to church on Sunday to pray for a crop failure is just one example of the Sunday Saint and Weekday Devil. The division is debilitating.

Not only is the double-truth theory intellectually divisive and psychologically corrupting, it ignores the overlap between certain revealed truths and certain reasoned ones. The existence and characteristics of God outlined in an earlier chapter could be called preambles to faith. If you followed the argument and verify the reasoning from your own experience, then strictly speaking you no longer believe in God, you know that there is one. Just as in mathematics, you do not believe that $2+2+2=6$, you know that it does.

The objects of faith are those which you could not know from experience; for Christians, things like the Trinity or the Incarnation are mysterion. Mysterion, the hidden design at which God gives believers a peek; even Moslems and Jews, things like the creation of the world, or of angels. Take the last example: reason might lead you to suspect that there is something on the evolutionary scale which is higher than man but lower than God (separated substances or angels) but that suspicion is unverifiable by reason alone.

46ST I-II,1,1,a.3

This philosophical attitude to revelation is not allied to a specific church or creed. It is the position of the Catholic Aquinas, the Jewish Maimonides, and the Moslem Avicenna. It is summed up in the story of Irish writer James Joyce when he was in one of his anti-Catholic phases. He was approached by a lady who had heard he had become a Unitarian. Joyce turned to her and replied, "Madam, I may have lost my faith. I have not lost my reason."

In the Middle Ages, there were three attitudes toward religion which still exist today. There were the Rationalists, who taught that everything, even the Trinity, could be explained by reason alone. There were the Fideists, who felt that "God has spoken, therefore I need no longer think, just follow orders." And there were the Moderates: some put faith above reason (Augustine), some treated faith and reason as separate disciplines, with their own subject matter, their own methods, and their own principles ... a type of home-rule subdivision-of-labor approach (Aquinas).

While the examples are Christian, the pattern shows up in Jewish Fideists (Avicebron) and Jewish Moderates (Maimonides); Arab Rationalists (Avicenna), Fideists (Al Gazel) and Moderates (Averroes). And it exists today. The third way has always been the most difficult. It has always walked a tight-rope between heresy and gullibility. But it is the only way for those who would not wish to surrender either their learning or their religion. And yet, the third way is the golden mean between: like all virtues, it is a balancing act but one which amply rewards the efforts.

In the academic world, there is a distinction made between Theology and the Philosophy of Religion. It required only brief comment here. Theology starts with the assumption that you believe and that you are interested in finding out more, that you wish to use reason to deepen your faith. (This is why theology professors have always been deserving of heartfelt respect and sympathy. Philosophers only have to assume that the student has a few gray cells to rub together to set off sparks of thought. Theologians have to do with students flying under false colors:

nominal, acculturated `believers' who take a course because it is required or because it fits into their scheduled quest for 120 credits. I do not envy them their task.)

The Philosophy of Religion does not presuppose faith, but examines religion as a phenomenon in the physical world which is to be analyzed. It sometimes studies types of mysticism or the object to which "god language" refers or it overlaps with rational theology and studies the proofs for the existence of God and the problem of evil.

The problem of evil is far too complex to undergo a brief analysis. It is not sufficient to say that evil does not exist. The best brief explanation ever offered runs as follows: The only way to eliminate moral evil is to abolish free will. Hence, the choice of the deity in preferring freedom is an act of choosing a greater good at risk of greater evils: to wipe out evil at the expense of human freedom is too high a price to pay for a purely ethical world. Such an outline leaves the problem of physical evil untouched: to say that disasters and diseases are opportunities for man is a hint of an explanation. The Chinese pictogram of `crises' as being composed of `danger' and `opportunity' hints at the possibilities for courage, but it is not by any means a conclusive solution.

If we return to the physical world, there are an immense number of disciplines for philosophy to study. Sampling the problems of each philosophical specialty and clarifying a very few terminological muddles is all we can hope to do in the brief space allotted.

Philosophy of Science studies the presuppositions of the scientific method in general. Where do the laws of science come from? What is the role of laws in a scientific explanation? How do we validate scientific generalizations (the problem of Induction)? Are there different types of explanation in physics as opposed to psychology of history?

The Philosophy of Physics is sometimes called

Philosophical Physics or Metaphysics. Right away you can see the confusion. This is a meta of physics, a study of physics, its basic terms, assumptions, and methods. You have to check whether a book is Metaphysics1 in the sense used above or Metaphysics2 in the sense used here by the philosophers of physics.

Apart from the terminology, philosophy of physics seeks to get a fuller understanding of the basic concepts which physics presupposes. If you open any standard physics text, you will find terms like space, matter, time, motion. They will have ostensive or instrumental definitions attached. An ostensive definition simply points to the thing; an instrumental definition tells you how to use the term; neither tells you what the thing is: an essential definition is not offered.

Space: is it something real or imaginary? A frame of reality or a mental construction?

Matter: is it the same as energy?

Motion: in the sense of local motion from place to place or in the broadest sense of any change of status possible? If everything doubled in size overnight (you included), how would you know it? Could you know it?

What is time? (Aristotle said it was the measurement of change. If nothing in the universe changed from now . . . until now, would any time have passed? There is no way to prove that time passed if nothing changed.) Of course a mechanistic physics is no proof of a philosophy called mechanism: Cf W. Heitler, a physicist who called such a confusion "a superstition far more dangerous than the one about the existence of witches: It leads to a general spiritual and moral drying-up which can easily lead to physical destruction.

When once we have got to the stage of seeing in man merely a complex machine, what does it matter if we destroy him?[47]

To move from the Philosophy of Physics to the Philosophy of Biology (Metabiology) [48]seems to skip over chemistry. When a chemist can tell me what chemistry is, I can include it. Right

---

47 Man and Science R Schlapp tr, NY Basic,1963 p97

now, physical chemistry is being swallowed up by the physicists, and biology is absorbing all the rest.

This concept of time sheds some interesting light on the notion of time and eternity. Eternity is more like a state of permanent timelessness, such as is experienced by children intensely at play or lovers at their games: a sense of permanent peak, which is different from an endless time-after-time. "Pleasure is not in time for what takes place in a Now is a whole"[49]

Preachers who talk of having endless heavenly bliss are not talking about an endless enjoyment so much as something so ecstatic that time is irrelevant. If this deity is that good, it says very poor things for both philosophers and theologians that they spend so little time making this goal as delightful and vivid as possible. Such is the state of being human that this one goal for the entire lifespan is the one which is least spoken of, the pleasures of which are least frequently looked forward to, and which is most easily swallowed up by the least distraction.

Of course, it also deserves more than a cursory note, but I am not poet enough to do it justice and theologians have more information about this goal than I do.

Metabiology explores the question of life and the characteristics which define a living thing. Biologists do not study "life", they study living things. Even if you remember that nutrition, growth, and reproduction are the essential characteristics of life, can you solve the following problems:

A virus can be frozen into a crystal; when defrosted, it can reproduce. Is it alive or not?

Is a fertilized human ovum a human being?

This last question takes on more force when we consider notions of justice and right. If biologists are to classify things taxonomically by the number of chromosomes, then no matter what your positions on social or ethical questions, the biological one is settled: genetically human, embryologically coming to

---

48JKonecsni.,<u>Biology and the philosophy of Science</u>, Washington 1978, Metabiology and Metascience NY& Ann Arbor 1973)
49Aristotle Nicomachean Ethics, X

fulfillment.

Before we go into the sciences of man, get clearly in mind that we are looking at roles played by people with certain formal viewpoints. Their science gives the shape or form to the questions and investigations within the format of their special science. The distinction between people and viewpoint (formal aspect) is important. Many a retired physicist has written a philosophy of physics book, just as biologists occasionally wax philosophical about their life in their field. Even granted the insights which they bring from their field to mine, there is a real difference between theoretical physics and the philosophy of physics. The dividing line is sometimes blurred by frequent travelers from one side to the other, but we have to clearly divide in order to see how all of the parts fit together.

Philosophical analysis is only half of philosophy: it remains a permanent invalid unless the task of integration, of putting the pieces together, accompanies it.

The Scientiae of Man are many and varied. Even the Philosophy of Man has gone by different names: Rational Psychology, the non-experimental investigation of the soul-psyche; Philosophical Psychology; Philosophical Anthropology: All have been fashionable terms at one time or another. In most cases the topics and techniques are similar: the broad outline of human nature, the questions of human freedom and immortality. Some, like Aquinas, suggest that the natural orientation of the human soul for the body through which it expresses itself and the soul's impoverished existence after death, give a hint of the future reuniting, what theologians call the general resurrection.

Philosophy and Anthropology share a common interest in man from slightly differing formal viewpoints. The philosopher is faced with the problem of evaluating the anthropologist's evidence as to whether he has discovered a man or merely an anthropoid.

Philosophical Psychology, in the sense of the philosophy of psychology, explores the basic terms of psychology. What is consciousness? Is the Id something real or a scientific theory? What is the responsibility of the insane? What is sanity/insanity? Mere nonconformity? It also on occasion challenges psychological theories which go beyond the limits of a strictly experimental science: thus the arguments about the behaviorist's denial of freedom or the arguments about the `worth' of a human with a possibly-inherited low IQ.or the description by APA of mysticism as a quasi-schizophrenic state

Physical Education comes under the view of philosophy. The status of the field in the minds of both academic types and the general public tell us something about the inarticulate philosophy of gym. The casual hedonist might pamper it into inertia; the Platonist might see it as a physical cage to be disposed of as soon as possible; most people think so little of it that they rarely think of it at all. The Manichees who starved themselves to death to escape bodily limits and the ascetics who waged the battle to mortify their flesh thought of the body as a worthy opponent. They cared enough about it to hate it. Does the fact that we don't care tell us something?

The Philosophy of Language overlaps with the discipline of Linguistics in attempting to find the general abstract laws which are the basis for generating a language and which analyzes the nature of man as the only animal which communicates with this very abstract system of symbols. Philosophy of Language can be more broadly defined to include investigations into the philosophy of authors who were expressing a viewpoint and the mechanisms by which they propagated their philosophies. The whole school of Linguistic Analysis is engaged in digging out clues as to what the nature of language tells us about the nature of reality.

The Philosophy of History, Metahistory, tries to find the pattern or patterns of explanation in history which will allow us to make predictions from the past to the future. What is the role of the hero in History? Do men make events or do the events make the man? How valid is the notion of causation in explaining the sequence of historical events? A history differs

159

from a chronicle in that the latter is just a recitation of facts and the former seeks to explain why. Is history repeating itself (cyclic)? Or is it the history of progress (evolutionary)? Or both (helical)? Such unspoken hypotheses color the presentation of facts in many a history book.

Aesthetics, sometimes too narrowly described as the Philosophy of the Beautiful or the Philosophy of Art, looks over the shoulder of the Art, Music, Dance, and Drama departments and tries to understand what they are doing. What is Beauty? Is it purely `in the eye of the beholder?' Is it merely the agreement of critics and creators? Is it the characteristic inside a performance or painting which attracts us with its order and affect? What is Ugliness? Why is something dowdy or dumpy? What is the basis for these value judgments?

Aesthetics and Ethics were once grouped together in the not too distant past by calling both part of Value Theory, because facts were assumed to be something different from values. Consideration of the next group of subjects will indicate the difficulty with that view.

Ethics is an organized body of knowledge which studies the notions of right and wrong as applied to the actions of human beings and attempts to generate from these basic insights general rules and laws of human behavior which will guide human behavior.

Ethics applies the notion of right and wrong to the individual; social philosophy performs an analogous function for groups of individuals. (analogous insofar as society deals with crimes and ethics with sins) Thus, Social Philosophy is intrinsically related to Sociology, Political Science, Business and Education in the academic world and to any human group in the real world.

Sociology is the scientific study of people in groups. Because of this formal viewpoint, psychology will emphasize heredity and instinct, while sociology will tend to concentrate more upon questions of environment: the formation of the individual into a membership in the group. While philosophers have been involved in this chicken-or-egg question of heredity vs environment, nature vs nurture, it is not the only area of philosophical interest.

To the extent that sociology claims to be a value-free science, philosophy is entitled to ask certain important questions: Are explanations in sociology as scientific as in physics? Does the element of human freedom impair accuracy? Or, to raise a sociological counter-rebuttal, if you play so many different roles in the course of the day, is there such a thing as a real you? If I can predict your attractions and repulsions on the basis of just knowing the roles you play, what does that do to your notion of freedom? Political Science can be viewed as a subdivision of Sociology to the extent that it studies people in specific types of groups, the formal groupings of organizational and political structures. Also claiming to be a value-free science, political science traces its foundation to Niccolo Machiavelli, who started his works by underlining that he was not saying whether certain behavior was good or bad, but merely describing the way things were.

Whether these two fields are value-free is questionable. The choice of a particular area of research implies the value judgment: you feel that is worth studying. The results of the research and its publication implies a value judgment: that all information should be openly discussed on all research. The publication of research may have value affects: "If this is what everybody is doing, maybe I should conform."

As we will see later in the section on law, there is a big difference between saying that something is statistically normal and saying that it is natural. The celibate clergyman and the homosexual are statistically abnormal in our heterosexually active society, but few from either group would appreciate being compared with members of the other group!

Business is likewise an area in which social philosophy,

ethics, and philosophy of man play a large role. The businessman in Marxist China obviously has to work with the limits of a different social philosophy from one in the United States. The bribery of a commissar in order to deliver the goods might well be ethical where it would not be here. Even one's philosophy of man will affect business: whether to feed the body or exercise the soul: either will effect purchases of TV-dinners or bibles. Should a businessman give the people what they want or what they should have: Do we trust humans to exercise their freedom responsibly or must people be protected from themselves?

Education is like business in some respects. To educate a student to fit into society demands an awareness of social philosophy; to teach each student according to his ability to learn demands not only educational psychology but a basic philosophy of man. Hence, the furor over sex-education as taught by a minister or taught by a materialist. The result: two different courses. In other respects, there was a medieval opinion that private property, governmental prisons, and the discipline required to get an education were the effects of Man's original disobedience. However, Aquinas saw education as a social sharing by which an idea is born in the mind of another. Just as a good teacher brings out the inner capabilities of the student so that the learner sees the truth as though discovered by the learner himself, so too the the mathesis or method of the learner and her docilitas, make the give-and-take of dialektos, dialectic, discussion, one motion like knife-through-bread.(Doesn't work on a week-old loaf, does it?)

I have barely touched on the ethics of the scientists, the philosophical implications of man's relationship to nature, the detailed problems of the educator, businessman, or social scientist. Since you can fill in the details from your first-hand experiences in some of these fields, you are well aware that each one of the disciplines can be the matter for a life's work.

The fact that it is enough for a whole lifetime gives new meaning to the medieval dictum, "Ens et verum convertuntur".

Everything that is, is intelligible. The problem of knowledge is not that something is unknowable, but that it is too knowable. There is too much there. All we can be assured of is that, while we may get tired or bored, the fault will lie in our limitations, not in the nature of reality. This is too much a place of variety and attractiveness with new things to inform and delight. It was just such an awareness that prompted Robert Lewis Stevenson to write

> The world is so full of a number of things
> I'm sure we should all be as happy as kings.

As a testimonial to reality written by a man dying of tuberculosis, it grasps just how much is in our stars and in ourselves.

CHAPTER IX
JUSTICE AND LAW

Right, law, fair, and unfair are words which are starting to lose their meaning because of overuse. The best we can hope to do in this chapter is put them in some kind of order and make them comprehensible.

You have a right to drive a car because you passed a test. The test was made a requirement of law by the state in which you live. It is the law which gave you the right to drive a car. Above the law stands justice as the yardstick which tells whether the laws measure up to standards of fairness. We can, therefore, begin in reverse order and consider justice, then the various types of law, and finally the different types of rights which we have because of different types of law.

A strict one-for-one type of justice is commutative justice or contract justice. In any business transaction of the normal variety, if you think an item is worth ten dollars, you buy it; if you do not think it is worth the ten dollars, you go shopping elsewhere.

The concept of fair price, therefore, includes a number of factors: are you paying for the object? Are you willing to pay extra for convenience? Speed of delivery? In short, what are your needs that make this thing worth the price that you pay for it?

From the viewpoint of the seller, the `fair market price' of the item has to cover cost of purchase and that includes the raw materials, labor, and shipping costs. Over and above that there are a wide variety of taxes built into the product at several points along the way. He must also add his costs of doing business: taxes, the rent, light, heat, salaries of his employees.

With this large combination of factors, it is rather amazing that there are any commercial transactions performed at all. In a real sense, you have a strict right to earn a profit because you have the right to earn a living. One of the differences between a salaried employee and an employer is that while the employee only has to please one boss, the employer has got to keep everybody happy if he wants to stay in business.

A more complicated problem of fairness comes into play with law enforcement. A policeman cannot possibly arrest everybody who has committed a crime. Given the limited number of resources available, how shall the police commissioner allocate his forces to ensure the best results and best serve the community which the police force has an obligation to protect? This problem is rather different from the first because it means that there will not be police on every block; they will be mostly assigned to high-crime areas. It may mean that pornographers, prostitutes, and pimps may go unmolested, while the police concentrate on crimes of greater violence.

If these two cases are so different, is there any definition of justice that will cover both of them? Yes and no. In general, *Justice means to give to another what is owed*. In the specific cases mentioned above, there are two different subspecies of justice involved. In the first case, there is a pure equality, *a one-for-one justice which is called commutative justice*. In the second case, there is a more sophisticated notion of *distributive justice which involves treating unequals unequally*. All three definitions require elaboration
.

If we expanded the original definition of justice, it would read something like this: Justice, a good habit (virtue) of the will which inclines us to give to another what is owed with greater ease and facility. Part of the definition shows how it fits under the general concept of habit and virtue, but some of the elements are new.

Justice is a matter of will means, it involves an action which we have to do whether we feel like it or not. Since will is not the same as emotion, our feelings are irrelevant: they may make the act harder or easier for us to do, but they do not effect the essentials of the act.

Justice is the most objective of the virtues precisely because it centers on the other and the rights of the other. It is the consummate social virtue, because its whole focus is based on the other human with whom we live. As Aristotle pointed out, "He who is unable to live in society, or who has no need because he is sufficient for himself, must be either a beast or a god.[50] It is only in society that we learn language; it is only because of the division of labor that we can develop our potentials to their greatest fulfillment.

Because of the existence of society, we can be poor hunters without fear of starving or poor builders without fear of exposure: so long as we bring to the society some skills or aptitudes, we can avoid want. But, the more we are aware of our worth as persons, the more we must also be aware of the obligation to respect that worth in other humans. This is the role of the present study: to see how we might best fulfill ourselves and others by dealing with them justly and being dealt with in a like manner.

The formulation of distributive justice must be at first shocking to a simplistic egalitarian. How can "to treat unequals unequally" be just? The examples come to mind so rapidly, it is hard to select the best one. Would it be fair if a teacher gave all students in a particular class F's? Probably not: in a class of any size there would usually be pupils of above-failure production. Would it be fair for the same teacher to give all the students A's? The A students are getting what they deserve, aren't they? What is the matter with the teacher giving the others a little gift? Several things.

First of all, you are treating grades as the private property of the teacher to be disposed of at will without respect to the recipient. If you grant that in the second case (A), then you must grant it in the first (F).

50Politics 1; 1253a31. Of course, religious hermits claim that they are NOT alone.

Furthermore, the student has contracted with the teacher, via the administration, to pay for a set of lectures (absolutely) and a grade (relative to the student's performance). If the student is measured relative to the group, then it has a right to a grade at the top, middle, or bottom of the group. If the student is measured relative to the total body of the knowledge presented, then the grade must represent their absorption of that percentage of the material. In neither case is the student at the caprice of the instructor.

In a (mythical) commune where each makes her own clothing, the one who distributes the yard goods would be unfair to give superskinny and superfatty the same amount of material because one would have a microskirt while the other would have enough material for two outfits. Or, again, the automotive permission given to the eldest child in a family does not require that, in the name of equality, we allow the five-year-old child to start the engine.

One of the social issues in education is the fair allocation of resources so that you do not slight the genius or the retarded. If all have a right to an education, then these last two are not receiving that which they have a full right to.

If justice is the yardstick by which we measure law, then we must also define the concept of law. First, an example, the local traffic light. What would happen if it were not there? Disorder. Who decided to put it there? The local authorities, probably after five people got killed at that intersection. Why did they put it there? Because it was a reasonable way to make things orderly and was cheaper than a crossing guard.

Law:
 a putting into order,
 by reason,
 by one having the authority,
 for the common good.

Despite the abuse of the phrase by political demagogues of all stripes, law and order have a close relationship even if they are not identical. It is other parts of the definition which offer more difficulty in explication.

What is the relationship of reason and power? "Let us face it, something is legal not because it is reasonable, but because those in power want it that way." Yes and no. The role of power and authority is there in the definition. The teacher who "lays down the law" in the classroom would not try to do so to the LEO who just pulled him over for speeding. In fact, even the concept of authority has to be clarified with a distinction. Someone is an authority in the field if a certain topic is the field of expertise; they exercise a certain dominion over it because they have earned that authoritative status. That is a far different type of authority than the one who exercises authority on the basis of sheer power. That is not authority, that is subjugation.

A rationalistic philosophy of law bases law primarily on reason; a voluntaristic philosophy of law bases it on power. Since orderliness proceeds from intelligence, it seems more properly intellectual than volitional. Both must function in this definition if laws are ever to become laws.

Last, but not least, is the purpose of law. No, order is not the purpose: it is the instrument for achieving something else. Not even in the tyranny of the ant-hill or the totalitarian state is order an end in itself. The function of this orderliness is to provide for the common good.

The common good does not mean the greatest good for the greatest number. If that type of statistical utilitarianism were the norm, then certain undesirable consequences would follow. If an act were judged on the basis of its utility each and every time we acted, it would inhibit action, create a radical instability in which nothing could proceed in an orderly fashion, and deny even the possibility of there being anything like a code of behavior. If it is a general type of rule-utilitarianism, its consequences are equally undesirable: for the sake of the stable rule, you might have to contradict your own utilitarianism and do something undesirable and the rights of the individual get lost in the general rule. On either account, utilitarianism is too simplistic.

The common good seeks to perfect the balance between the rights of the individual and the rights of the society. On the one hand, society, as a group of persons having rights, has the right to defend itself against those who would destroy the collective rights of the individuals: from this source arises laws constituting armies to protect us against alien invaders and internal thugs. On the other hand, the individual person is the primary and first bearer of rights; the spiritual side of man is of a qualitatively different order than matter; therefore, the rights of the person must also be considered and protected: the purpose of all liberty is ultimately personal liberty.

Because one spiritual man is superior to all of material society, the Russians had to exile Solzhenitzen: he was a spiritual one-man government of opposition. Because the demands of liberty and order require constant examination, there is a wide range of possible ways of ordering a society: so long as the rights of both sides are balanced, the choice from among socialism, fascism, democracy, republic, aristocracy or limited monarchy is more dependent on the needs of the locale than anything essential to the human condition.

The first two on the list are economic theories and the rest are political ones, but, since the first two presently have political platforms and run as organized parties, the meaning of the terms seems to have changed. The exclusion of Nazism and Communism from political discourse is just insofar as both systems have so systematically destroyed the rights of the individual that it is impossible for either to be an ethical system. While similar charges can be leveled against the governmental ownership of industry (Swedish socialism) and government dirigisme against private corporations (U.S. Facism), the dignity of human rights is far less threatened.

The levels of law differ according to the authority of the

lawmaker and the jurisdiction over which the legal body has competence. As can be seen from the following chart, there are two different hierarchies of law, both of which ultimately stem from the different relationships of faith and reason which man has with God, the primary Lawmaker of the Universe.

Since the deity has made the universe, he would also have the reason, power, and authority to pass the laws. Since we come to know them through the different channels of faith and reason, this bifurcation creates different but overlapping societies organizationally, even if all the people in a given area individually belong to both societies.

Natural law philosophy asserts the existence of laws of nature which are more or less discoverable with differing degrees of difficulty. It is the difficulty of discovering the natural law which raises the problem of promulgation.

When the Federal Government of the United States lowered the speed limits in 1975 for the purpose of conserving fuel, you would have had to be blind and deaf in order not to know about it . . . in which case, you weren't likely to be driving a car. In the case of the natural law, there are different degrees of obviousness, depending on the size of the print, as it were.

The primary laws of nature are fairly visible: the law of gravity in physics, laws of nutrition in biology, "do good and avoid evil" in ethics. (As argued earlier, this last is just as much a part of our psychic makeup as gravity is of our physical makeup.)

Imagine two large isosceles triangles with the base on top and the point on the bottom: such is law the higher the law the more general; the more local the law the more particular.

The secondary levels of natural law are almost as clear. "Virgins don't get pregnant" is an axiom of the most primitive biology; the broad outlines of the Ten Commandments are found in all societies, at all times and places.

In fact, it is just this universality which argues so forcefully for the natural law. If cultures which have never contacted each other have broadly similar laws regarding worshiping a deity, honoring parents, protecting the family, against first degree murder, theft, and lying, if they have all of this in common, it is quite fair to conclude that these laws are intrinsic to human nature. The cultural relativity of the early anthropologists turns at its deepest level to show the unity of humanity as much as its diversity.

It is when we get to the tertiary level that some things get blurry. One society worships its deity with bread and wine, another prefers human sacrifice. One society honors its ancestors by burning incense to them, another floats the aging out to sea to allow them to die with "dignity." Two tribes ban homicide, but one practices abortion and infanticide (because "they are not human") while another cheerfully slaughters adults from another tribe (because "they are not human"). One tribe has community property and community wives, another kills you if you touch another's property or wife. The Natural Law is not that obvious to all. (Is it any wonder in this context that some oppose abortion? In regard to something as valuable as human life, they would rather give the benefit of the doubt to too many beings than to too few. In an older tutiorism, as today, the rule is `be safe.')

On the tertiary level, the sheer amount of knowledge available plays a role. If anything, heightened knowledge should increase the awareness of responsibility, but this is a generalization allowing for emotional exceptions to the intellectual norm.

Continuing now with the chart, one finds under Natural Law, the jus gentium, the old Roman law of the nations, is a historical accident which contains a philosophical truth. When the great organizational ability of the Roman Respublica was carried over into the expanding Roman Imperium, the Romans found themselves in control of vastly different tribes with vastly

171

different codes of law. The Roman genius was to compromise: "We Romans have taken a least common denominator of all the laws of all the provinces. We will administer this jus gentium and your local authorities will enforce any of your specific laws." Thus, every country within the Roman Empire was under twin rule. But this historical accident contains a historical truth.

Thus: certain things appear which, while not essential to the nature of man, seem to be the concomitant rule rather than the exception. The best example of this is the right to private property.

By nature, a human being has five basic rights: the right to live, the right to food, clothing, shelter, and education. The right to live because it is given by biology, as it were: the laws of Nature and Nature's God, as Thomas Jefferson expressed it.

The other four rights follow with immediate speed upon them. Life will indeed be mean, nasty, brutish, and short without food, clothing, and shelter. And man is the only animal whose instincts are so poor that it needs education in the broadest sense of training, exposure to the information necessary to fend for itself.

These are the five things the offspring has a right to demand of its parents. (This demand must be even more insistent in an age with a contraceptive mentality. Now more than ever before the child can insist, "You wanted me, now you've gotta take care of me.")

The jus gentium suggests a solution to the question how best to provide for these human needs? It is the common historical experience that what belongs to everybody, everybody wants to use and nobody wants to take care of. The members of Plymouth Colony starved their first year because of the rule, "From each according to his abilities, to each according to his needs." Result: few worked, most ate, then everybody starved. The next year the rule was "if a man will not work, then he shall not eat."

Private property has in it the elegant simplicity that people take care of what belongs to them. Efforts at "community-

172

building" are spotty at best: cars are cleaned, washed, and polished while buses get dirty, rusty, and rot. Time share apartments deteriorate faster than condominium or co-op. The Post Office charges 13 times what it did 50 years ago because it is a government corporation while a phone call from home still costs less than a dime because it is a private corporation. Historical wisdom seems to back daily life.

Now that we have two different levels of law and two different types of right coming from these two different levels, a general principle of law (and ethics) can be enunciated. In case of conflict of rights, the right coming from the higher law takes precedence.

Textbooks of a century ago used to use the example of people shipwrecked on a private island. While the owner under normal circumstances had the right to his island and all it contained, the rights of the shipwrecked took precedence. They had a right to food, clothing, and shelter, provided they exited as soon as possible and did as little damage as possible.

That ancient example has been relived and brought home with new force because of the survivors of the Andes plane crash in the 1970's. In the normal course of things, your dead body is the property of your next of kin. In the case of the Andes survivors, there was no choice but to cannibalize some for the carcasses. Dead muscle tissue is less important than keeping the living alive. Interestingly enough, they too, placed restrictions on themselves; they set aside the carcass of any relatives, lest they hurt the surviving relative. Again, private property took second place to survival.

The rule is recognized in the enforcement of certain laws against theft. For a hungry man in pre-welfare days to steal bread for his family was not always treated with the same severity as the mugger who stole a blind beggar's cup.

The United Nations and national treaties between sovereign states give rise to international rights of commerce and travel, in the name of International Law, a bruised and battered thing, more breached than observed.

Once inside a country, the United States, for example, the levels of laws and the conflicts of rights become more complicated: to the point where we need a Constitution and all of its amendments which remain superior to any other federal laws. In fact, it becomes so complicated that we now need a lawyer.

Federal law supersedes state law, except where the states are sovereign under the Constitution. States may suspend local laws because of emergencies, natural disasters, and the like. And the local legislative machinery regulates the purely local concerns.

If the last paragraph is a bit vague about the rights conferred by each jurisdiction, I can only plead extenuating circumstances: the number of laws and restrictions requires an immense legal library and is so detailed that it defies even outlining. The very complexity of the laws on this level raises some interesting philosophical questions.

The application of this mass of laws requires the existence of equity and someone to apply it. Any law has within it the possibility of injustice: humans not being omniscient, the cases arise where hard cases make bad law. To avoid some of the more harmful effects, society can appoint people whose sole function is to see that the law is applied equitably in each case. Not equally, but equitably: not every felon deserves the same sentence. The first offender has a greater claim for leniency than the three time loser: to give both the same punishment, depending on the circumstances, might be grossly unjust.

The role of the police, legal professions, and judiciary is to see that the laws are applied equitably. In America the jury system adds to the process: juries, like the cop on the beat, have been known to turn someone loose if they felt the projected punishment was too severe for the case.

Religious law is a totally different kind of law in its origins, in its interaction of levels, and in its treatment of its domain. The basic divine law, rooted in some extraordinary type of experience, is more sacrosanct of its nature . . . if you believe the original revelation.

On the secondary level, the interpreters of the law are a mixture of Written Words, Oral Tradition, and Leadership (Bible/Tradition/Pope; Koran/Tradition/Grand Mufti; Torah/Midrash/Rabbinate).

Frequently, there are rules for the application of the revealed truth to the conditions of the believer's country, locale, and parish.

Unlike the policeman and court system which disillusions idealists with grimy realty while it dispenses equity, the believer is the ultimate applier of the law to his own situation. This is the role of the much abused term conscience: to apply all of the higher levels to the concrete situation. This con-scientia is usually a knowing-with process which agrees or conforms to higher intermediary authorities. Even within religions which are based on the primacy of conscience, if your conscience disagrees with that of the group, then God go with you, but go, anyway: the church or sect is built upon the shared aspect of the belief.

On the one hand, conscience is the most regulated of things in the moral order, it is superseded by all of the laws of the ecclesia, scripture, and God; on the other hand, it is the court of last resort, the conscience is absolute and even if totally wrong, ignorant, and misguided, it must be followed faithfully if the truly well-meaning are to remain in good conscience. How can they both be true at the same time?

The contradiction is only apparent: in the objective order of things, our action might go against all of the laws of God and man; in the subjective order, the fact that we see the act as something good or necessarily inevitable makes it in our eyes something at least blameless and possibly even praiseworthy.

175

Secular law has difficulties with this notion of subjective responsibility. The definition of insanity is wrangled over continuously, and the maxim of the law in more usual cases is "ignorance of the law is no excuse." Yet, even secular law is not totally unbending in this matter. The charity which runs a rummage sale and forgets to charge sales tax, might well be let off the first time with just an admonition from the officer or the court. The international conglomerate can expect no such leniency. The rule is not capricious: people in certain positions are expected to know things which are not expected of others. Businessmen, business law, etc.

If it is understood that secular law can only regulate our actions in the external forum and that religious law binds primarily in the internal forum of our internal thoughts, then it follows that civil law is not co-terminous with ethics.

It is possible for something to be legal but not ethical (confiscatory taxation) or for something to be ethical but not legal (use of alcohol during Prohibition). It was the opinion of Aquinas that, since justice is the measure of law, an unjust law was not a law at all!

Before we all go out and start disobeying all of the idiotic laws that we dislike, take note of the fact that this is nothing less than a call to civil disobedience. Civil disobedience is nothing less than a nonviolent act of civil war against one's own society. Like any war, it could only be ethical if (A) all other means of righting the wrong peaceably had been exhausted, (B) we are clearly in the right, (C) with a reasonable chance of winning, and (D) The good we seek to accomplish is sufficiently sizeable to justify all of the social dislocation and other evils which will follow upon our action. Declaring a civil war in Nazi Germany is one thing, starting a civil war over parking meters is another.

This notion of social dislocation is important to complete a theory of law because of the role custom plays in society. Custom, the un-institutionalized behavior patterns in society, is the lubricant which makes for smoother interpersonal exchanges, which oils the social machinery. The British habit of standing to the right on an escalator so that someone in a hurry may pass; or the New York habit of walking on the escalator; please, thank you, you're welcome, sir, ma'am, hello, how are you?: all the little courtesies which make life a little more bearable.

"But this is the way we've always done things!" Granted it is a cry which can stifle creativity: we are back to the problem of balancing the rights of the individual against those of the whole. If a Western Electric scientist creates a new gizmo which speeds up telephone connections by 1/2 a second, but it would cost a trillion dollars to reorganize the entire system, then it seems reasonable for all of us to wait that extra 1/2 second.

There is a good conservative case to be made for custom. Customs continue only so long as they have meaning for somebody. True, the meaning might change from generation to generation, but something about the regularity of the customary ritual carries within itself a factor of anxiety relief. How many people do you know who always prepare for bed the same way every night? Or must comb their hair just so? Put on one specific shoe before the other? The ritual gives meaning, creates and imposes order on the potentially chaotic life of human beings.

The conservative continues tradition because he sees it as a good which is worth conserving. If democracy implies the equality of all voters, prostitutes and politicians alike, then tradition is the widest democracy, for it includes both the living and the dead. If a tradition survives, there must be something in it: that is a possibility worth investigating.

The prudential judgment is, in the last analysis, the only protection against a neophilic society discarding something just because it is old, or against a stagnant society discarding something just because it is new. What matters is that it is true, not new . . . or old.

If you count equity and conscience as law-like things, and include the hosts of customs which loiter about the fringe of law, we have seen fourteen different types of law. And there is one topic on which they all have something to say: marriage. It is as good an example as any to see all of the different levels of law working in concert.

In keeping with the notion of law, let me offer a natural law definition of marriage. Marriage is a contract between a man and woman, a contract of its nature sacred and unique, by which each mutually gives and receives the body of the other for those acts appropriate for procreation.

The definition needs explication. Begin with the elements of contract: under the general understanding of the contractual relationship, a valid contract does not exist if there is force, fraud, or an inability on the part of one of the contracting parties to fulfill the contract. Therefore, neither the shot-gun marriage nor the marriage bunco racket qualifies as a marriage: in many jurisdictions, proof of either constitutes grounds not for divorce but for annulment: the law is saying that a marriage never existed.

Inability of the partners to fulfill the contract is more subtle. On the gross anatomical level, someone who was impotent or minus genitalia would have difficulty contracting marriage. On the psychological level, there are people of forty who aren't mature enough to enter into a marriage relationship.

To insist that a contract be between a man and woman, while it might cause indignant objection from male and female homosexual communities, is merely to follow the proper use of the language. If this highly political group succeeds in changing the meaning of the language, then the above definition will only apply to heterosexual marriages, as should be obvious from the remaining parts of the definition.

A contract is always a contract to do something. In this case, its purpose is sex. Not necessarily in the narrow context of the `missionary position': the "sex act" can be broadly understood to include all of those gestures, positions, preliminaries and after affects which accompany the vaginal reception of sperm. It might be reasonably objected that this section says nothing about love and makes sex the only thing the parties agree to do together.

The objection is a reasonable one. If philosophy were restricted to our own age and own country, the objection would be decisive. If a natural law definition is going to follow the law of nature, a lot of the accompanying features which we culturally accept as the `normal' part of marriage are going to appear culturally relative. Arranged marriages are the historical and statistical norm globally. The attitude toward them was a business contract to continue the family name, hand on the patrimony to another generation, and provide for future workers for the family farm. If love entered into it, fine; that was a bonus. In the early romance literature in Western culture, it was assumed that the only person you could not have a romantic relationship with was your legal spouse.

To say that it is a contract to engage in `those acts apt for procreation' implies several things. First, despite the objections of women's lib, it is not a relationship designed for 1 1/2 people: there is no stunting here of the role of one of the partners for the sake of the other. In fact, just the opposite is true: by restricting the relationship to the conjugal bed, it puts restrictions on the demands one can make on the other. Each has a legal right to the other's body, but not in a relationship of total slavery.

Secondly, the phrase, `for those acts apt for procreation' is at the heart of present attacks on natural law. Because humans are spiritual things due to their intellect, there is a conflict in each age caused by those who want to destroy part of their bodies for the sake of their mind. While a sane approach to pleasurable bodily functions must await discussion of temperance, it is still a law of biology which links sex and offspring.

Notice, however, the definition does not say "for the

179

purpose of having kids." There is still a valid marriage if one or both is sterile. (A case can be made for fraud, however, if this is known before the marriage, but not revealed to the prospective partner. Generally, impotence invalidates, sterility doesn't.)

That introduces the role of man to nature. If medicine and medical knowledge have a function, it is to supplement nature, to make up for the defects of biological irregularities. One of the ironies of our time is the natural-foods faddist who will not eat any artificial chemicals in food, but will take pills to induce temporary sterility. We are biological animals; tampering with a sexual cycle which has taken millions of years to evolve for the sake of transient convenience sets a smaller good against a potentially larger evil.

Another irony of the contraceptive obsession with security comes also from this last century's medical advances. The ovum can only be fertilized on two days out of the 28 1/4 days of the menstrual cycle. It implies interesting things if people set on avoiding pregnancy feel they cannot bring their genitalia under their conscious control for 48 hours. Within the definition now under discussion, there is little reason not to enjoy each other 26 days a month, except for considerations of abstinence due to occasional physical or psychological indisposition.
When Natural Family Planning, properly taught and properly understood has a 98.6% success rate, chemical or mechanical methods have no ethical justification.

There can be no hard and fast rules about child rearing decisions. Possibly there are married couples who should never have any children, but psychologists indicate that these cases are rare. Whether most people have children as a visible sign of their love, to carry on the family name, or because it is the thing to do, no matter what the motive, I suspect that a childless couple with no overwhelming reason, physical or other, for childlessness might indicate a narcissism a deux.
No matter how many angles are examined on the definition, one is inescapable: only women get pregnant. Until some genetic engineer solves that one, we have to include the

difference between men and women in any philosophical system which claims comprehensiveness. Seeing how past and present ages have stated the difference is almost laughable. Which is the more startling: Aristotle's opinion that a female is an embryologically defective male who did not reach maturity before birth, or the assertion of modern embryology that males are just oversexed females who overdeveloped?

Biology has done much to cut down sexual stereotypes. All humans are hormonally bisexual, with bodies containing both estrogen and progesterone, but the proportions are different in males and females. If boldness and activity of the irascible orexis is in part hormonal, then we might expect women to be capable of great daring, but men do it more frequently: if it happens differently in society, then nature is being overcome by nurture. This is one of the difficulties in designing a society: a society which represses almost to extinction any part of the human organism is visiting upon the individual increased tensions and upon the society a potentially explosive situation.

If the Freudian insight has done any service to society, it is to show the pervasiveness of sexuality upon the personality of the individual. This is not to dictate what roles one sex must play, but to suggest that whatever role sex plays, it will bring its own style to fulfilling that role.

Thomas Aquinas' biology was a generation behind his own time, so that we cannot expect much help from him in the face of the increase in biological knowledge. He could hardly have been expected to single out the role of the Y chromosome in inclining males to greater physical violence, or the role of the XX chromosome in giving females greater stamina. However, Aquinas offers one suggestion which is at least worthy of investigation.

Aquinas suggests that, on the whole, males are more inclined to indulge in speculative knowledge, while, by implication, the female intellect is more practical. Since it is only a generalization, it will not be an argument against great speculative females in mathematics or theology or highly practical males like the local repairman or mechanic. Today it would only be a suggested direction for possible research and further investigation.

A reasonable approach to the intellect must be asexual. There is no suggestion of a difference in the intellectual capacity between the sexes. A certain intellectual humility and truthfulness is needed on the part of all researchers into this area, lest ideological preconceptions preclude the discovery of further similarities or differences. Humans have nothing to fear from truth except the loss of some comforting lies that they are better off living without anyway.

In the context of the marriage relationship, there are still to be considered the real differences between the sexes during pregnancy. To the extent that there is a physical incapacity during pregnancy, childbirth, and after care, there exists an inequality between the sexes that requires that unequals be treated unequally. The woman has the greater right to be provided with the necessities dictated by her condition, and in the usual course of things, the male would have the obligation to provide them. Both are doing hard work, only the nature of work differs because of the structures of biology.

One phrase in the definition has been left until last: the contention that this contract is sacred and unique. By sacred I do not mean necessarily something in the sense of formally religious. Religion adds to our awareness of the importance of the event, but even in nature this relationship has a numinous or awe-inspiring quality about it. The relationship is unique because there is no other contract which demands an act which swallows up a human being with all their abilities in one act.

Coitus is a peak experience. Not only does it call forth the total involvement of our physical and hormonal systems, at its best this includes an ineradicable psychic union. Since sexuality is the most forceful internal experience which a human can experience, it is unforgettable. Medicine shows that the force of a strong emotional experience impresses itself indelibly upon our memory. If a person's first sexual experience was a type they would rather forget, they probably will, but not without recourse to repression mechanisms.

Psychically, our first sex partner has ineradicably changed our lives and our memories of sex will forever be bound up with that person to some degree or another. Superficial sexuality, "It's just another itch to be scratched" is purely and simply a lie.

There are, have been, and probably always will be persons of so fearful or stupid a mentality that they cannot enjoy sexuality to its fullest. There is no justification for making these cripples the guide of what sex is or can be at its fullest expression. Paradoxically, it is the natural law "Puritan" who argues for the sex-act to be enjoyed in marriage so that it can be enjoyed to its fullest without regret; it is the "Puritan" who argues for the enjoyment of an act which is so overwhelmingly good that it naturally overflows into the existence of new creatures capable of enjoying this fullness of human life.

Coitus is the high point of nature: only damned fools would screw up their opportunities for enjoying it at its best in exchange for some lesser good.

As the whole presentation suggests, it would be difficult to make a case for divorce under natural law. Annulments, the statements that a true marriage never really existed, are more likely. Divorce, the assertion that a full marriage existed but no longer does, rather recalls the married lady who would like to kill her husband, but, "Divorce him? Don't be silly!" If she can't have him, nobody can. One spouse can't live with the other . . . or without the other: that is not material for the divorce court, but for a full-out argument after which they can reconcile, kiss and make out.

Philosophy has no answer to the problem of the couple who cannot live together. To impose celibacy on both might reconcile them but that is hardly guaranteed. The case of the abused partner is worse: why impose further suffering on someone who had to get a separation because of previous suffering? Eventually, enough cases can be collected to create a hole-in-the-dike situation. If the family is the basic unit of society and the place where we all first learn to act like humans, and if modern psychology has shown the need for children to have the role-model example of their own mothers and fathers (and of the need for seeing parents love each other): if all these things are needed, if the child has a right to these things, then what percentage of the population can divorce without wrecking the psyches of innumerable future citizens and thus deteriorating the society? What does one do with a 50% divorce rate or a 60% illegitimacy rate?

Other levels of law admit of a briefer exposition because they add the necessities of the smaller society to the broader demands of nature. The jus gentium indicates that people raised in a clearly defined family have a clearer sense of their own worth than those raised in a commune who do not know who their parents are. The UN has set a minimum marriage age of 14 (protested by the Arabs, who thought that fertility at 12 wasted two good years). The Federal Government of the United States banned the admission of Utah to the Union until the Mormons made polygamy illegal. The state government sets laws for the protection of the woman, reflecting a society where women would be the objects of injustice and possibly wards of the state if deserted. Even the county gets in on the act in letting the Parks Commissioner set the restrictions for sunrise weddings in the local park.

In natural law, given the sexism of biology, polyandry would be unethical if the child has a right to know who its parents are. Polygamy would not only be ethical, some today are arguing for it as a way of solving the problems of unliberated women, liberated women, too many women, and the economic strains of the atomic family. My only reservation to a solely biological natural law's liberality concerns the possible exclusivity of peak sexual relationships to two and only two people. This is an argument now used by educated Moslems who see Mahomet's rule that all wives be treated equally as a psychological reductio ad absurdam requiring monogamy.

Divine Law in Torah, Bible, and Koran has commands concerning marriage and divorce, which the leadership of the religion interprets to the congregation of the several organizations. Thus, for example, the Bible condemns the remarriage of divorced persons; while the Roman Pope opposes the marriage of divorced Catholics to another spouse, the Canterbury Convocation (Anglican) allows it. As always, one's acceptance of his faith is the binding force on accepting the subsidiary regulations.

The National Conference of Churches and the National Conference of Catholic Bishops have their own ways of adapting the general regulations to the situation in America. (Try to get a Catholic wedding without producing a freshly-issued Baptismal Record that says your single.)

Each diocese can require a pre-nuptial investigation. They would rather a child be born a canonical bastard than perform a shot-gun wedding. To give a Church blessing to both fornication and violence they view as being an accomplice to something they should not sanction.

Each pastor can set restrictions because he must keep in mind the needs of his entire parish. Strewing rose petals in the path of a bare-foot bride is one thing, performing a wedding in church with the wedding party in swimwear might be treated differently.

In the last analysis, conscience decides. Only the individual in the depths of his mind can testify as to his intention to live up to his promises. Once that is done, custom simply adds the finishing touches. Something old, something new, something borrowed, something blue; the bride in white; throwing (uncooked) rice. (In ancient times intended to symbolize fertility, today it gives the assuaging of anxieties because it makes us aware that it has all been done before, we are not alone. It is also the churchman's nightmare of liability for

185

somebody slipping on the rice: some require cleanup fees to protect themselves.)

And how many guests at an Irish wedding have listened to the strains of `Danny Boy' or `Mala femina' at an Italian wedding? What is a Jewish wedding without a Hora, or a Polish one without the Polka? While fulfilling all the customs sometimes increases the strain on the couple at the time, it is amazing the numbers who look nostalgically back and enjoy in retrospect the things which annoyed them at the time.

All of these laws have the simple intent of spelling out the requirements which each partner fulfills to the other in justice. Two cohabitors might be fulfilling the definitions of natural law without benefit of church or state and be truly married; the case of the two students awaiting graduation before fulfilling the legal requirements is far more a marriage than two casual lechers. But the memory of the earlier question relating love and justice still nags at the back of the mind: if love is to will good to another, and do it; if justice is merely to give to another what is owed to them; then how do we comprehend your lover, who professes to want to give you all good things but is not willing to do or give you the minimal to which you are justly entitled?

AFTERWORD ON JUSTICE

Since the bulk of this chapter was written (1976), a large amount of literature has been published on Church-State relations. Its contemporary nature is not worth discussing. Presidential candidate Jesse Jackson raises campaign funds in churches. Israeli war bonds are sold by U.S. temple/synagogue officers. Clergymen argue for (and against) just wars/nuclear weapons, the rights of women and/or their fetuses. Who cares? It would be terribly hard to build a case to say that religious people have fewer political rights than atheistic citizens.

Nor is the history of bigotry relevant. It is clear that the antisemite wants Jews dead, that the white racist wants blacks to be subservient, and that the anti-Catholics wants those

186

religionists to abandon their leaders and their beliefs.

The chart on levels of law implied a level of interpenetration between church law and state law that may be construed as an ideal. It is that interpenetration which this afterword seeks to address.

Ancient Greeks and Romans and Barbarians possessed a religion which was simultaneously personal and civic. Household gods of the fireplace and the larder coexisted with major seasonal feasts like the Saturnalia (which is still celebrated in the week or two before Christmas!)

This natural religiosity failed to distinguish between one society (secular) possessing a terrestrial common good and another society (religious) seeking to help its members to an eternal common good. For their failure to worship the state god, countless Jews, Christians, and Moslems have been killed for their `atheism and treason'. If you do not worship the state god how can you wish the state well?

Space forbids repeating the historical conflicts of Henry II of Germany with the Pope at Carnossa, the multiple kidnappings and exiles of Popes by Emperos, the death or exile of Thomas a Becket, Anselm of Canterbury, Thomas More and countless others. History aside, how shall/should these two societies co-exist?

Werner Stark, in his magistral five books on The Sociology of Religion, outlines the options for this type of social philosophy as three: State Religions, Sectarian Religions, Universal Religions. In a State Religion, king and pope are mixed into a Caesaro-papism: where the state supports and controls the church. Psychologically it is a religion of the status quo and those content with their life in this world. Sects on the other hand, arise out of dissent from the dominant society and, in a strict sense are caused by the state church. The psychology of the malcontent is fed by the reversal of values in Western Religion where the meek shall inherit the earth. Finally there is Universal Religion where the foundation is "Render to Caesar what is Caesar's and to God what is God's." This sublime indifference to secular government was the hallmark of Calvinism and Romanism. Indifference becomes political action only when the religious freedoms of its church members is threatened and that is the history of the modern age: universal religions seeking the liberty to preach, teach, marry, and perform its other functions in the face of antipathy or a hostile indifference.

Less cosmic is the example of the U.S. Supreme Court which has given `humanism' and `atheism' the protection of religious sanction or which has permitted Sabbath laws and Christmas cribs because they `serve a secular purpose' or do not violate a mythical `wall of separation' between Church and State. The transition of American history from the 1815 requirement of Connecticut office holders to be Congregationalists, through John Kennedy's 1960 willingness to resign if his religion barred him from discharging his official duties, to Ms. Ferraro's 1984 willingness to reject her church in her quest for office--these and other examples may show how difficult it is to do full just to both societies, to distinguish the legitimate claims of each society, and to secure the full rights of believers and non-believers alike. Only with justice can a civil (or ecclesiastic) society be civil and civilized.

SINCE THIS CHAPTER WAS REVISED FOR THE 86 VERSION: The issues of what constitutes sexual harassment has gone from being a topic used by the left end of the political spectrum on everybody else to being a topic used by the right end of the political spectrum against a self-described new liberal president. Ignore the personalities: focus on the principles: Equity, the fair application of the law to the particular case. In "he said- she said" cases, the limits of the human mind are such that third parties are reduced to character judgments and /or the seeking of corroboration. Needless to say that if the principles applied to the example of marriage obtain, the argument for premarital virginity and marital fidelity dispose of all of these cases because they violate one or the other standards of chastity. For more on which see the chapter on temperance.

IN 2012 HOMOSEXUAL MARRIAGE IN NEW YORK AND FIVE OTHER STATES RAISE THE ISSUES:

•How does State law apply to the Federal Defense of Marriage Act?

•How are you married under NYS income Tax law but not the IRS?

•If Marriage is not about reproduction, is Bestiality legal?

•Is everybody else obligated to give you 'your' right as a gay couple?

CHAPTER X: THE POTENTIAL PARTS OF JUSTICE

Some real obligations do not fall under the strict definition notion of justice .

"To give another what is owed to them." You cannot be just to the household which you head. In what sense is your mate somebody other?   Or your children? Imagine a family constructed on legalistic lines where the laws were justly enforced and reward and punishment were doled out with complete equity! Even assuming such a cold-blooded group could be assembled into a `family', could you call it a family? I would definitely not want to visit it, much less live in it!

There is an old "problem case" which points up the problem quite well. It is the sort of thing to not only cause fist-fights at a party when charades pale, it forces one to consider what comes first in one's own life. Rules: read the following paragraph then close the book. Further instructions will be given at the end of the paragraph.

Case: You are the captain of a boat of considerable size which sinks in the Pacific, off the usual sea routes, and before you can radio for help. In the huge life boat with you are the following people: your father-in-law and your mother-in-law, your husband, your child, a paying passenger, a stowaway, your cousin, your mother and father, and yourself. As Captain, you not only are legally in charge of the life boat, you also have the only gun: therefore, you have the right to rule and the power to back it up. You take inventory of the life boat supplies and discover that there is no way to feed ten people for any extended length of time. What do you do?

Question: Can you resign as Captain? Let's assume that individualistic war would break out, therefore, you can't resign.

Question: Does survival of the fittest mean that you throw the weakest overboard? But society's civility is measured by the care it takes of its weakest. Further, on the basis of the above information, you couldn't decide who to get rid of.

Question: Why get rid of anybody? Either we all survive or we all die? Very noble, but do you have the right to do that? Isn't that nobility disguising a rather unreal and, therefore, unethical romanticism? Isn't it just survival of the fittest in pretty words?

Question: Does it matter how you get rid of them? Is there a difference between shooting them and giving them a life jacket and letting them swim? If you shoot them, couldn't you cannibalize the corpses and stay alive longer? Does the end justify the means? Would it be right to kill someone just to prolong your own life? If you let them swim away, would you be doing the same as killing them or would they still have a chance at being saved?

Question: Let us assume that there are no volunteers to go overboard. Let us further assume that you opt for swimming rather than shooting. If supplies force you to chuck overboard one person a day, who goes first?

Last problem: Make a list of who goes in what order. Do it by yourself without consultation. Then compare your list with a group of five others. Each must explain why they chose as they did. In the face of a better argument, you may change your ordering. Then come back and read the solution proposed by the Middle Ages.

First of all, note that while we have certain obligations in justice to some of these people, most of them fall under the greater obligation of blood relationship or love.

Second, a utilitarianism of survival could only be ethical if one of the crew were a navigator or had some special skills; otherwise strength is irrelevant to the problem.

Third, the end does NOT justify the means. Everybody has an equal right to life. Nobody made us God with the power to decide that someone also had outlived their usefulness. Even a normal society only uses capital punishment on humans who have deprived others of their right to live. Here you would be killing the innocent.

Day one: The stowaway goes because there are no obligations to him; there is no contract with him; he takes his chances in the water.

Day two: The passenger goes because he has contracted for normal services, not for guaranteed delivery.

Day three: Now we are into the area of love and blood relatives. The cousin has the least claim on either.

Day four: I pass along here without comment the argument of my students that, if you get rid of your in-laws, you do an injustice to your husband; if you get rid of your own parents, what has become of your obligations of gratitude to those who gave you life? Therefore, "Wait four days and chuck all four overboard."

Day Eight: Choosing between your mate and your child is the most difficult of all. There are those who would say, "You can always get another husband, but your child is part of yourself." On the other hand "You can always get another child, but your mate came first; it was because of that primary love that the child developed in the first place." To dispose of the mate is the decided preference of, most Americans: it implies much about the `childolatry' of the society. The Medievals would have chucked the child, feeling that it was inordinate to put your children above the mate who helped generate them.

Let's consider another problem!

Problem: Another shipwreck. Five survivors make it to two small tropical atolls which are within sight, but not shout of each other. On Island A, we have John alone. On Island B, we have Nicky, Wayne, Mary and Albert. Mary and John were fiancees on a shipboard cruise. A storm arises and the people on Island B see a palm tree fall on John. Mary, frantic with anxiety for John's fate asks Nicky, who has just finished building a boat, to ferry her over. Nicky, a firm follower of the Playboy Philosopher and a fraternity brother of John's, eyes Mary's body, leers, and suggests that they make a deal. Mary refuses and seeks out the help of Wayne, who is working on a half-finished boat of his own. Mary wants Wayne to get Nicky's help without her having to sleep with him. Wayne refuses, "You have your troubles, I have mine. I prefer not to get involved in private arrangements between consenting adults."

Mary capitulates to Nicky's demands. The next morning Nicky ferries her over to Island A where she saves John's life, nurses him back to health, and brings him back to the group on Island A.

Things will slip out in conversation and John discovers Mary's infidelity. He confronts her with her infidelity. She denies it. He confronts Nicky, who grinningly compliments John on his choice of women. John returns to Mary and breaks off the wedding plans, because, "I could never marry a slut, and a liar."

Mary, heartbroken, cannot change his mind. Finally, she tries to get Albert to intercede, "Please, make him realize that I only did it for him." Albert is a good-natured slob, short on brains but long on muscle. He tries to reason with the adamant John and finally, in sheer frustration, Albert beats the hell out of John.

There is John lying on the ground, bruised, bloodied, and probably a few ribs broken. Mary comes along, sees John lying on the ground. She walks over, smiles at his predicament, and says, "Good. You had it coming." She kicks him in the ribs and walks away

.

Given this unlovely group of people, which of them is most reprehensible? Who is best or least reprehensible among them? As before, put them in order of dastardliness, then confer with others. The book will be here when you come back

This time I have no intention of choosing between them. I will only point out previous ideas that "the end does not justify the means" and remind you of the modifiers of behavior, like fear and other emotions which inhibit our clear perception of things. I will only add that the notion of "choosing the lesser of two evils" implies that one should choose an evil--better no choice than an evil one.

There are so many things which elude the generalized framework of law. For example, what is the relationship between justice and mercy? A family which is overmerciful to an overindulged child generates a selfish monster; a society which forgoes the demand of justice and punishment, generates a society of criminals. An overly strict family nurtures a child without any compassion; an overly strict society creates a cruel populace.

The habit of mercy seeks to immediately relieve the wrongdoer the instant the demands of justice are met. Justice without mercy is cruelty; mercy without justice is irresponsible.

Applying mercy and justice in each case is fraught with problems for the equitable judge or parole board. In some cases a prisoner might be so rehabilitated in just one day in jail that the punishment has forever frightened her into acting better: more incarceration given human adaptability, might only produce a worse felon. Another prisoner might have to remain incarcerated for life, mercy can only try to improve the conditions and rehabilitate the person if not free him.

There are still other obligations which elude the definition of justice. How shall we return to God all that he has given us? How shall a person redeem his debts of obligation to Someone Who has given us all that we have, Someone Who has given us the very abilities with which we could seek to pay him back?

LATRIA is the name given to the worship to which this Being has a right because of all its past goodness to us. While

194

philosophy cannot specify when, in what manner, or how frequently, it can point up the obligation of religio which all societies have felt. Because the debt is strictly unpayable, because we cannot give to this Other what is owed to Him, therefore, this is called a potential part of justice, because it does not fall within the actual definition.

DULIA is the name given to the obligations of respect which we owe to superiors, officers, and those in authority. Let us take them one at a time. The American tradition of individualism tends to downplay the respect which is owed to superiors and public officials because of their office. We all know some truly rotten human beings in positions of authority. Nevertheless, that does not excuse us from respecting them because of the position which they hold. Not a hypocritical subservience such as students flattering teachers or employees seeking to impress their employer. I am referring to the awareness that the office which they hold is structually important to the institution and society, and that it is the importance of the office in its service to the whole which makes it worthy of respect.

DULIA extended to parents (pietas) will change its application relative to their position and ours; its necessity never changes. The child has the obligation of obedience to them, the adult has the obligation of respect, and, as time goes on, may also have the obligation of supporting and caring for the aging parent.

Pietas never changes in itself, only in its expression. Any cult of convenience or cult of youth which will take the experiences of age and consider them fit only for deprivation and death is purely Darwinian. Maybe the eskimos of an earlier age were more mercifully misguided in their motivation when they put the elderly out to sea on an iceberg than the Americans are when they institutionalize the elderly in ghettos or slumlord nursing homes. In either case Man cares where apes don't.

GRATITUDE is the obligation which we owe to those who have done good to us. If you borrow money from a bank, you have discharged your debts when you give it back with the stipulated interest. If you borrow money from a friend who charges you no interest, have you discharged your obligations when you return it? Not at all. There may be no clear and easy way of discharging that obligation, but sensitivity to the obligation will frequently recognize the occasion when it arises.

BENEVOLENCE is the obligation which we owe to others who are in need. Do you pick up hitch-hikers? What do you do if yours is the first car at the scene of an accident? May a doctor's car ethically keep going if it is the first car at the scene?

The obligation to help our fellow human being involves three factors which have to be balanced against each other: the extent of their needs, our ability to help, and the cost of that help to ourselves. Apply it to the last question listed above.

If a body is slumped in the car, the need is apparent. The doctor is able to help. Cost determines this case: May a doctor legitimately endanger his expensive training against a possible malpractice suit from treating a patient in the dark, under the worst possible conditions? If the state has a Good Samaritan law which renders the doctor immune from lawsuit, can the doctor in any way justify refusing to help? The morality of the action might well change according to the circumstances.

Circumstances so affect the morality of an action that equity and conscience in a well trained individual are the only things capable of deciding a particular case in all of its concrete details.

An elderly couple comes to a clergyman seeking a secret ceremony. Both are on Social Security and a state-licensed wedding would halve their income. Even though the clergyman is under law as a justice of the peace to report all weddings he performs, it is more important to let the couple set themselves at ease with their God than to obey the injustices of the Social Security law.

Likewise, a physician whose conscience and whose views

of natural law will not allow him to take a human life when he has spent his whole life saving lives might well have to resign from a hospital rather than engage in performing euthanasia or abortions.

The case of Karen Ann Quinlan has become a shorthand for all of the problems of balancing obligations in complex circumstances. We all have an obligation to take reasonable and normal care of our health. That means different things to different people in different circumstances. Running out into the snow without a coat would be a minor negligence . . . if you can afford to own a coat. Normal self-care in terms of food, drink, and rest means different things if you are (a) a starving native in the Sahel desert, (b) an obese American, (c) a doctor working around the clock during an epidemic, or (d) a nine-to-five employee.

Normal is not only determined by the health care available, but our ability to pay for it. Does the hemophiliac have the right to bankrupt friends and family for a clotting factor which costs $100,000 a year? Can a millionaire hemophiliac justify not taking the factor? This last example bridges the gap between benevolence and self-care. A father who sacrifices a kidney to save his son's life is doing something which will not cripple himself, but will save another. The millionaire might feel that given the limited supply of serum, someone else has a better claim on it.

This sacrifice differs markedly from the suicide. In the first case, there is no desire to take life, even if nature will take its course, disable the father and kill the millionaire. It is the very frustrating fact of human existence. It is the frustration which keeps researchers working to end the evils of physical illness, that calls forth some of the greatest sacrifices and dedicates some of the highest abilities of man. The suicide, the mercy-killer, and the abortionist in their tasks of destroying nature and people are not even in the same class.

The very hard cases summon up all the prudence we can

muster to make the best decision we can with the facts available. But prudence is not enough. A great respect for the dignity and immeasurable value of a single human life imposes the obligations of justice upon us if we wish to consider ourselves truly human and humane beings. The courage and perseverance necessary to complete these difficult tasks will be considered in the next chapter. To see a situation in the true light of all its circumstances, to exercise true justice and courage, requires that we finish up this chapter with a consideration of truthfulness.

The obligation to tell the truth falls under the potential parts of justice because of all of the shadings and refinements which are needed to fully understand the nature of the obligation.

Have you ever told the truth and it turned out to be incorrect? Were you, in that case, a liar? Did you ever tell something which you believed to be a falsehood and only by accident have it turn out to be the truth? Were you, in that case, being honest?

Lying can be defined as speaking contrary to your own mind. You may be wrong, but honest; you cannot be lying and truthful. Before the definition's implications slide by too quickly, stop and think about the nature of speech.

Humans are the only animals which have elaborate systems of artificial symbols or language systems. Animals communicate with natural sounds, which indicate pain or pleasure, use body language to indicate more complex behavior, but only humans can lie. It is the defect which our Intellect and Will allow to us rational animals.

To appreciate the full horror of lying would require a deep understanding of our position at the top of the evolutionary pyramid, the highest creature in nature. It would require that we fully appreciate the closeness which intellect gives us to approaching the god-like. The fact that we are incarnated gods only makes the perversion of our intellects the worse. By this standard Aquinas find seduction even worse than rape because intellectual perversion is worse than brute force.

The added realization that we are incarcerated in bodies adds to the enormity of the crime. Speech is far and away the greatest means we have at our disposal to share the fruits or our thinking with others. Moreover, not only are we perverting the function of speech to truthfully communicate our minds, we are destroying society.

This last statement is no poetic flight of fancy. A society of liars cannot exist. No one in such a society could dare act on anything which was told by another. The great co-operative efforts of mankind in medicine, construction, in all of the co-operative ventures which have made life more truly human, all of these would be impossible.

"But we lie all the time, don't we?" It depends on what you mean. Language is a supple tool, always changing to meet the increasing needs of people to communicate new things. Don't get caught in the myth of monomeaning: the fallacy that words have only one definition. One of the longest definitions in the Oxford English Dictionary is for the word "set"-- in length it is 2/3rds that of *Paradise Lost*. (Get set to set the table after a few quick sets of tennis and put away that damn erector set!)

Back in the days when dictionaries were prescriptive, i.e., when they set the standard of English as used by the best writers and speakers, they told the tale of the young lady who corrected an eminent Victorian Clergyman on his pronunciation only to be reminded that "My dear dictionaries exist to record the pronunciations of people of education like myself." The New OED is descriptive merely recording anyone's usage − "to google" something is in the OWD now..

One reason to unpack the definitions of Aquinas is to avoid the problems of misunderstanding which would result if you understood words in a different sense from my intention.

Words can take their meaning from their context. Anthony

199

Burgess did something like that in creating a futuristic vocabulary in his book *A Clockwork Orange*. We do it every time we use words like "fast": something is *fast* if it moves quickly; something is color-*fast* if it resists running; something is *tied down fast* if it cannot move at all; someone might go on a *fast* for religious reasons but you wouldn't say that someone who was *fast* and loose was particularly religious. In Japanese which is an even more elusive tongue, seikan may mean, among other things, serene contemplation, can manufacturing, naval construction or sexual feelings.[51]

A basic five-hundred-word vocabulary might have 15,000 definitions for those 500 words. Yet, we rarely get confused because the context usually indicates what we mean.

Another trap to avoid is the fallacy of literalism. Drama is not a lie, fiction is not a lie, fairy tales are not lies, poetry does not lie. Even an ancient Irishman telling a monstrously tall tale is not a liar. In none of these cases do we expect a literal narration of descriptive truths. The liar who is thus gifted, but who perverts fiction by attempting to pass it off as fact is the greater abuser of his abilities than the prostitute because of the misuse of a greater thing than sex is involved here.

Since the meaning of words is determined by their context, a variety of things which are called "white" lies can be seen as being not really lies at all. The salesman who, seven days in a row, hears the same secretary tell him that her boss isn't in or is in conference is a moron who had better find a new line of work. Convention has made "the boss isn't in" mean "the boss isn't in TO YOU" where the last part has been suppressed as a part of business courtesy.

This is nothing so strange. Somebody who says, "Hello. How are you?" would usually be startled if you said anything other than "Fine, thank you." It would really disconcert them if you gave them a detailed report of your last physical. Likewise, it is a wise spouse who knows whether the mate inquiring about

51Robert C Christopher, *The Japanese Mind*, Simon & Schuster,1983 p.42

dinner is asking for an honest opinion or fishing for a compliment.

Circumstances arise in which we are caught between two conflicting obligations to tell the truth or to keep a secret. Consider the rights of the second element before we explore the conflict.

In the ordinary course of things, there is such a thing as a natural secret. Sometimes the confidences which a friend imparts to us are such that we might just naturally not want to go blabbing them about. In other cases, the request for secrecy might be explicitly, albeit casually, made, "This is just between us you understand."

There are circumstances where we would be ethical in violating the confidence for the sake of some greater good, but only with a full knowledge of the circumstances and a highly developed sense of prudence. When you know both sides of the story between two feuding friends, your role as intermediary might justify your confiding to one what the other has told you. Since you run the risk that both will wind up hating you, the role of peacemaker requires skill, tact, and sound judgment as to whether or not it is even possible.

Even in the natural conversations of daily life, so much gossip is unethical that Spinoza was right when he said that, "History shows that there is no organ over which man has less power than his tongue.[52]"

Students come to class for the first time prejudiced against a teacher because of the grape-vine, or RateMyPressor.com. School gossip ruins the reputation of teacher and student alike. Lawyers' gossip undercuts confidence in professional secrecy. The list is endless.

Whether we speak the truth (back-biting) or a lie (slander) about another, we are depriving someone of the good reputation that they have a right to . . . whether they deserve it or not. As

---

52The Ethics

Shakespeare summed it up, ironically in the mouth of his most serious defamer Iago:

> Good name in man and woman, dear my lord,
> Is the immediate jewel of their souls.
> Who steals my purse steals trash; 'tis something, nothing;
> 'Twas mine, 'tis his, and has been slave to thousands;
> But he that filches from me my good name
> Robs me of that which not enriches him,
> And makes me poor indeed[53].

The confidences which people confide to the practititoners of the traditional profession of religion, law, medicine, and teaching are of even a more serious nature.

We willingly impart to our clergymen things which we do not expect them to repeat. In the case of Roman Catholicism and Eastern Orthodoxy, what is told the priest in the confessional is a matter of absolute secrecy. They may in no way, by word, sign, gesture, facial expression, or body language impart to another their knowledge about a penitent . . . even to their bishop, even to save their own life, a fact which Alfred Hitchcock played upon suspensefully in an old movie called "I Confess", in which a priest was tried for murder himself because he could not reveal his own knowledge of the killer's identity. (Of course, priests who write textbooks for seminarians to guide them in hearing future confessions may describe the case if all identifying elements are removed.)

The confidences which we extend to professionals always suppose that we are in a clearly understood professional situation. While the discretion of the professional is his greatest asset, something told to even a priest outside the confessional is not under the strict seal of the confessional.

This establishment of a professional relationship occurs in the case of a patient and the company doctor. A policeman sent

---

53*Othello Act 3, scene 3, 155–161*

down to the medical office for a physical does not have the right to keep the results secret from his department. The Police Department is the employer of the doctor not the individual officer. Many an employee has been placed in an embarrassment because they were not aware of the non-existence of the relationship.

Where a doctor-patient relationship does exist, an ethical practitioner does not have the right to withhold information from the patient or give information to the next of kin that he will not give to the patient. Psychological circumstances might allow for some time delay to prepare the patient for the bad news, but that is all.

Doctors have the obligation to divulge their confidences only in highly restricted circumstances related to the performance of a greater good. Doctors are obliged under criminal law to report to the police gun shot wounds which they have treated. They are obliged to report to the Public Health Service cases of highly communicable diseases to avoid their further spread. They are also allowed to use confidential information to protect themselves against civil suits, but with certain restrictions. The psychiatrist whose patient alleges rape, may defend himself by disclosing the delusions for which he has been treating the patient (assuming that the doctor is innocent).

What obligations a doctor might have in regard to giving testimony under other circumstances is dependent upon the relevance of the information. If he is giving testimony about a gunshot wound, the patient's other ailments, if irrelevant to the proceedings, are still protected.

An attorney has a twofold obligation: he is the representative of the client and an officer of the court. In the first relationship, he is obliged to respect the confidentiality of a client as regards past crimes. As an officer of the court, he is obligated to present to the police whatever information he might have with regard to future crimes or crimes being planned by his client.

The conflict of obligations can lead to some interesting conflicts of interest. Take the case of the attorney whose old client has called to say that she just put poison in her husband's medicine. The lawyer tells her to sit tight and he will take care of everything. If he calls the husband, he is admitting his client is guilty of attempted murder, and has violated her right to confidentiality. If he does not call the husband, he has violated professional ethics by not telling the police about a future crime and, in fact, he has become an accessory before the fact. (In the actual case, the legal firm chose to have the husband called anonymously.)

The ethics of the teaching profession are also twofold: As an employee, the professional has a contract with the administration, and as an instructor he has an indirect contract with the students. Confidences here admit few hard and fast rules, and are mostly contingent upon the nature of the case, but to politicize students, using them as tool against the administration, or to jump contract without prior notification, are clearly unethical.

Having explored the requirements of the different kinds of professional secrecy, we can now explore the conflict-of-rights problem between the obligation to tell the truth and the obligation to maintain secrecy. There are ways of keeping a secret without telling a lie. Ambiguous answers, answering a question with a question, changing the topic, or just plain silence will work most of the time if we are quick-witted enough to use them. In the face of some direct questions, we might be able to say, "I'd rather not talk about it."

There remains the case of being given the ethical choice of ethical violation or punishment. If the situation involves a sufficiently serious matter, the integrity, the wholeness of the ethical individual is at stake. Some may be unable to keep themselves and their ethics intact under attack. It is a great choice: honorable unemployment or a dishonest prosperity.

Ethics isn't easy just essential. The person who refuses to capitulate to injustice is the only bulwark against both the disintegration of society and the materialization of man. In the face of those who feel that man is nothing but genes and conditioning, the just stand witness to the wholeness of the person and the superiority of the spiritual life of the intellect to the vast armada of physical things. In the face of liars who surround and flatter those in power, he defends society by sometimes speaking the unpleasant. Will the liar help society by saying, "Good," to its illnesses? Can a tyranny be improved by merely populating it with liars? God help the social animals who follow that route. It is rapidly becoming apparent that ethics requires courage. That is where we shall turn next.

CHAPTER XI: THE COURAGE TO BE

Courage is the virtue located primarily in the irascible appetite which allows us to get the greatest good out of those appetites. Hardly a stirring definition, but the implications are wide-ranging.

Recall the object which these emotions seek. Generally speaking, they involve going after objects which are difficult; more specifically, things like money, power, fame, honor, glory, reputation, things which involve great risk.

Recall the mechanism of the human emotions when faced with difficulty: the adrenalin starts flowing, our hopes rise up in anticipation accompanied by the darker fears, we can be driven to extremes of daring or despair or furious anger.

How do you train somebody to handle difficulties? In a perfect moral pedagogy, each individual would be given tasks just a little beyond his present ability, rewarded when he achieved them, boosted and encouraged to go on to the next. The factor at work in building self-confidence is more than anything the conquest of fear. It could be argued that, while a healthy fear often keeps us out of trouble, it is probably the greatest single factor in stopping us from all that we could become--for better or worse.

The Boaster, who is constantly telling us about the greatness of personal and mythical achievements, is merely another version of *the Self-Belittler,* who is constantly telling us about the miserable defeats and failures of his unworthy self. Both never let us see their faces. Both are hiding behind a mask of lies: only one is a mask of comedy and the other of tragedy.

Both are fishing for compliments. Both are afraid that if we could see them as they really were we would not like them. And they so much want to be liked. Yet, how can we ever know them if they will not allow themselves to be known?

The self-revelation process, while strictly a part of truth-telling, is also largely involved in this notion of courage. It requires courage to take the chance, to risk ridicule or contempt, because we open up to others a part of ourselves, whether it be the most superficial political opinion or one of those things which is deepest to our heart.

Love may have been known to inspire some courageous acts but *we are not really looking at courageous acts but the habit of courage.* It is important to recall that, because these habits are habits, the mere act on one occasion does not show the virtue.

We do not call the village idiot a prudent man simply because the idiot occasionally comes up with an astute observation. If anybody talks long enough, he is liable to say some very profound things. Even I could do it.

A person of remarkably shrewd judgment is able to make a mistake. The greatest rational detective in all fiction, Sherlock Holmes, was once defeated because he could not tell that a woman's "brother" was really her husband. The perfect thinking-machine failed because he was all head and no heart. Nevertheless, that one mistake hardly allows us to call him the idiot of the Western world.

Likewise, a judge of remarkable fairness, of such impeccable justice that he never convicted an innocent man, never freed a guilty one, was never reversed on an appeal to a higher court: even such a man might perpetrate a massive injustice without ceasing to be considered a just man. We judge people by their everyday, habitual behavior: the good thief may have done a good deed, but he was still a habitual thief.

The relationship between act and habit takes on a new force when we consider the notion of courage. The humor of Paul Gallico's book, The Adventures of Hiram Holiday, takes its force from the unexpected expertise of an encyclopedic book reader, who never before had shown off his abilities at daring-do because there had never been the opportunity before.

It is like that with many of the things we consider acts of bravery. As Shakespeare put it,

> "Nothing in his life became him like the leaving it; he died as one that had been studied in his death to throw away the dearest thing he owed, as 't were a careless trifle"[54].

All fears pale before the fear of death; if we do not fear death for some reason or training, then the other objects which cause us fear are small matter.

To study death, whether as Socrates or an ancient Christian, or as a modern thanatologist or a student of Ernst Becker's <u>Denial of Death,</u> is mental health. Only someone with a well-integrated personality could make Thomas More's jokes at his own execution. Only a person who knows what meaning death has in his own life can live that life to its fullest.

When we hear of the one final grand act of a soldier throwing himself upon a grenade in order to save the lives of his compatriots, we may reasonably expect that a deeply ingrained habit of courage secretly growing inside him was the only thing that could have caused him to act with a promptness which those less habituated could never achieve.

It is of philosophic interest that the ascetic and the athletic both seek the same goal: training the body to obey, bringing it under the control of the mind and will so that it will perform to the limits of its capacity. It is as much an attitude of mind as of body: the more-than-sensual satisfaction that comes from climbing a mountain, getting an M.D., coming in first in sports or politics, the `feeling good' that comes from an activity which engages all of your activities to their fullest, which is rough and demanding and difficult and the greatest fun in the world because you are aware that you are doing it and doing it superlatively.

54William Shakespeare, *Macbeth. Act I, scene iv*

Maybe the only safe rule is to assume that "if it isn't difficult, I'm not working to the fullest of my potential." Here it is sometimes safer to overdo rather than to underdo. As soon as that last is stated, it must be qualified: as in all other virtues, there is no virtue without prudence.

For an external observer, it is never easy to tell courage from its related vices. The `coward' who flees a battle may have panicked or, seeing the odds against him, may have decided to risk the opprobrium of his buddies to go get help. The `hero' who fights off an army single-handedly may not be a coward but a moron who did not have enough sense to be afraid. The psychopathic `war lover' is not courageous but is a reckless nut.

Since moral good and evil reside in the human will we may never know the motives of another. Thomas More, a judge who sent felons to death or imprisonment because of their actions, summed it up neatly when he said, "I have no window to look into another man's conscience. I condemn no one." Because we might only see the one good act of another without knowing why they did it, we cannot objectively praise or blame their conscience. We can praise or damn their action, but only God and the person himself can know its true motivation. To quote T.S.Eliot, "

The last temptation is the greatest treason:
To do the right deed for the wrong reason."[55]

While objectively we are agnostics with regard to the motives behind the actions of others, we are all too conscious of the motives behind our own actions. Ben Franklin once commented on the similarity between a clear conscience and a bad memory. Francis of Assisi, a man of honest memory, once uttered what on the face of it was a massive self-belittlement when he called himself the greatest sinner he knew.

55MURDER IN THE Cathedral 1935

Assisi was doing no inverted bragging, but stating a literal truth: because he knew his motives for some of the actions he performed, he was all too clearly aware of the monstrous lording it over another which can inspire a kind of act of true contempt. You may know of others who have acted more badly than yourself but do you know anybody who has been motivated by as dark a set of motives as those which guided your worst act.

As we survey the parts of course, we shall, of necessity be forced to assume the motives of the people whose actions have been observed. The only alternative would be to visit upon you a series of autobiographical anecdotes which illustrated the vices and the virtues: something devoutly to be avoided. I also am the worst sinner that I know.

While the newspapers report the great acts of courage, cowardice, and recklessness, there are acts of courage over a protracted period of time which rarely if ever come to our attention. Some involve sustained activity over a long period of time, others involve "putting up with" great hardship.

Perseverance describes the first, and patience the second. Its related vices, like all vices in relation to their virtues, are a matter too much or too little. Fickleness reflects the choice of its practitioner not to put up with anything which takes too long. It is the mentality of the reader who could not comprehend an author's statement that it had taken five years to write a particular book. The reader was too accustomed to never waiting more than fifteen minutes for a bus or fifty for a TV dinner.

The people with too much "perseverance" are usually called, more accurately, "stubborn." There are times when the only sane thing to do is to give up. Where do we draw the line? The stories of a blind man finishing his medical schooling and getting his M.D. inspire and frustrate those who are aware that they are not living up to their own best abilities.

This 'total self-actualization' is rather a matter of what you have to begin with. When viewed from the outside, the opinion

210

of others might over-or under-evaluate you. Balance this off against the lies we tell ourselves about our `self-image,' and you have the newspaper editor who had two different word-lists, one for his friends and one for his foes. His friend was "persevering", his foe "stubborn"; his friend "courageous", his foe "a reckless damn fool".

While the virtues are worthy of admiration and their related vices can be pleasantly ridiculed, their presence or absence is no joke. It is not insignificant that the virtus for the Romans was courage: the virtue most becoming the adult man (vir)---the most conspicuous virtue. A few moments ago it was suggested that it might be safer to overdo it in being hard on yourself. It is one of the observable facts of life that it is easier to lower one's personal standards than to raise them, it is easier to create a self-indulgent society than an industrious one: for most people to give up than to expend the energy to succeed.

It is wrong to convey the impression that courage only has its highly active and visible expressions. The courage of the person putting up with evil when there is nothing they can do about it is the least attractive virtue to those who dislike being `passive'.

The element of passivity, which patience requires, makes the ailing doctor a hospital's worse patient. He can't get sick! Or so he believes. Patience can be very closely linked to both notions of gratitude and humility. If we have an honest awareness of ourselves, we must of necessity become humble: not groveling, like Uriah Heep, of Charles Dickens's David Copperfield but striking the golden mean between boasting and self-belittlement. Humility is truth: remembering those who excel us in many ways will avoid swelled head; remembering how we excel in our own special ways will avoid a shrunken confidence. Humility treads the fine line between the 'Great I' and `poor little me'.

Patience is the form of courage for those who must endure being the recipients of others when they would rather be left alone, self-sufficient, and on the giving end of the equation: you're damn right it is more blessed to give than to receive--it is also easier.

Patience is not in any sense an ultimate virtue: it too can be carried too far. The gray-faced commuters whose suburban railroad had broken down for the fifth time this week might well emulate the Japanese commuters who several years ago demolished an entire train because it was late. It was never late again.

The awareness that there comes a time to give up being patient and blow your stack, turning your fury loose on the deserving object of your wrath, is the province of prudence. You pick your target, you pick your time, you pick your issue, and then you blow them out of the water. "The worm turns." "Beware the wrath of the patient man." There are countless epigrams which testify to the limits of patience.

In America, anger is "not done". In the words of the Brooklyn politician, "Don't get mad, get even." And, yet,...isn't there something more honest and tension dissipating about a truthful confrontation than the cold calculation of revenge? Given the structure of the human frame, with the capacity for anger built in, the options are limited: we can choose to swallow our anger until it yields angina or ulcers; we can express it openly and precisely as the occasion arises; or we can follow the 'kick-the-dog' theory.

The `kick-the-dog theory' is an everyday occurrence: the breadwinner comes home from a frustrating day at the job and vents all sorts of unjustified anger at a mate who will sit there and take it; Mate then leaves the room and takes it out on the kids; It passes from the oldest child down to the youngest; Youngest finally starts screaming and hollering at the family dog, who looks vaguely perplexed at the whole furor.

There are times when an honest man has to tell the boss to stop. There are times when fighting or quitting are the only mature things to do. But what about the person, swift to anger, who is trying to control some of the more excessive outbursts? A hint of a solution is contained in the kick-the-dog theory. Whereas the abuse of an undeserving person is both unjust and unworthy of our anger, the redirection of the anger into more productive channels might well let off steam and at the same time get your body in shape, make that new bookcase for the home, or turn the yard into a farm.

This redirection of anger, the great insight of sublimation, makes anger a truly useful good because it is being put to use, being burned-off to produce something. The suppression of anger or its kindred emotions is something else: the autarky of the self-sufficient stoic who has eliminated all emotions is a fraudulent amputation of our emotional life.

Seneca, Cato, Spinoza, and various Stoic Oriental Cults have their followers. Why? Because societies of great complexity require the intellectual workaholic. Advance cultures have habitually required a work-ethic of the "talented tenth" to carry the remaining 90% of slobdom. The Stoic of Rome, who had conquered (killed) his emotions, was the natural, detached, intellectual administrator to supervise the bread and circuses for the mobs.

Herman Wouk, in The Caine Mutiny, said the same thing: "The navy is a system designed by geniuses to be executed by morons." The great concern of the academic/governmental neo-Wasp who works 18 hour days providing a womb-to-tomb, abortion-to-euthanasia, security system for those who need not work at all merely continues the system. The middle class work ethic is turned against its practitioners, who hold down two jobs to support the 'deserving poor' through taxes because they live in horror of not having autarky, of not being economically self-sufficient.

Yes, there is such a thing as being too patient. It is called insensibility. It is the numbness of the overworked. It is the rat-race. It is the man who is too busy pleasing one boss to go look for a better job. It is the overextension of stamina which robs people of their intellect. It is the thing which destroys homes, shortens life-spans, and creates alcoholics, addicts, compulsive gamblers, and compulsive eaters. It is the thing which drives people to Transcendental Meditation, or Pentecostalism, or anything which offers the promise of relief from strain. The impatient man who is "as even tempered as the next guy, provided the next guy is Donald Duck" may have no patience. The laborer who has only the energy to work and to sleep may be far too patient.

It may seem strange in this context to talk of gentleness, but, in a real sense, *gentleness is the fullness of courage and patience*. The nice, easy Casper Q. Milquetoast is not gentle, but effeminate. The rough, tough, beat-em-up character is the ungentle Neanderthal of women's lib comics. Gentleness is more accurately ascribed to figures like Kojak or Christ, Captain Kirk of Star Trek or Moses: people of immense personal power capable of great anger. It is in the expression of gentleness by this type that shows the shining forth of true mastery of self and the fullest expression of the human character.

You can see it at work in the *manganimous man. Literally, the term means great-souled, high-minded, large-hearted.* The daily pettiness of the day tends to grind down the average person unless they are sufficiently vigilant and courageous to overcome them. If we allow it, we can be pecked to death by a gaggle of geese. The hintergedanken, the gremlins of buried fear which slither out of our mind at two in the morning when we are overtired and too edgy to sleep, can undercut our humanity as much as anything else. In the words of the Roman motto, *nihil illegitimi carborundum* (Don't let the bastards grind you down). That requires courage.

The Mr. Great-Heart of Pilgrim's Progress, the Atticus Finch of To Kill a Mockingbird or even the person who "can't be bothered" to take revenge, or who refuses to waste time on that trivia: all of these have grown to such a control over their lives, and, more importantly, a control over the objects which impinge

214

upon their lives, that their magnanimity is a type of mental courage. They have acquired the knack of keeping first things first.

Of course, this ability to keep things in their proper perspective is prudence; to keep them there, unswayed by the pressures and fears of others, is courage. Those who cannot achieve this are the *pusillanimous, literally, the small-souled,* the petty-minded, who are truly the obsessive-compulsive neurotics who can only get their security from fulfilling the last little dotted i or crossed t in their contracts, instruction manuals, or rules of bureaucratic procedure. This is the type that created the notion of `the right way, the wrong way, and the Army way.' This group assumes that laws were passed, not for the common good but for the generation of red tape, the bow on their gift-wrapped package of neuroses. Bureaucratic rationality is to reason as military music is to music. If a bureaucrat can function `without fear or favor', we must also note that all too often he functions without knowing or caring

.

Needless to say, while the great-souled seek and desire large goals worthy of their talents, the small-souled greet all such projects with, "It can't be done", "I never get involved", or, "That's too preposterous for me to consider." While the great-souled man disregards trivia, giving it as little attention as it deserves, the small-souled man glories in it. Be careful not to confuse attention to detail with pettiness: there is no such thing as a great accountant, proofreader, editor, typist, or artist who does not pay attention to detail. In execution of these jobs, the littler the mind the better. Notice that we are not talking about precision workmanship, but the obsession of the petty-fearful with petty things.

Magnificense, literally magna-facere, is the doing of great deeds. The great-souled man requires, not only the desire to do great things, but in the executing of them must also be able to bring the work on the grand scale to completion efficiently. The small-souled man never accomplishes anything great because he never even thinks of trying to.

Vainglorious individuals are not so much, magnanimous as 'keeping their eye on the main chance', thinking about great projects primarily because of the glory it promises them. Where the magnanimous man's mind is primarily focused on the desire to be engaged in a worthwhile project, the gloryhunter merely seeks the reputation or glory which accrues to accomplishment.

When the desires of the magnanimous and the glory hunter are translated into action, two different results ensue. The act of magnificence may be admired for its greatness of vision and simplicity of execution as much as for its precision and economy. To the glory-hunting president or prelate, it can be as wasteful as is necessary to assure them of the splendor they desire.

Since the vainglorious man frequently generates a self-deceptive self-image, he is most liable to deceive himself into taking on the ambitious project which is beyond his means, overambitious, and open to the further psychological suicide which comes from greater fear of failure. The magnificent man can quell his fear of failure only because of the accurate assessment of the situation and of his own powers.

This attitude extends even into *a lesser virtue, like liberality. It is the least of the varieties of courage because it only extends to courageous control over our desire for getting and spending.* To control our appetites in all spheres, to make ourselves large-minded, to be patient with others (and ourselves) to persevere in the fact of difficulty: all of these are more important than liberality.

The magnificent man throws himself magnanimously into a project; the merely liberal man only gives of his property, not of himself. Because of the nature of a capitalist society, and especially because of the Horatio Alger Americanism of the self-made millionaire, our attitude toward possessions is sometimes blown so far out of proportion that it becomes necessary to give this virtue more emphasis than it might be worth in itself because it is more important in our present society.

Your car is involved in its third collision in three months. The last rainstorm has just wiped out your basement and ruined all its contents. Somebody just stole your coat, your money, and the report you finished working on. On a day like that you might well ask whether you own things or they own you. To keep a sane perspective on the matter might indeed require some form of courage.

How reasonable are our desires? Would we want a million dollars if it meant working an eight hour executive week? Do we sometimes sneakily pass off our green as `wanting the kids to have all that I didn't?' That last is a marvelous way of passing the buck. "But I'm only thinking of them." Nonsense. You were only thinking about the reflected praise of what a good provider you were to your daughter the engineer, your son the doctor, with you basking in their achievements.

The other extreme is more reasonable? The bank clerk who deserts wife and children to become a Gaugin on some tropical island in the irresponsible self-indulgence of self-induced poverty is a more noble type?

The spendthrift squandering of resources by the `idealistic' anarchist, communist, fratricelli, communard, or hippie is no more reasonable than the miserliness of the `founding father' of wealthy dynasties. Liberality, like all other virtues, seeks to keep reasonable balances.

The freedom of the irresponsible (with no cares because they do not care about anything) may sometimes be the wistful object of admiration by the overworked, but the importance of our liberty lies in what we do with it. It is conceivable that one tribe would prefer a governmental dictatorship which insured personal liberty rather than a democracy which severely restricted personal freedom. Luther's <u>Liberty of the Christian Man</u> is of greater worth than the license of the porno shop simply because the use of the liberty was aimed at a different goal. Is the free butterfly really able to enjoy the satisfaction of the frazzled parent who has produced good work and upright offspring?

Sober analysis once separated from the romance of rags, might indicate that the expensive library is necessary for the research scholar locked in a small town, that the horrendous expense of a car is less expensive of more precious time and energy on public transit, that a higher priced quality purchase is less expensive in the long run than cheaper goods which have to be replaced more frequently. The unreasonable element might more likely come into the American obsession to own the `complete' everything, where a single missing book halves the cost of a set, or a single missing tool halves the cost of a toolbox.

The whole force of liberality as a type of courage comes home to us only if we realize that we sometimes confuse what we have with what we are. The pitiful miser's spiritual impoverishment stems from the equation of `my importance' with `my income'. Possibly, the child of poverty is no more responsible for acquisitiveness than the child of affluence is for wastefulness. But once the misuse of objects is seen as reflecting a lack of discipline, order, and courage, once the lack of true liberality is seen for the character flaw that it is, only then do we become fully obligated to change our ways.

Societies are much like people in this respect. The state squanders its resources and then tries to compensate by nationalizing private property or appropriating the holdings of foreigners. It is no different from the wastrel who squanders savings and inheritance and then turns to theft. Likewise, the country which, in the name of nationalism, hoards its resources rather than improve the living standards of its people in international trade is little different from the miser who lives in rags: both have made money, a means of exchange, into an end in itself.

Possibly, the most frightening thing is to see the formation of these traits in children. What kind of monstrously greedy future lies in store for the little glutton who demolishes not only his piece of pie, but that of his little sister? Or who steals the toy of another? What kind of minimal self-esteem will be found in the grown-up who, as a child gave away his toys "so the kids will play with me"?

The corporate executive who grasps for more, or the "Good Fellow" who always grabs the lunch check is little different from the children. The only difference between the men and the boys is the size of their toys.

If we truly concentrated on the immense value which we have by nature, invested as we are with the dignity of being persons, if daily we meditated upon the Being Who has such immense love for us, would we really seek to compensate for our lack of self-esteem by hoarding or squandering mere externals?

With respect to courage as with all the other virtues, our happiness lies in ourselves. The sanity of the prudent, the clear conscience of the just, the serenity of the courageous: all of these virtues hang together to help us live a truly "good life" which is also a happy one. Because these virtues stand in the primary relationship to ourselves, nature, and God, those who possess them can be sick, broke, and slandered, and still be happy. It is even possible to be Olympic champion, a millionaire, and enjoy the esteem of one and all--and still be happy.

Without the virtues, one can be at the top of the heap--or at the bottom--and still be an unhappy human of diminished humanity. The choice is ours. As the signers of the Declaration of Independence knew, there are certain things worth the courage necessary to pledge "our lives, our fortunes, and our sacred honor."

CHAPTER XII
PIZZA, LIQUOR AND LIPSTICK, SEX AND SLEEP

There are fewer abused words in the American vocabulary than temperance. The Women's Christian Temperance Union, Carrie Nation, and Prohibition have permanently warped our appreciation of a temperate person.

Temperance is the good habit, primarily located in the sensual orexis, which helps us to get the greatest good out of our sensual drives. Abstinence is doing without something totally: it bears no more relationship to temperance than cannibalism does to vegetarianism.

While the general virtue of temperance covers all the sensual drives, there is another sense in which the special virtue of temperance applies to food and drink.

It is a biological truism to define eating as taking something into your mouth, then swallowing it, with or without chewing as needed. It would be unnaturally narrow to see food in its biological context only. All societies have their special customs and rituals surrounding so important an act as the one which keeps us alive.

Only special reasons of health could really exempt us from the sociable sharing of Thanksgiving or Christmas dinner with family and friends. Even the business luncheon or the "Let's discuss it over a cup of coffee" testify to the social uses of food and drink.

Because of this BIO-social combination with respect to food and drink, it admits of a wide variety of misuses. The ancient Romans, in order to enjoy three-day feasts of gluttony, sometimes had a room set aside as a vomitorium. The function of the room was to let overstuffed guests vomit up the contents of their distended bellies so that they could have room for more. The custom continues among the chic super-thin models in today's fashion industry.

Because food is sometimes used as a way of expressing love and affection, we sometimes have to choose between being overfed and being rude. The rightness or wrongness of that decision is far less clear than the case of the grossly obese who have misused food to alleviate boredom or who have settled for the warm comfort of a full tummy in place of the more delicious warmth of being loved.

Because alcohol has become part of our rituals, it too admits of abuse and of reactionary abuse in the other direction. Even ancient scriptures refer to the wine which gladdens the heart of man, while simultaneously describing the horrors of the drunk. The greater confusion requires greater explication.

Because alcohol is a depressant of the central nervous system, it is often mistaken for a stimulant. It stimulates sociability because it depresses the tensions, anxieties, and memories of the work day. In the over-pressured executive, it might be more beneficial than any of man's wonder drugs in coming down from the high pitch of the work day. For the coward fleeing the realities of a world he hasn't the daring to face, it is pure poison.

Because of the abuse of alcohol, many have made temperance synonymous with abstinence, which is rather going to the other extreme. Some people might have a genetic defect which makes them unable to drink; after one drink, they are either drowsy or drunk. Others have a psychological inability to drink without going to excess. In both these cases, the only reasonable thing is total abstinence.

To assume that total abstinence is necessary for all humans not only flies in the face of all history, but more dangerously implies a very low estimate of the human race. If to be human means that we have intelligence and free will, then the Total Abstinence Society is saying that we are inherently imprudent, unable to treat ourselves justly, and lack even the most rudimentary courage to discipline ourselves.

To do justice to the Temperance Union, however, requires the objective realization that 150,000,000 Americans are either obese or drunks or both. The concern of philosophy differs from the social reformer in refusing to ban either food or liquor, in refusing to admit the culpability of that 100 million. Temperance is something different from a concern with just the manipulation of objects.

In the case of temperance, something other than a healthy body is involved. Public Health statistics could be trotted out which show that moderate drinkers outlive drunks by 3 to 1, and also outlive nondrinkers by 2 to 1. At the risk of being blasé about it, so what? We are all going to die eventually; what is at issue is how we live, not just how long.

The gourmet is just as much an intemperate person as the gourmand. The little old lady who doesn't want "to be a bother, dear. I'd just like a piece of dry toast and a cup of tea," can be truly intemperate: she neglects to tell you that the toast must be a chromatically measured shade of brown and that the tea must brew for exactly 3.957 minutes. This lady is investing too much of her life in what keeps her alive rather than just enjoying the fact that it does keep her alive. A 2012 story is making the rounds about the model for <u>The Devil Wears Prada</u>: she has a color swatch above the coffee maker for those who fetch her coffee so they match the creamer.

Another difference in relationship to food appears in the difference between dieting and fasting. Fast, if used to mean zero calorie diet, is just another diet. Fasting when used a day or two before a feast might well be an imaginatively ethical way of enhancing your coming feast by increasing your appreciation for food's taste and by allowing you to eat without guilt from fear of eating beyond the needs of nutrition. In older parlance, you diet for the good of your body; you fast for the good of your soul.

The social barbarian who rejects an exquisite dinner (which took the host six hours to prepare) is just as intemperate as the host who spends six hours getting every detail `just right' for a simple supper for two people. The first has no appreciation of the sociability of dining and the second has no sense of proportion.

"Recreational drugs" are as old as alcohol, as medieval as the Crusader's pouch of hashish, and as modern as pharmaceutical chemistry. Used in a medical context to restore the person to optimal health, they are an undeniable good which fills up the defect called illness. Even the psycho-pharmaceuticals which curb our hysteria or elevate our mood or stimulate us out of narcolepsy or lethargy are clearly beneficial. It is the sheer power of these things which poses the problem.

As one VP for research in the pharmaceutical industry said, "It takes ten years to discover what a drug can do *for* us but twenty years to discover what the drug does *to* us." Based on the ravages which non-medical use causes to the brain and other organs and to the risks of breeding mutants and causing cancers, it is hard to consider marijuana, cocaine, heroin, amphetamines, and tranquilizers as suitable forms of `recreation'. Legality is not the issue; the overall good of the whole person is. To seek death in this fashion, even, under the disguise of temporary oblivion or `recreation' is a defeat for the dignity of the person and the power of the human will to bring external things under our dominion--not us under them.

The one sensual appetite which can divide an entire country more than drugs, is sex. As I have indicated in the sections on the love of a mate and on the nature of marriage, I have a high regard for human sexuality: it brought me into existence and for that I am deeply grateful. It also is one of the most deeply pleasurable experiences of the human animal.

Anatomically, sexuality relates to the primary genitalia which generate life. Physiologically, it includes the various stimuli and reactions which occur in and on the body of a human. Hormonally, it includes the sensations in the bloodstream which increase body heat and enhance the final surges of coitus. If it were a simple biological function, there would be little to discuss; we would only need to consult the biological sexperts, study their results, and that would be the end of it. It would be then just a matter of scientific research.

Anyone over the age of puberty can tell you from the testimony of their internal experiences that it is not quite that simple. Custom and culture have cluttered the topic with a collection of clichés ranging from the sublime to the ridiculous. Buried beneath the debris are a few truisms about men and women.

According to Masters and Johnson, the arousal time of a female is more prolonged, the peak is longer in duration, and the gradual return to a lower energy level is slower. In the male it is a matter of rapid excitation, quick ejaculation, and rapid deflation. According to St. Augustine, a saint not without his own sexual expertise, "After coitus, all animals are saddened" (by the letdown of sexhaustion).

The data not only implies the sexual superiority of the female, but also gives some indication of a sophisticated sexual ethic. The human use of human beings (to steal cyberneticist Norbert Weiner's title) would make some of the more outrageous aspects of female flirtation, especially those which result in male erection without possibility of release, to be unconscionable acts of cruelty. This is the more true insofar as sexuality is not merely a genital phenomenon, but one which involves the whole person.

By the same standard, the male in intercourse who climaxes and then slumbers without regard for his partner's desire for love and affection is abusing the partner's sexuality to strictly personal gratification.

We are confronted here with the fact that sexuality is inevitably an other-directed phenomenon. The adolescent who is not given any preparation for the onset of physical changes will be totally at a loss to understand the fact that the changes are biologically related to a thrust in the direction of the opposite sex. This awareness of the other carries with it two implications for the nature of masturbation and heterosexuality.

In the case of masturbation, the private arousal of one's self for the purpose of self-gratification, there is the danger of a totally narcissistic, inward-turning state of mind which might make one less able to relate to another only with difficulty because the pleasure has been experienced as a mostly private experience rather than a shared one.

Sociological studies (which indicate that the practice is `normal', i.e., is statistically practiced by a majority of the population) have often been used in justification on the grounds that "everybody does it". Such a justification makes about as much sense as a referendum to repeal the laws of gravity. Just as the lawyers argue that a political offense might be common but still illegal, so too the philosopher of natural law can argue that the misuse of biology might be statistically `normal', but could never for that reason become biologically, psychologically, or ethically normative. If anything, the statistics admit of another explanation: it might well testify to the diminishing of the pleasure bond which had made marriages in the past more firmly cemented together under the heat of passion.

That the other-directedness of the sexual drive argues for heterosexuality is a position which has fallen on sad times in large urban centers in the Western world. It is relatively easy in such areas to find urbanites to argue for homosexuality. (Farmers sodomizing sheep are rather more reticent, and probably more rare).

Discussions of homosexuality must proceed with a clear separation between the objective order and the subjective order. The homosexual cannot be assumed to be in bad conscience. Some studies argue for a surplus of the other sex's hormone in the body of the homosexual. Other cases are recorded of genetic females possessing the male genitalia and secondary characteristics. Still other cases argue for the limited freedom of the homosexual to be a heterosexual because of a wide variety of physiological and sociological conditioning factors.

225

Members of the homosexual community often take offense at studies like those listed above. They assert that they are the talented top of the society and therefore have the intellect to break out of the biological and cultural stereotypes of heterosexuality. Furthermore, they assert that their love is other-directed and beneficial to population control.

The ancient tradition concerning chastity, the virtue which regulates sexual activity, involves the proper use of the sexual functions. It does not mandate that they be used at all. It merely indicates the best way in which sexuality can be used and enjoyed to secure the greatest good from it. Under this definition, chastity applies to the unmarried and the married, the virginal and the sexually experienced. We will return to that in a few minutes: for the moment let us continue with the arguments of the homosexual.

There is a basic bias within natural law which the ecology movement has revived with its concern for the natural way of life. It is philosophically similar to the position of this entire work. Unlike the Promethean theories of the 19th Century which culminated with Nietzsche and the Nazis and which preached the power of man to bring everything under the power of his mind for the purposes of control, the naturalist--both in natural law philosophy and the sociological sciences--professes a realistic materialism.

Man is a part of nature and therefore there is a certain biological wisdom in conforming to nature. Since Man's mind is a part of nature and the only tool with which man can really defend himself against some of the more destructive aspects of nature, intelligent conformity to the ways of nature wherever possible should be a basic guide.

In the case of medicine, man deliberately sets out not to frustrate nature but to supplement what is lacking in nature which could contribute to the well-being of nature. Man's relation to nature is as guardian and protector, as cultivator and shepherd, who, with the power of the mind, makes nature produce more abundantly than she would have under non-human conditions. As arguments over additives in the food supply show, there is a constant measurement of the risk against benefit balance. We contravene nature at our own risk. It's not nice to fool Mother Nature.

In the context of the homosexuality argument, non-human homosexuality only occurs in nature under unnatural conditions. Caged monkeys and overcrowded rats also practice homosexuality: the aberrant conditions of both hardly argues for the homosexual as being a natural product.

As to the other-directedness of the action, biological considerations seem to make this more a matter of mutual masturbation among narcissists rather than true intercourse.

Finally, considerations of population cannot be dismissed at all lightly. Even aside from the fact that the starvation of the globe is more a matter of political selfishness than limited resources, the problem of population admits of solution in other ways. The Irish have long solved the problem culturally by making late marriage (age 30) the social norm. Other societies have created attractive alternative conditions for those who would practice celibacy. A case for premarital or perpetual virginity will be considered later.

It is significant to recognize in the American culture that our sexual expectations far outstrip any possibility of realization,. Even as late as 1900, 20% of the population spent their whole lives as unmarried individuals: in 1976, only 5% could be expected to hold to such a lifestyle. All of these different styles argue for the non-necessity of the homosexual option. As a member of a fertility religion, I will only briefly mention my preference for the option of colonizing outer space because it would relieve the population strain, commit the best resources of the planet to a worthwhile effort and would provide indirect inventions which would improve the quality of life on the planet itself.

Before leaving the topic of homosexuality, it is important to remember that even if the action is objectively evil, and the person is possibly non-culpable in the subjective order, the rights of the person as person are not at issue.

The question of discrimination against homosexuals is too tangled a problem to develop in this limited space. A brief recitation of the factors involved in the rights of homosexuals would have to include the rights of a person to seek employment on the basis of their ability to perform the task, the right of every human to the necessities of life, the right to protection against the invasion of privacy. It also includes the rights of a society to produce a future generation and to educate them as whole people in the society. Questions of the role-model influence of the homosexual teacher, the morale effect of homosexual soldiers on their heterosexual companions, the sanctification of homosexual alliances in the various churches, the right of a home-owner to refuse rental to a homosexual: all of these questions require objective analysis detached from the ideological homosexual or the ignorant passion of the homophobe.

I said earlier that the definition of chastity included both the virginal and the married. Let me explain. Since chastity includes all questions of usage and attitude to sexual expression, it would cover both classes of people but in different ways.

In making a case for premarital chastity, we must have recourse to the pervasive role which nature has given to our sexual makeup. A sexuality limited to primary genitalia is a cheat and a fraud. It suffuses our whole being, each body cell, and literally has a power which carries to the depths of our soul.

Since it is something which includes all types of biology, all cognitive and appetitive powers, the sex act at its fullest is the merger of two bodies biologically, emotionally, and psychically. Any sex act that does not allow itself to come to this full fruition is so crippled and defective a thing that it must be considered evil.

Given all of the insecurities attendant upon premarital sex, given its abuse for purposes of experimentation or as the expression of casual affection, Chastity merely insists on virginity so that the person will not shortchange themselves of all the joys attendant upon the act at its best.

A good case can even be made for premarital virginity as the enhancer of marital sexuality. Even in the first chapter we saw that the power of memory leaves a far stronger imprint upon the emotions than does imagination. A pair of married virgins might imagine what another sexual partner might be like, and these fantasies might even enhance marital play. The case of the memory is rather different in so far as the memory of the earlier partner will always be there as the basis for implicit comparisons which can ultimately poison the free fun of the marriage and undercut the entire relationship.

You will notice both partners are described as being virgins. There is no double standard with respect to chastity. As to the clichés about an experienced partner being a better lover, that is nonsense. This game for two improves with knowledge of the partner. Just as the style of two chess players can be totally different from two others, the style of two lovers is not transferable to other players except insofar as the mechanical basics of the game are concerned. Anyway, think of the fun two virgins can have exploring each other in full fun and clear conscience!

Obviously the act cannot merely be construed so narrowly as to mean just the deposit of sperm in the vagina. That is a part of it, indeed that is so essential a part of sexuality that mechanical contraception would diminish the act to mutual masturbation. But that is not the only part of it. The imaginative capacity of the lover to both delight and enjoy the partner might well call upon all the imaginative powers one can summon to keep the partner continually off balance with new and ever more delightful surprises. The rest is up to your imagination. Enjoy yourself.

The only restriction which chastity places on the married

are the restrictions of prudence. It can be argued that sexuality behind closed doors has value in not distressing the mind of a child who only sees the violence of the act but not the affection. It can be argued that a decent respect for the condition of one's partner might dictate the frequency and style of sexual activity. It seems unreasonable and unethical to force some types of sexual activities upon a partner who is too tired to enjoy it right now or who finds a particular sex practice bizarre and repulsive. A mutual consideration dictates the sexual manners and morals of the marriage bed better than any mechanical marriage manual, even though they too might have their place in finding new and imaginative ways to pleasure your partner

After all that purple prose about the delights of heterosexuality, it will come as a shock that a case can be made for the perpetual virgin. Such a case can be made on a variety of levels. Integritas carnis, the integrity of the flesh which was part of the medieval definition, while at first blush a physical definition aimed at females, nevertheless, indicates something more basic.

It should be fairly apparent to anyone who walks down Main Street, Megalopolis, that sexuality is sold at a rather cheap price in our society. When it comes to sexuality, it is easier to find out the market price than the real value. In this kind of society, the ability to "get your head together" and keep it becomes the psychological prerequisite for any Integritas carnis.

Such a person who desires to practice virginal chastity is in quite a different psychological boat from those who are frightened into frigidity because of the fear of intimacy or the fear of venereal disease. The chaste virgin is not running away frightened from evil, but rather has the head set on the hope of some good from which sexuality would distract them. Without sleep we would not live a week; without water, we would not last a month; without food we would not live a season. But genital activity can be deferred for a lifetime without harm to one's physical or mental health.

Freud abstained from sex in his last years because he found it distracted him too much from his work. Some career types prefer to make their name in the world before they `settle down' to married life. Some have found their job too strenuous (work in the jungle, perpetual travel in the service, too demanding in terms of hours) to even have the energy of sex much less the fullness of a relationship. There are even still religious people, including priests and nuns, who find that their religious work is a jealous mistress of their time and energies.

While not passing judgment as to the value of any of these lifestyles, none of them seems unreasonable on the face of it. The publicly known celibate even serves a positive function in our society by showing that a continued sexual presence is possible without genital activity.

One of the subsidiary virtues under chastity is modesty which is the rational regulation of the accouterments which are designed for purposes of attractiveness. The clothes you wear make a statement about yourself to the outer world. The 'slob' and the 'sport' are just as likely to be making a statement about themselves as they are trying to construct an image of themselves for others.

Even Jansenistic morals texts from an earlier age assumed that clothing has purposes of sexual attractiveness over and above the need for protection from the weather. Some of the books from the early 1900s even tried to legalistically divide up the parts of the human body into public parts (face, hand, feet), semi-private parts (arms, legs, breasts), and strictly private parts (genitalia).

While there is value in the notion of dressing for attractiveness, this legalism borders on the absurd. No person in their right mind could hope to spell out for all times the proper length of a skirt or the number of square inches of material needed for a bathing suit. I leave it to those with greater knowledge (and courage) than myself to even attempt a contemporary code for modest clothing.

231

The ampler mind of Aquinas saw things in simpler outlines when he suggested that dressing for sexual attractiveness was primarily something which concerned people who were married and wished to keep the mate interested, those who didn't yet have a spouse but were looking for one, and those who still had an open mind on the subject. (Of course, even his catholicity of interest didn't anticipate the development of mod ministers and stylish sisters, but then he usually wore the white sack of the Dominican priesthood.)

The business world is less reticent in such matters. John T. Molloy's three best-sellers (<u>Dress for Success</u>, <u>Women's Dress for Success</u>, and <u>Live for Success</u>) dictate the office uniform, their means for projecting a woman's sexy vs. successful images. He even tells job candidates what to order at lunch! Obviously, the old morals books knew something that the rest of the world is just catching on to.

One trivial argument about modesty as applied to cosmetics might be of contemporary interest. It was the opinion of St. Augustine that cosmetics were unethical because they were a form of deception, something like counterfeiting. Today we could call it a Truth in Packaging Law or the Law against Deceptive Advertising Practices.

Despite the modernity of Augustine, I prefer the more liberal opinion of Aquinas that such things--from cosmetics to cosmetic surgery--are quite legitimate to remedy a defective physiology, to provide the support for one's self-esteem, or to attract others.

If you have read your way to this part of the book, dear reader, then it is time we took some time off. Yes, philosophy has even something to say about work and play, about labor and leisure. It comes under the heading of temperance because even our attitude to work and to time off should be moderate.

The Virtue of Eutrapelia is the part of temperance which regulates the balance between and among work, labor, leisure, and recreation. Some stipulative definitions are necessary at this point. Let `labor' refer to the kind of work which has little or no `job satisfaction'; the kind which is primarily aimed at providing for the necessities of food, clothing, and shelter, but you would rather not spend the rest of your life working at it. Let `work' designate the type of activity which not only provides for the necessities but which does confer some job satisfaction. Note that these differences are more related to one's attitude to the work than to the work itself.

The person who was forced by family pressure to become a lawyer might consider it pure labor while they work incessantly at developing a new profession. Likewise, given a favorable reaction to the job, anything can be a `profession', a person who gets great satisfaction out of his work might well be a truly professional gravedigger, waitress, or even teacher.

Let `leisure' designate the activity which we do for its own sake. In this case, leisure might not be leisurely but it provides us with the refreshment necessary to get back to work with a cleared and stimulated mind. To say that the purpose of leisure is work might throw some people in this age of the 35-hour work week. Let it stand for the moment.

Let `recreation' have its literal meaning `re-creation' and you can see why it can be defined as a state of rest which allows sleep to knit the unraveled sleeve of care. The sheer physical exhaustion or mental exhaustion of the misnamed `nervous breakdown' is simply an extreme form of exhaustion where our intellect and will have pushed our physical frame well beyond their physical limits. (`Nervous breakdowns' in animals is a misnomer: the average animal has more `horse sense' than to work itself to death. Most neurotic mice and psychotic rats were created in the laboratory by man).

Eutrapelia seeks to govern the relationship among these four parts of human activity. It is no accident that you can drive the streets of New York and find corporate executives and city officials jogging, bicycling, or coming out of the athletic club at

6 or 7 a.m. Sustained physical activity is sometimes the only curative for sustained mental activity. It is no accident that those professions which are the hardest working generate personalities which also play hard.

Where to draw the line between reasonable and unreasonable extremes in any of the four is a difficult matter. When the "charitable cause" interferes with performing our job commitments then that hobby has gone too far. When you live only for your golf game, playing 18 holes every day, summer and winter, and 36 holes every day off, which either indicates that you are no longer rational about your hobby or that you had better change jobs if you have to play so hard to flee it. (During the 1980 Israeli-Lebanon war the Beirut golf course was in use every day--despite the war going on around the borders of the golf course.)

On the other extreme is the workaholic who can be communicated with 24 hours a day , 7 days a week. This kind of workaholic is not so rare or so laughable as first sight indicates. If they were honest, how many students would admit to `getting edgy' around the middle of August and (horrible dictu) were glad--or, better, relieved--to get back to school.

In both cases, the executive and the student have over-identified themselves with their jobs and thus feel that their lives have no meaning apart from their jobs. This is idolatry of the rankest sort: we have so identified what we are with what we do that we have reduced ourselves from full human persons to a mobile something which just performs certain functions.

The real concerns of "practical people" about training for a productive job has been swallowed up by a series of "practical" or "worthwhile" activities. Your actions only have value because you are doing them: person is more important than function. It is to refute these very practical people, who will ultimately toy with throwing all sanity and ethics out the window in the name of practical efficiency, that philosophers have constructed philosophies of play and it is just against this overabundance of "practical business sense" that a defense of nonsense is necessary.

Sports, play, leisure activities are in the order of ends: they are not the means to anything else. They are speculative activities in the sense that they seek no other purpose than the activity itself. Moscow perverting the Olympics of 1980 into a political event, like Berlin in 1936, or merchants who can only see the economic impact of the misnamed "leisure industry" have lost the whole point of the thing.

In the final analysis, the workaholic may be a variety of things; the one thing he cannot be is fully human. There may be people for whom their job is labor, work, and leisure all rolled into one but they are a small segment. The old man who founded his company 55 years ago and still will not surrender the family business to his 50-year-old sons is a man obsessed with work because he is fighting off death. Or worse, the uselessness which makes death look pleasant.

It is one of the saddest things in our society that we cannot give meaningful occupations to people forced to "retire" because an aggregation of youths is pushing them out of the way. Hard cases make bad law. There are those who die mentally at 30, there are others who will not hit their prime until 80. Just as the physical capacities of one man will allow him to thrive on four hours sleep while others have nervous collapses, so too a personalistic philosophy would seek to set up the work to the ability of the individual. As someone once remarked, unless you discriminate between people, you discriminate against people.

Rather than end on such a grim note, let us turn back to the people who have totally thrown themselves into their play. The sense of timelessness, the strict sense of eternity, the total commitment to what you are doing at your maximum cruising speed, the taste of bliss so sweet that it almost blocks out the niggling fact that it must eventually end, truly a taste of heaven. Maybe it would not be too farfetched to say that God created the world in one day simply out of a sense of play.

AFTERWORD

Now that this little book is approaching an end, I realize that there are a million other things that could and should have been added and much that should have been deleted. If I forget thee, O Aquinas, may my word processor lose its cunning or clumsiness, as the case may be . . . for you see I have totally left out the man whose thoughts this book outlines.

To outline the man would rather be like outlining a mountain--he was not called the "Dumb Ox" because of his daintiness. There are a variety of good reasons for sparing you further optical hardships: Aquinas himself sought anonymity almost as strongly as he did God, Father James Weisheiphl has already painted the most thorough portrait in his 1974 biography Friar Thomas D'Aquino, and I would find it impossible to write about the man without mentioning the theology which is his greater achievement. I promised at the outset to merely sketch the outlines of his philosophical system and the philosophy starts here, with the end of the book.

I do not mean the trivial list on the next page with its references for further reading; rather I would ask you to consider your own life and your own world. Has Aquinas really said anything which contributes to your understanding of your life and that of the world around you?

If so then this is only
THE BEGINNING

Appendix I: GLOSSARY:

chapter one

1.absolute skepticism: asserts that "you cannot be certain of anything."

2.All names are proper names

3.all words are less specific common nouns

4.Ockham's razor: Never multiply explanations beyond necessity

5.Intuitio entis, The intuition of being is the necessary and reasonable, but unprovable, assertion that our senses make contact with reality more or less accurately.

6.KNOWLEDGE IS THE UNION OF THE KNOWER AND THE THING KNOWN

7.Hot/cold, rough/smooth, hard/soft: the proper sensibles which our tactile abilities reach

8.SWEET, SOUR SALT AND BITTER the proper sensibles which our TAST BUDS REGISTER

9.Color is the proper sensibles which our eyesight registers

10.Sound is the proper sensibles which our hearing registers

11.sensa communis" more accurately a coordinating sense: the physical, chemical ability of the brain to reassemble the data made available by the particular senses. This ability to combine and distinguish sensations is what the modern psychologist calls perception.

12.Sensation and perception deal with the outside object while it is present to our senses

13.imagination and memory are the internal senses which help us to handle things when they are no longer present to our external senses

14.In a hierarchy of senses, the most limited would be taste, then touch, smell, hearing and sight

15.Imagination is the physicochemical ability of the brain to reassemble the image of an object no longer present to our senses

16.Memory is the physicochemical ability of the brain to reassemble the image of an object no longer present to our senses with a clearer image and a sense of time

17. the estimative sense, the knowledge portion of instinct

18..potential intellect: the sum total of all our concrete particular experiences: Sensations, perceptions, memories, imaginings, and instincts are all particular, all revolve around concrete, particular objects.

19.Ideas don't have parts: they are simple, discrete insights which are quite separate from all their instances.

20.If ideas do not have parts, then they are something simple which cannot fall apart. Since everything which is physical has parts, therefore, ideas in the sense of universals, generalizations, concepts cannot be physical.

21.The active intellect draws out of the potential intellect the concept which the passive or possible intellect rests content in understanding.

22..The passive intellect rests content in understanding the concept.

23.Creativity can be defined as the power of the intellect to take apart and reassemble into new arrangements the images stored in the imagination.

24.Mnemonics is intellect + memory

25.Observing=seeing +intellect

26.Listening= hearing +intellect

chapter two

1.Orexis: any drive or motivator; emotions plus will in humans

2.concupiscible appetites, AKA the sensual orexis, the broad category of sensual motivation and motivations

3.Love: a positive attraction to an object under the aspect of good

4.Desire: love for a future good not yet possessed

5.Joy-satiety: rests content in possession of the good which we desired

6.Hate is the negative reaction to something which you view as evil;

7.Aversion is the turning-away from some easily-avoided thing which you view as an evil in the near future;

8.Sorrow is being stuck in possession of a sensual evil

9.(Pain is a sorrow localized in a particular organ).

10.the irascible appetites, or the utility motivators involved in those acts where we value something not for itself but for its ability to get us something else

11.Hope is the irascible appetite, utility motivator, which helps us to some hard-to-attain good which we might not be able to get.

12.Fear is the irascible appetite which helps us to avoid some hard-to-avoid evil which we might not be able to avoid

13.Daring is the irascible appetite, the utility motivation, which drives us to take urgent (and, yes, daring) action in order to secure some imminent but very difficult good in the very near future.

14.Despair is the utility appetite which makes us resigned to a hard-to-avoid evil whose seeming inevitability in the near future is almost certain.

15.Anger is the utility orexis which seeks to secure some hard-to-attain good by attacking a difficult evil which stands between us and desired good.

16.admiration is a form of fear

17.The arc of the emotions begins with love and ends with love possessed or lost

18.*Will can be defined as the intellectual orexis.*

CHAPTER THREE

1.Hylomorphism: physical objects are made out of the union of form (shape) and raw materials (matter),

2.Form and matter are not something static as much as something relative

3.In Greek, psyche or soul was used by Plato to mean mind.

4.In Latin, anima is the word for soul and this follows. Aristotle. having a soul means being alive.

5.Accidental change; The apple goes from green to red, its accidents (appearances) have changed (accidental change), but it is still an apple

6.prime matter would underlie any change from one substance to another.

7.Aristotle's soul is what the scientists today call homeostatic equilibrium.

8.In humans we have the most complex balancing problems, not only a homeostatic equilibrium, but also a psychosomatic equilibrium

9.What's it made of?, is a request for information about the material cause, is asking for data on raw materials.

10.What is it?, is a request for information about the formal cause, is trying to find out about the shape or format of the finished product

11.How do you make it? constitutes the search for an efficient cause; it is the nuts and bolts, practical, mechanical question.

12.Why did you make it? For what purpose? This is the search for reasons, for motives, for purposes, FOR FINAL CAUSES

Chapter four

1.*the difference between the natural and the praeternatural*: maybe something different from our limited notion of what the physical is but hardly supernaturallike radio waves v. ESP

2.An orchid that could talk would be *supernatural in the strict sense: something impossibly beyond the nature of the flower as flower*

3.*the transcendentals of being* has the following five characteristics on it: *essence, existence, unity (unum), desirability (bonum), and intelligibility (verum)*

4.*When a word is univocal, or unequivocal, it says one and only one thing.*

5.*When a word is equivocal, it means two differing things which have no apparent connection one with the other.*

6.*there is a similarity, and even a strict proportionality (hence the technical term analogy of proportionality)* between the foot of the mountain and the foot of the man.

7."Health" is the primary analogate which permits us to speak of healthy foods and vitamins (causes) or healthy blood or urine samples (effects).This is the *analogy of attribution.*

8..*Unitas, unity: everything that is has its own unity and self-identity as this particular individual*

9.*Verum, intelligibility, or to spell out the idea: everything that is, is true. That is, everything is capable of giving us information*

10.*Bonum, desirability: everything that is, is good*

241

11.all things are good in themselves but, when some of the goodness is destroyed, they turn into a crippled good called evil

12.Strength, speed, smarts are personal goods;

13.peace, order, justice are social goods.

14.structural goodness, the notion that everything that is, is good is called transcendental goodness.

15.A proper appreciation of the relation between good and evil requires that we recognize four types of opposites:

16. Contradictories ("A or not A" or 0,1 binary logic),

17. Contraries ("Some are, some aren't"),

18.Relatives (you are parent to your child but child to your parent), and, finally,

19.Privatives. In any pair of privative opposites, one item is the primary partner (light, eyesight, health) and the other only exists by absence, defect, or privation (darkness, blindness,

20.EVIL WHETHER PHYSICAL, MORAL, OR SOCIAL IS A PRIVATIVE

21.Essence is simply stated: everything that is, is a certain kind of thing

22.Existence: everything that is, is

23.In logic, if A implies B, then B is dependent upon A, A is necessary for B, B is contingent upon A.   This relationship of contingency and necessity

24.the existence of the contingent universe depend upon some kind of Necessary Being.

25.Godel's theorem any counting system (and the universe is a system of things which can be counted) cannot be consistent and complete at the same time.

26.G is so immanent that G is "more intimate to me than I am to myself".

27.ZG so transcends is that it says 'My ways are not your ways. My thoughts are not your thoughts'

28.God is not just within us (extreme immanence or pantheism)

29.or just outside of us (extreme transcendence as in the 18th Century Deism).

30.As the formula says: "God is in us but not shut in; outside us but not shut out".

31. St. Augustine's argument from universal assent--that everyone everywhere has always believed in God's existence

32.St. Augustine's argument from universal assent--that everyone everywhere has always believed in God's existence

33.The five ways or quinque viae that Aquinas used to show the existence of God

FURTHER READINGS

Chapter I: Knowledge
Pieper The Mystery of Knowledge
Aquinas. In de Anima . De Veritate
Aristotle. De Anima
Osborn. The art of Creativity
Phillips. Modern Thomistic Philosophy, Vol. II
Pieper. The Mystery of Knowledge
Plato. Timalus

Chapter II:Orexes
Becker. Denial of Death. Angel in Armor. Escape from Evil
Farrell. Companion to the Summa.
Gaylin. Feelings our Vital Signs.
Hoffer. The True Believer.
Morris. The Naked Ape.
Royce. Man and His Nature
Terruwe and Baars. Loving and Curing the Neurotic

Chapter III
Aristotle> the physics. The Metaphysics
Aquinas In de Metaphysica. In de Anima
Plato. Apologia. Crito. Phado

Chapter IV
Bochenski. The Logic of Religion
Stevenson. Ethics and Language
Sayers. The Mind of the Maker
Maritain. Essence and Existence. Existence and Existent.
Moore. Principia Ethica
Oesterde. Logic
Owens. The Doctrine of Being in Aristotle's Metaphysics
Aquinas, Bonaventure, and Seger of Brabant. On the Eternity of the World
The Baltimore Catechism.
Bourke. The Christian Philosophy of St. Augustine
Darwin. Origin of the Species
Fabro. God in Exile
Freud. Future of an Illusion
Moses and Monotheism

Greeley. Sexual Intimacy Sex and the Single Christian
Jung. Ego and Archetype
The Terry Lectures
Answer to Job
Leibniz. Monadology
Marcel. Homo viator
Morris. The Discovery of the Individual: 1050-1200
Pius XII. Humani Generis
Plato. Republic
Rescher (ed). Leibniz.
Stark. Sociology of Religion. 5 Vol.

Chapter V
M. D'Arcy. The Mind and Heart of Love
Lewis, C. S. Pilgrims Regress
The 4 Loves
Aquinas. DeVeritate. Summas Theologiae I., QQ 1-5

Chapter VI
Caponigri. History of Modern Philosophy
Copleston. History of Philosophy, 9 Vols.
Descartes. Meditations. Rules for the Direction of the Mind
Gilson. Descartes to Kant
Heiddeger. Sein und Zeit
Hume. An Enquiry Concerning Human Understanding
Treatise on Human Nature
Jones. History of Philosophy,4 Vols.
Konecsni. Scotus to Kant
Locke. An Essay Concerning Human Understanding
McInerny. History of Medieval Philosophy
Ryle. Dilemmas. Concepts of Mind
Geach. Histpry of Western Philosophy
Chesterton. Orthodoxy. The Everlasting Man
MacIntyre. History of Ethics.

Chapter VII
Augustine. On Free Choice of the Will
Bleich and Rossner. Jewish Bioethics
Fagothy. Right and Reason
Wojtyla. The Acting Person

Chapter VIII

Aquinas. On the Division and Methods of the Sciences
Aristotle. Nicomachean Ethics. Metaphysics
Hempel. Aspects of Scientific Explanation
Konecsni. Biology and the Philosophy of Science
Lonergan. Insight
Maritain. The Degrees of Knowledge
Nagel. The Structure of Science
Pieper. The Cardinal Virtues
Plato. The Symposium
Russell and Whitehead. Principice Mathematica

A BIBLIOGRAPHIC ESSAY on the divisions and methods of the sciences:

There are so many places to begin, that, like the chart of the separate disciplines, I will start at the bottom and work upward. The physical sciences are so admirably handled by Jacques Maritain in THE DEGREES OF KNOWLEDGE and Ernst Nagel in THE STRUCTURE OF SCIENCE that most other surveys almost parody one or the other. Prentice-Hall paperbacks has provided an extensive series of works ranging from Hempel's PHILOSOPHY OF SCIENCE to W. K. Frankena: ETHICS that a glance into Books in Print can supply a full listing. To biologists I would especially point out Morton Beckner's FROM THE BIOLOGICAL POINT OF VIEW, Simon's THE MATTER OF LIFE, and my own BIOLOGY AND THE PHILOSOPHY OF SCIENCE.

On the level of man in general, Fr. Royce's books are uniformly excellent in combining philosophical anthropology with the latest work of the specialties. In aesthetics the work of Emil Fackenheim is a good beginning but do not overlook Maritain's ART AND POETRY AND THE FRONTIERS OF SCHOLASTICISM or the massive STRUCTURE OF ESTHETICS by F. E. Sparshott. In metahistory, not only is there Nagel and Prentice-Hall as mentioned above, but also work by Sidney Hook, especially, THE HERO IN HISTORY.

For some of the more delightful insights to social thought, the immense number of works perpetrated by a factory called Andrew Greeley range over society, politics and religion with no sacred cow unburned.   In that treacherous borderland between philosophy and theology, A. J. Ayer the linguistic atheist, Schuber Ogden the process philosopher, Lonergan the transcendental Thomist are all represented, introduced and synthesized in David Tracey's BLESSED RAGE FOR ORDER. Since each book has an ample bibliography, ENJOY, ENJOY.

APPENDIX III: AN EXISTENTIALIST PHENOMENOLOGY OF HUMAN SEXUALITY

A. O Introduction

When I first published while dinosaurs still walked the earth, it was a rare philosophy book which dealt with human sexuality. If it showed up at all, it was usually within the format of the schools which taught and fought over substantive ethical issues, and even there it was done in the most covert terms and almost never in print, except under the rubric of an ethics course in philosophy or a marriage course in theology. Today, there are almost no Introductions to Philosophy Books whose selection of readings do not include something concerning sexuality. For that reason, this appendix has been added to the present volume. If more justification were needed, it also provides us with an opportunity to consider the phenomenological method at work on a level more concrete than its in globo application in the earlier chapters.

The following pages are not intended to be comprehensive. The number of different perspectives which philosophy brings to the study of sexuality are too large for a simple appendix. There are books of reading available whose only topic is philosophy-and-sex or philosophy-and-women. To my own knowledge, there does not yet exist a book, written by a single author, which attempts to do a philosophical analysis of all the different approaches to sex. There is a gold mine of material awaiting the philosopher who will tackle the philosophical critique of the sociological approach to sex, the limitations of the psychological models of sexuality, the philosophical integration of the Masters and Johnson mechanics of biology into a larger perspective of the whole man, the work of social philosophers on sex roles, the shrewd observations of the philosophers of law on the question of sexual equality, differences, and dynamics. The number of philosophical dimensions of human sexuality is indeed large.

The only purpose of the following pages is to try to present one of these dimensions, the view of the embodied consciousness of human sexuality as seen in the perspective of an existentialistic phenomenological technique.

We have the common experience of being part of an intellectual community, any study group is. The basis of our sense of "community" is based, in the present case, on a) our common experience as sexual human beings, b) our common understanding (to know, if not to agree), and c) our common will to unite in agreement upon a common judgment.

The present inquiry is purely philosophical. Biology and

psychology are assumed, theology will only be allowed to the extent that it provides cultural documents for our reflection.

Philosophy is reflective thinking about human experience, a reflection upon the pre-reflective. Therefore, we must first describe the pre-reflexive experience of human sexuality. That task creates a problem because of the difficulties of description. Will not any description presuppose our implicit philosophy? It damned sure will color our experiences. What will we be trying to describe? Our own experience? Who is "our"? You or I may be immature, narrow, or sick. But is there any other perspective which is possible? America in this decade? A large task! Other societies in other times? Even if Augustine, Luther and the Victorians formed one tradition, that is too much. Even the term "experience" is ambiguous.

The term "experience" is ambiguous--it can be limited to the brainless sensual or broadened to include sexual mysticism. Are dreams experiences? Influence of the co-existing unconsciousness? From the range of intrauterine conception to mutual heterosexual orgasm and/or beyond (if there is a beyond), we must select a "field."

Therefore, we will describe, in order to sharpen, what we will philosophically analyze. We will explore the nature of the phenomenological method used, the phenomenological thesis on what human is, and then study the relation of sex to total reality. Notice carefully that we are using a Western thought-process to analyze an a-Western, a-local experience.

All that follows will flow from Merleau-Ponty's definition: MAN IS A BEING-IN-THE-WORLD, WITH OTHERS, FOR A PROJECT, WITHIN ONE'S POWER.

A.1 A Being-In-The-World, A Body-Subject
A being-in-the-world, a body-subject: not the body as object. Man is a subject of so many disciplines which tend to view him as an object, as in the objective model of physics which uses objectification and abstraction. Objectification has, as its ideal the total separation in the scientist of data from data-gathering-consciousness. Their output is usually statistical data with a theory to hang it on. Man as subject is man as subjective and self-aware, as he discovers himself, as she finds her autonomy by freedom and self-determination. The existence of the person, male and female, is a becoming. One is not one-self. One becomes one's self: not a `body // subject' but a `body-subject,' as in Aquinas where human is one substance consisting of matter and form, body-soul. Both Aquinas and the phenomenologists are in reaction to the old dualism which was not reality itself but merely a way of looking at reality.

248

Your presence to others is a bodily one. There are degrees of being a subject: the baby is less a subject than the fully matured genius who has mastered both self and specialty.

Needless to say, the definition is purely descriptive. As Alphonse De Waelhens puts it in his "La philosophie et les experiences naturalles", We experience our subjectivity in some thing-like dimension, e.g., I share in the thing-ness of adjoining things, exist and suffer causality on and from things. cannot absolutely reject this thing-like reality. My interiority is linked to an inexorable exteriority.

Let us see if we can analyze this statement of transcending-self-de-facto into a statement of greater existential importance.

Objective space can be defined as parts outside of parts in geometrical space. Things are entities whose properties we discover, which are identifiable by measurement, and ultimately are governed by the laws of mechanics. That "object-experience", when applied to man, can be undercut by considering the a-mechanical physiological structure of the human nervous system--such a system cannot be understood apart from initiative and self-organization.

Another way is the phenomenologist's description of her own body: "I do not experience myself as two things." Classical psychology (Descartes), did recognize that the status of the body is not the same as other objects. I cannot get the distance from my own body to study it objectively. "To say that the body is with me and near me is to say that it is never in front of me; it is always on the fringe of my perceptual approach." Thus, says Merleau-Ponty. I cannot make my body a spectacle on which I can freely take any perspective.

Body, as the necessary pre-condition for approaching things, is therefore not a thing. The body is an object that is imperfectly objectified. "I do not see my body insofar as it sees, but only as it is seen by another, and then incompletely and from a different perspective." It can become an object insofar as it is able to be another's. This will involve us later on with the concept of transcending one's own body; likewise, "for me" and "possibility of projection" will be locutions which will require study.

The subjective is from any individual's perspective. Subjectivism, which is not the same thing, denies that two individuals can ever get the same perspective. Subjectivity: I am a condition for meaning to come in from the object to me. Subjectivism: I am the total cause for that meaning. While we consider terminology, let's add a few more. Affectivity: classical psychology would say the body was an affective object; a knife-like object causes pain but in itself is not pain-full, whereas no causal effect of pain is produced in a finger apart from the finger itself. Movement is observed from others by trajectory study because a subject has kineasthetic perception.

Interim Conclusion

Based on the above considerations, the body is not just a thing. Can we attribute to the body geometrical spatiality? Yes, but not as fundamental characteristic because there is another more basic spatiality. I cannot say that my body is "there" in the same way. It is a fundamental here; a peculiar kind of space: non-geometrical, "body-image". Body image is not equal to the sum total of all the images I have gained of myself. It is what Gestalt psychologists call a form, a whole, which is prior to its parts in the perceptive field. "The body is the darkness needed in the theater to show up a performance," said Merleau-Ponty in the Phenomenology of Perception. The origins of even the geometer's geometrical space comes from body-space via abstraction.

Corporal-schemata, body-outline, body-image, background of behavior, background out of which we act, a subjective reality which orients our behavior: consider the phantom-limb of the amputee whose presence is felt until the patient adjusts to the new condition. Only the possible allows us to pass from the abstract to the concrete: for example, map-reading involves certain real motions which are not for themselves alone but whose meanings come from the actions in the mind. You have to see the possible reality in the reality of the map by using your body imaginatively. Thus, the possible is a third term which is intermediate between the parts-outside-of-parts space and pure intentionality. The possible is the median power which can abstract us from geometrical space. The body dwells in space, it is not contained in it.

As we have said of space, so too, of time. It is the original "now" from which we abstract "time". "Now" means we are perpetually inaugurating a new beginning. It means this new beginning is an arrangement of the surrounding environment as well as of the past. This beginning is never an absolute source but is rather a re-commencement within a horizon of total finitude, radical limitation.

Reality for me begins today and here but is also a hold on reality that synthesizes previous acts. I never have an absolute mastery over that in which I find myself.

Being-in-the-world does not mean being-in-the-world as an island, or any inanimate or unintelligent thing. Thus, the idea of a universal container, which is in no way perceptible, can only be conceived by a being who is simultaneously located in the whole and is effectuating the whole: Persons "add up" the world into a totality. Humans seems to grasp the whole, but at first darkly. The whole as a horizon, as a boundary of the known, implies that beyond our horizon there is a different grasp of the "beyond" as the not-present or as possibly known. Being-in-the-world means that man exists in such, is sharing in it, and is totally in the real, that she is that member of reality that has as her ability and task to recognize that reality   Heidegger: "Man is the only being that knows he will die." Thus, also Pascal.

There is a dialectic at work here in the broad sense of opposition between facticity and transcendence. Facticity is the thing-like dimension which makes us purely and simply associates of all that is real. It is not identical with the reality of things because it does not end as a blend with itself but as tending to a transcendent access-as-known. Transcendence involves intentional beings which surpass every reality which is closed in upon itself, which rises to a mode of presence capable of opening out on something more than itself. The dialectical analog "proper objects" for the human intellects are quidditates materialis rei (the what-ness of the material thing) which allow us to abstract the idea of ens simplex (simple being). Dialectic is broader: it includes all modalities: intuition, action, sensation. The structure of human existence is this dialectic. Facticity is not identical with body, nor is transcendence identical with consciousness. The structure of human existence implies an ordered plurality of things which is rather dynamic in humans and which goes all the way back to Plato's dialogue the Philebus. "Body" and "consciousness" are abstract limit concepts; in the concrete, the body has transcendence while the consciousness is loaded with facticity.

Pre-reflexive behavior implies total identity and yet distance. Here we have an opening to criticize Sartre's concepts of nausea and pain, where he maintains that body is utter non-meaning, has no significance, and is pure facticity. (Therefore, he has the paradox of saying that its meaning is meaningless.) Pain tends to make the body just a thing but we never reach that state until death. We cease to be in the world, our world disintegrates under pain and it more and more ceases to be. (As C. S. Lewis points out in The Problem of Pain, Christ under maximum pain surpasses all insofar as he is conscious of doing it for the world.)

Idealists push transcendence to its limits in reflection. But all reflection implies a non-reflective moment which is 1) like an act of faith in the being we experience and 2) always implies the non-reflective on which we reflect. Aquinas is admittedly reflecting in doing philosophy which gives him an advantage on the phenomenologists who seek to describe the pre-reflective and get tied up by the problem of "how do you reflectively say something that is pre-reflective?"

Sense requires organs, signification and direction. Organs are effective and material causes which put us in relation to others. Signification provides the form under the aspect of thought content. Direction is the drift of discourse, the purpose, the orientation, the end or goal to which we are tending. A sense datum, something given to the senses, appeals to a certain structure by which we are adapted to the world. A datum has a sense because it has a possible elicited response from us and orients us, and our bodies especially, in a particular direction. Thus, the sensory qualities as objective or subjective is a false problem: the human is the revealer of sense. Nothing makes sense except in appearing to a rational subject who is a lumen naturale, a natural light who is the source of the birth of the thing in the world. Like light, it does not create color but births it. If we are to look for the bearer of intentionality, we must look to none other than behavior as the bearer of meaning.

Consciousness is affected by the world. The body has an intentional, or mental element about it. The body is a dynamic dialectic, not composite, not mixture. The sense of things presupposes in its appearance the existence of a human being which is significative. The human being is the only revealor of sense, by word or deed or silence. Nothing has sense except insofar as it appears to a being who constitutes its sense. This giving of meaning isn't just done in human knowledge. meaning is brought by sexual activities: only the Bible recognizes this as a type of knowledge.

The three dimensions of sense are revealed by some encounter which touches the organic, the signification is given and a direction implied. Encounter means that both realities bring something to put together meaning and that neither element can be reduced to the other. There is no absolute realism either: I do not require the world to prove to me that I exist. Intentionality: every thinking act is a consciousness of something other than consciousness itself, hence there is a facticity involved in conscious thought. There are many diverse modes of intentionality. The medievals centered on the intellectual but we recognize the intentions built into the world of tools, the world of inter-subjective relation, the world of values.

A.2 World

It is quite a problem to say that the world is. Is it something "out there", a sum total of things? No, because it is the knower who totalizes the world. Maybe each has his/her own world rather than the world? To answer that question we need two concepts of the world: 1) the world as the locus of behavior, the place where we behave and 2) the world as horizon.

The world as horizon: is the limit which encloses the world for me and which also implies that there is something outside the limit. Horizon implies a totality only one part of which is given explicitly, a cosmos, not a chaos, an ordered sense of things. The world is not explicitly given in each experience but we realize that the individual objects in the world are limited because of the beyond which is implicit in the horizon. The horizon depends on the things around me. Our world depends on both our stand-point and the things out there. The world is a real and formal a priori which man establishes as the being who signifies. The world is real, not the total creation of the subject, yet is somehow brought there by man (formal a priori). The world--the horizon of all things.

The world as a locus of behavior where we exist. Locus is the matrix of meaning, the womb of behavior, Mother Earth. Our encounter gives birth to meaning. Because there are modalities of behavior, we behave differently; the world is a source of correlatives to meaning to the human who makes meaning arise.

A.3 With Others

The body's personality, the human subject, develops out of the behavior of some other interpersonal relationships and is influenced by that relationship. But for our purposes there is a distinction, to use Heidegger's terminology, there are two ways of "being-with".

1) Existential (existentiell): that mode where there is an intimate involvement of men with one another which has its part in the creation of free relationships.

2) Existentiary (existenital): the fact of being with others. This extentiary mode emphasizes that, in principles from our beginning, we are made of the same stuff as other's being. It is a prime fact of every stirring consciousness. Humans are immersed in a community which we do not choose. Only in this pouring-in from outside of a milieu do we get the intellectual framework in which every free decision must be made. We come into existence as a focus of actions from the outside. This Existentiary mode is antecedent to any decision and it is the base from which we will make our decisions. Your decision to accept or

reject your society is what makes you autonomous. The human makes herself a personal center of being. The person is a free self-positing: therefore is not yet in being as such. The person is not yet fully existing until the sense of personhood is formed by personal fellowship, communion with others. Thus it is in the gift of love that we become a person. To keep our better existential self from degenerating into a mere Existentiary being requires a constant renewal.

This distinction is useful for sexuality study because probing the unconscious involves studying that which is Existentiary. Recalling earlier chapters, you are aware that the unconscious cannot be called `a thing which is the cause of conscious acts' but rather it is something which involves an unarticulated meaning. The study of the unconscious will strive toward the goal of articulation.

A.4 For A Project
The intentionality of a person's behavior constitutes the self. Since the self is an entity ascribed by time (past-present-future), the element of a pro-ject emerges. The designation in general of a future action which depends on me and which is within my power, makes project the intentional correlate of decision. Noesis (decision) has as its object the Noema (project).

A project is one type of judgment. Judgments which involve wishes, commands, statements of existence have nothing to do with the project judgment. A typical project judgment ("I shall go tomorrow") involves something to be done by me. Concrete images are not essential to a project judgment which is expressed in an abstract or empty designation, as opposed to a concrete or filled designation. A "so-be-it" attitude is not a vague wish concerning some act in the future; pro-ject involves future temporality, anticipation, the future-as-intended.
We leap from project to project over "dead time". I pick the end before the means and then add on secondary projects. The time projected is discrete and reversible; lived-time is continuous and irreversible. We think of the future as an expectation which is within our power in the case of a project. You usually think of an expected future into which you project yourself. The expected time seems to be at first in the world of cause and effect. But you do not foresee the future you foresee in the future. What permits us to say that there will be a future? Is it not just an extrapolation of past causes into future acts and effects? No. Rather projections presuppose the existence of a being who is capable of being-for-a-future, a consciousness which

makes the future ahead of time, or a consciousness which is strictly atemporal. Thus there is the temptation to tend to the other extreme and try to say that the future is a pure projection created totally by the consciousness. Anticipation of the future occurs in modes of behavior which are not `project'. Even the preliminaries of a sneeze anticipate its resolution: which may be why Pascal thought the sneeze worthy of philosophical analysis.

Reference to the future is not an act: it is a fundamental situation which makes possible both expectation and projection. Consciousness is carried along into the future; it is powerless in its drift; the future is the condition of the action. I do not decide the future, I consent to it. Decision is to project as consent is to involuntary being. I consent to the tempo of duration. Sexual relationships have a tempo of growth unique to itself, which can only be dominated, pushed, or slowed at cost of destroying the relationship.

Within One's Power: is a notion which requires the distinction between theoretical and practical possibility. Practical possibility is what I make possible by my project. Possibility has its own feedback to me. I am the realization of my own being. I make my own mind.

A.5 Project and Values

Projects are efforts to achieve that which we value; values are the goals of projects. We are primarily interested in fulfilling our own existence, finding happiness. Every being is given a positive or negative value in relation to yourself, values reflected in our attraction or repulsion relative to them. Good is the value. Value is whatever helps us to be. Values are multiple: therefore the character of value is not unique: there are moral, religious, aesthetic, social, and biological values. The concrete realization of value is never exhausted in our finite existence. An absolute experience of any value is not within the present abilities of the being know as human.

In summary, then, You are always a human substance but it is only when you are experiencing that you are also a consciousness, a knowing subject. For this reason people who do not succeed at biological sexuality usually fail because they are not successful as whole people.

A.6 Gabriel Marcel.

For Marcel, there are three levels of existence. On level one, there is consciousness, lived experience, pure empiricism, the unreflexive. On the second level, we hit the first level of reflection, the level of objectivity, of science, of technology. Here our aim is to control. On the third level, we reflect on our reflections. This is the level of philosophy, wherein we try to reach the core of our own being and indeed the core of being itself. Usually we concentrate on level two because we are afraid to pass on to the conversion required to make it up to the third level. This fear is that which enriches science but which impoverishes the humanities. Survival has taken us from level one to level two but to go from level two to level three requires a profound turn of mind, but most especially a turning from the self as selfish!

This desire of the philosopher to confront being on its terms and not ours is unique. It means life. In order to love I must surrender self by my belief in the other person. The third level is the level of mystery which is opposed to the inauthenticity of the scientific model. Others on the second level are merrily problems to be solved or objects to be manipulated. Problems call forth solutions, mysteries of existence do not. Mysteries are penetrated, little by little, felt, personally involve us. Our body is a `be' as well as a `have': hence the mystery of be-have-iour. What does it mean for one partner to be present to another? Love, like evil or knowledge, are not problems to be solved but mysteries to be shared in as lived experienced. Being present invites the pun on your being present and your being a present to your lover. "I am and you are only because We are."

Sexual desire, which shows the obscurity of the body-subject to another body-subject is a force but not a push in the sense of a mechanical force. Sexual desire is not conscious, it is a new concept of one's own body, and a new way of viewing another. It is experienced in viewing others in its most brute-like expression. A young girl's first experience can be frightening and yet seductive because of the realization of the inner response which is triggered. Freud recognized sex as a cause of hysteria, just as much as The Vital Force, the Life Urge, or some of the other names it has gone by. Behavior has replaced the idea of Instinct as a way of demonstrating the heredity vs. environment interplay. Imprinted behavior represents both an abyss and a foundation for the human species.: it is unlimited and yet it is also foundational.

The first and proper meaning to sexuality was the attribution of cosmic forces in the life and death cycle, in the manner of the Phallic

257

cults. Sex as sacred, as man's communion with nature more than even human communion between man and woman. In agrarian cultures, the male would have intercourse with the female in a furrow of a just-planted field, only without the horrors of Tom Tryon's novel, Harvest Home. It was for the same fertility functions that the institution of temple prostitution existed. This sacredness is even observed in our orderly urban rationality by the ritual of the spring break. "It happens every spring", this renewal of the sacral sex even if modern society insists that this sacral content remain covert rather than overt.

Our attitude to the other changes when our sexual desire is aroused. Arousal increases both the substantiality, density, and obscurity of the body of the other. The other is the offered possibility of satisfaction. The desiring being always anticipates the "I-know-not-what", still less does he or she know what awaits in the initial encounter. It is not the same as the logical anticipation of an outcome where you know all the facts. It is more a felt anticipation of the unknown, more psychological than biological in the desire it proffers to satisfy.

Sexual desire is quite different from affection or sympathy insofar as sexual desire centers on the BODY- subject. Body is not a transparency through which I get to something else but it is rather a density with its center within that every opaqueness

A.7 The Invasion of Existence by Impulse

The other reveals itself to us as both carnate and desirable. The infantile libido discovers the body as a resonance in his own body and of the pleasure which the other takes in his body. The boy plays at male aggression, the girl plays but does not LIVE her sexuality in the specific sense of female fertility. Puberty dictates a new style of presence over and above mere physical maturation. The body possessing the adult secondary sexual characteristics becomes a stronger presence and acquires certain rhythms in the more obvious forms of menstruation and nocturnal emissions as well as the biorhymic hormonal cycles. Added to the biology and the psychology, there is also the society which dictates in part the role model of male and female to every member of the society.

Sexuality is at the center of existence but not merely as an instinct, more like a human product which is invested with

258

meaningfulness. What does desire seek or expect from the Other? The desire is not simply oriented to reproduction or even to the new person as novelty. Desire tends to seek its own gratification by means of the other. Desire in quest of satisfaction-as-such is eroticism; desire in quest of the-other-as-such is love.

The quest for sex pleasure and that pleasure alone is eroticism. Thus it is self-defined to include self-satisfaction, at least superficially. The instant of pleasure is not in time but rather is a creation of time. Loss of consciousness in orgasm with its ego-regression is thus an analog of death. Rigid people who fear loss of absolute self-control find the results of that self-control in frigidity and impotence and the other psycho-sexual repressive diseases. If the other is not important to you, then the results are not fridigity but self-eroticism. Masturbation as a substitute for manipulating others has its own sadness because it is our contact with the other which gives a psychic rebirth, even if the other is viewed as an it, a disposable Kleenex.

Every Kiss, Caress, or Intercourse Act can be ambiguous. Self-eroticizing, like gourmandizing, has the effect of making us feel that our bodies are prisons. We live sexuality by living it in the conscious or spiritual sphere which constitutes and supports the person as personal presence. Our desire is expressed in the gesture of the caress, a gesture which can show either the erotic thrust to possess or the sense of submission which makes the other susceptible. The caress has meaning even before the caresser can fully realize it. The simpler the language the more ambiguous the meaning. The more primitive the experience the more we bend signs to our intentions. In short, sex brings us to the realization of a paradox of communication: if I do not put too much of myself into what I say, then I stand the best chance of being understood. If you have ever tried to tell a lover something that was deeply and personally important to yourself, you know the difficulty of the paradox.

Caress is a non-verbal medium of communication that involves more than just two persons. Inherently, it seems to involve one person more than the other. "Am I seeking myself or am I seeking fusion with the other? A question is always present that must be answered. What grounds this experience? If the experience does not abolish the solitude, does not establish communion, then there are grounds to suspect that its thrust is selfish. Therefore the rest of the subject's life must be examined to verify the validity of the initial judgment of selfishness.

259

One does not know what will satisfy the desires we feel. We are fulfilled and yet not fully satisfied. he caress is ambiguous precisely because it involves the body of the whole person: the caress is a form of carnal speech which is never just the mere transfer of a conscious content from one to another. The act, encounter, process itself has given new meaning to the experience. The meaning changes as the encounter is experienced, and a relationship is established. Self-eroticism never reaches the depth of experience such that it can be considered an encounter with another. A certain self-discipline is required if one person is not to lose the communion with the other in the pleasurable solitude of one's own body. Only tenderness and solicitude can overcome sexual solitude. Sex as a philosophy of communication thus has all the material of symbolism fitted to it. A reciprocal causality between caress and caressed, each action changes with each response.

In the act of intercourse, we bring all our inner personal relationships to that marriage bed. Each person is a secret; what is attempted most specially in sex is to understand that secret. Sex makes us pilgrims questing after the unlimited: sex, desire and love with its own infinite boundaries are the basis for a whole philosophical tradition from Plato, through Bonaventure and Pascal, to Marcel. It is separate and complimentary to the tradition of knowledge which runs from Aristotle through Aquinas to Modern Science.

Thus we have a three cornered relationship: he and she and this absolute drive. Children will change this situation, as we will see later. Sex may well be one of the few experiences which still speaks meaningfully to modern man about the existence of God, simply because this experience has so much the taste of the absolute about it. In such a context sexual ethics may only be the attempt to make our sexual communications coherent and truthful.

There seem to be at least three facets of sexual responsibility:

1. The content which approaches ontology: to be responsible means to be the source of one`s actions. To act in any less a manner, means to act in an inhumane and impersonal manner.

2. The existentialist's view is to accept the ontological content as one's own "the cause may not matter so much as the commitment to take risks and carry them through." While such a view does allow

responsibility, there is still lacking a norm outside the person by which the person can test the act planned.

3. Responsiveness: our actions are responses to the world working on us, hence response-ability. We can appreciate the objective values in a situation: we are not solitary agents to our interconnecting rational mesh with others.

Humans are the shepherds of being: we are summoned by being, reality, to respond to bring and to promote it. To educate a person to the ultimate claims of reality, to give a scale of values for lesser norms that are objective, to show that lesser values dissolve in this context: that is one of the better statements of the natural law when it is properly built upon a personalist hypothesis.

Any personalist ethics gives a strong position to the intellect. The full sense of things cannot just be seen in terms of what happens in biological processes. The importance of the natural forces does not lie in their brute factuality. The sense that it is not `out there', the sense that it is completed by human minds in the light of the personal vocation to create being is the force which completes the schema, your mind is the faculty in the work of love which opens it up to the possibility of integrating sex into the work of love. Sex is a process for engendering offspring, thus we must never forget that making babies is a part of sex. The embodiment of mutual self-giving is the most intimate expression, the incarnation of love is the offspring. Sex as a human phenomenon transforms intercourse into pro-creation.

Sex at its most human is the family with all its possibilities. Sex remains symbolic of human promotive love. Any separation of sex from family violates the sense of this, and is a failure to face up to the full and integral meaning of human sexuality. It is immoral not because it interrupts a biological function but because it is unfaithful to the full and whole meaning of the act in its human context. Male and female intervention in natural processes is only valid if it enlarges the possibilities of living for yourself and for others. To act in a way which contradicts possibilities which are already there is to destroy being and to violate the natural tendencies of our own intellects.

A.8 Modern Dilemmas

In a real sense we must explore the extent to which man has divorced sex from its context and the extent to which sex has divorced man from his context.

A.8.1 Man has alienated sexuality

The primitive placed sex with fear, anxiety, terror, and anguish. We now realize that this context is neurotic. But, since we now laud our sexuality, the balance of the human is disturbed: anxiety overcompensated for by the debauching unavowed flight from love into the panic of conquest is Freud's fear-of-death syndrome all over again, and yet it is subscribed to by many in the society.

Sex also diverts the mind to the outside world of objects. In western capitalism sexuality is a status symbol for the mistress who represents the buying power of her master.

For the poor it remains the only distraction from the burden of their labors.

The openness of current sexuality has, as one of its consequences, the de-dramatization of sex from the level of mystery to that of pure functional organicism. Thus, the mastery of sexuality becomes self-defeating as the adolescent wounds himself trying to avoid sex traumas. Ejaculating becomes as non-joyous or as non-aphrodisiac as urination: no fuss, no frills.

The generation of the 1960's and 1970's has desacralized "untouchable sex" but this "sex as it is" is ultimately a despair camouflaged by all sorts of statements. "I'm not afraid of sex" all too often means "I am afraid of love."

A.8.2 Sex Alienating Man

The two great factors of modern estrangement or alienation are work and sex: the productive function and the reproductive function. The first has been critiqued by Marx and there is a connection between the two: the price tag on sex. Both men and women have been alienated from their sexuality.

In the area of advertising, women are used to sell machinery, allowing their bodies to be viewed with an equally mechanical eye. Sex is used to rivet the population to the necessities of the market. We alienate ourselves from ourselves with unneeded commodities.

In the army, men and women are now mutually accomplished in

262

the arts of destruction. Women at home did not attain a warlike mentality, which today's veteran females [1 OUT OF EVERY 7 SOLDIERS IN 2008] now carry into daily life. Predictions in this area are still nebulous. Equality in sharing in destruction is equality by degradation. It is not that much different in medicine: men and women are now accomplices in death. Medicaid abortion mills speak for themselves.

8.9 Final Thoughts

The old distinction between the sacred and the profane only meant that which separated the sanctuary from the courtyard in front of (pro-fanum) the temple. Mircea Eliade in his works on sacred times and places, Joseph Campbell's quartet on Mythology, even Tolkien's Hobbit and Lewis's Perelandra are all attempts to reconsecrate, re-sacralize . . . all trying to remind us that there is something MORE.

If Springtime is only the time when you can hear the adjacent car's radio, If nature's seasons cannot penetrate uniseason office buildings, If even day and night disappear from midtown Manhattan and the Vegas strip--If we are indeed facing increased self-isolation from Nature, then a thoughtful sexuality can not only introduce us back to both love and play but has the capacity to reintroduce us to the love of nature and even the God of love.

Made in the USA
Lexington, KY
13 September 2019